BREAKFAST COOKBOOK

Favorite Recipes From America's Bed & Breakfast Inns

Phyllis & Tracy Winters

Winters Publishing
P.O. Box 501
Greensburg, Indiana 47240

Printed in the United States of America

PHOTO & ART CREDITS
Front cover: By Andrew Haltof, from Snowvillage Inn, Snowville, N.H.
Back cover top: By Joan M. Busta, from Maple Leaf Cottage Inn, Elsah, IL
Back cover bottom: By Judy Cheney, from The Waverly Inn, Hendersonville, N.C.

The information about the inns and the recipes were supplied by the inns themselves. The rate information was current at the time of submission, but is subject to change. Every effort has been made to assure that the book is accurate. Neither the inns, authors, or publisher assume responsibility for any errors, whether typographical or otherwise.

Library of Congress Card Catalog Number 90-70150
ISBN 0-9625329-0-8

Dedication

With Love,

to our parents,
Wilbur and Marianna Mozingo
and
Jack and Shirley Winters
for their love and support
through the years

and

to our 1 year old daughter
Rebekah Ann
for her patience while Mommy and Daddy
were on the phone, at the computer, or typing.

Acknowledgement

Many thanks to all of the innkeepers,
including the hundreds whose recipes
do not appear in this edition,
who took valuable time to select recipes
and fill out questionnaires.
It is because of their efforts that we
were able to make this book a reality.

Preface

When we first mailed our letter to the inns requesting recipes for a new Bed & Breakfast cookbook, we wondered how many replies we would receive. We soon had our answer, as many mornings brought 30-40 new recipes to the mailbox. Then began the process of sorting the recipes into categories, searching out duplications, and verifying information from those that were selected.

From the hundreds we received, we have included just over 300 recipes. We believe they best represent the wide variety of delicious breakfast dishes available at Bed & Breakfast inns nationwide. Geographically, 48 states are represented. Many dishes are distinctly regional, some are exotic, and some are just good home cooking. All of them are special though, as they have been tested by time (and lots of happy customers) at inns that are famous for breakfast.

Although this book is primarily a cookbook, we have used a format that features details about each inn that supplied a recipe. This was done not only to give credit to the inns, but also to provide you with a directory of fine Bed & Breakfast establishments across the country to assist you in selecting accommodations when you travel. An index at the rear of this book lists the inns by state.

When you decide to stay at one of the inns included in this book, please call ahead to check on room availability and to verify the rates and other information. Although the rates listed were accurate at the time of submission, they are subject to change.

We have certainly enjoyed compiling this book. Through correspondence and telephone calls with the innkeepers we feel we've made many new friends. We hope that you enjoy reading about the Bed & Breakfast inns and preparing the wonderful recipes.

CONTENTS

MUFFINS

ACORN MUFFINS

2 eggs, beaten
1 1/2 cups sugar
1 cup prepared acorn squash
1/2 cup salad oil
1/4 cup water
1 2/3 cups flour
1/4 teaspoon baking powder
1 teaspoon baking soda
3/4 teaspoon salt
1/2 teaspoon cloves
1/2 teaspoon cinnamon

To prepare acorn squash: Wash one acorn squash, cut in half and bake cut side down on a cookie sheet in 350° oven for 45 minutes. Let cool slightly, then scoop out pulp from shell, discarding shell. Mash pulp with fork into a smooth consistency. To make muffin batter: Mix eggs, sugar, squash, salad oil and water together. Sift together remainder of ingredients and add, blending well. Fill 12 muffin cups 3/4 full and bake in 325° oven for 30 - 35 minutes or until tested done with a toothpick. For cast iron muffin trays, use less batter for each and bake about same length of time.

Origin: Lynn came up with this recipe after receiving Grandma's old acorn shaped cast iron muffin pans. The taste is similar to pumpkin.

Submitted by:

Greene House
Bed & Breakfast
R.R. #2, Box 214
Whitewater, Wisconsin 53190
(414) 495-8771 or outside Wisconsin (800) 468-1959
Lynn & Mayner Greene
$39.00 to $75.00

Full breakfast
6 rooms
Children, over 5
No pets
Restricted smoking
Mastercard, Visa, Am Ex

1848 farmhouse in southern Wisconsin allows you a trip back in time. Lynn, a caterer, will delight you with unusual breakfasts, while Mayner plays soothing guitar music. Collections of musical instruments, handstitched quilts, rag rugs, old books, and historical photographs.

APPLE CHEESE MUFFINS

- 1/4 cup bran
- 1 1/2 cups Kellogg's All Bran cereal
- 3/4 cup rolled oats (not instant)
- 2 1/4 cups milk
- 4 1/2 cups unbleached flour
- 1/2 teaspoon salt
- 1 tablespoon baking powder
- 1 tablespoon baking soda
- 1 tablespoon cinnamon
- 3/4 cup corn oil
- 1 1/2 cups sugar
- 6 large eggs
- 7 large tart apples, peeled & diced
- 2 cups grated sharp Cheddar cheese
- 1 1/2 cups toasted walnuts

Soak bran, cereal, and oats in milk for one hour or more. Sift dry ingredients. Blend oil and sugar. Beat in eggs. Add dry ingredients and soaked cereals. Mix just until blended. Fold in fruit, cheese and nuts. Fill muffin cups 2/3 full and bake at 350° until done, about 25 - 30 minutes. These freeze well and keep well. Makes 2 dozen large muffins.

Origin: Original recipe by Chef Marcia Dunsmore.

Submitted by:

The Settlers Inn
4 Main Avenue
Hawley, Pennsylvania 18428
(717) 226-2993
Jeanne & Grant Genzlinger
$55.00 to $75.00

Continental breakfast
18 rooms, 18 private baths
Children allowed
No pets
Restricted smoking
Mastercard, Visa, Am Ex

A lovely Tudor manor beside the park in the village of Hawley. Elegant dining featuring regional cuisine. Afternoon tea by the fireplace or on the spacious porch. A great example of 1920's hotels.

APPLE CINNAMON MUFFINS

1/2 cup butter or margarine
3/4 cup white sugar
1 egg, beaten
1 cup buttermilk
1 teaspoon salt
1 1/2 cups diced apples
1 cup all purpose flour
3/4 cup whole wheat flour
1 teaspoon baking soda
1 teaspoon cinnamon

Topping:
1 teaspoon cinnamon
2 - 3 tablespoons white sugar

Blend margarine, sugar, and egg until smooth. Add buttermilk, salt, and apples, and mix well. Stir together white and wheat flour, soda, and cinnamon. Add dry ingredients to liquid, stirring only to moisten. Spoon into greased muffin cups and sprinkle with topping. Bake at 375° for 20 minutes. Makes 12 muffins.

Submitted by:

Patchwork Quilt Country Inn
11748 County Road 2
Middlebury, Indiana 46540
(219) 825-2417
Maxine Zook & Susan Thomas
$39.95 to $49.95

Continental breakfast
3 rooms
Children, over 5
No pets
No smoking
Mastercard & Visa

Patchwork Quilt Country Inn is a centennial farm, tucked away in northern Indiana country. Patchwork Quilt offers fine dining and is rated one of top 10 restaurants in Indiana, with overnight lodging and tours which will take you to meet our Amish friends.

APPLE NUT MUFFINS

2 cups flour
1 cup brown sugar
1 teaspoon baking soda
1/2 teaspoon salt
1 teaspoon ground cinnamon
3/4 teaspoon ground cloves
1/2 teaspoon ground nutmeg
1 cup chopped walnuts
1 cup raisins
1/4 cup milk
1/2 cup vegetable oil
2 eggs
1 cup unpared, grated or finely chopped apples

Preheat oven to 400°. Lightly grease bottom of muffin pans. In large bowl combine flour, sugar, baking soda, salt, cinnamon, cloves, nutmeg, walnuts and raisins. In separate bowl, combine milk, oil and eggs; beat well. Stir in apples. Add liquid mixture to dry ingredients. Stir until dry ingredients are just moistened; batter will be stiff. Fill greased muffin pans 3/4 full. Bake 17 to 20 minutes or until tops are lightly browned. Remove muffins from pans onto wire rack; serve at once, or keep warm by leaving in cups, slightly tipped to allow steam to escape. These muffins keep well. Yield: 18 muffins.

Submitted by:

The INN at Honey Run
6920 County Road 203
Millersburg, Ohio 44654
(216) 674-0011
Marjorie Stock
$60.00 to $150.00

Continental plus breakfast
36 rooms, 36 private baths
No pets
Restricted smoking
Mastercard, Visa, Am Ex

A contemporary country inn - wonderful staff enjoys serving guests. Heartland cuisine, made from scratch in our kitchen. Fresh fruits and vegetables, fresh trout, Amish bakeries, wood-burning fireplaces and whirlpool baths. Quiet, serene on 60 acres of woods and pastures.

APPLE OAT BRAN MUFFINS

2 1/4 cups oat bran cereal, uncooked
1/4 cup brown sugar
1 1/4 teaspoon cinnamon
1 tablespoon baking powder
1/2 cup skim milk
3/4 cup frozen apple juice concentrate
2 eggs (or substitute Egg Beaters)
2 tablespoons vegetable oil
1 medium apple, peeled and chopped
Optional:
1/4 cup nuts
1/4 cup raisins

Mix together cereal, brown sugar, cinnamon and baking powder. Blend milk, apple juice, eggs and oil. Add to dry ingredients. Fold in apples, nuts and raisins. Line muffin cups and fill to the top. Bake at 425° for 17 minutes. Store in plastic bag to retain moisture and softness. Yields 8 - 12 muffins.

Submitted by:

Harborside House
23 Gregory Street
Marblehead, Mass. 01945
(617) 631-1032
Susan Blake
$50.00 to $75.00

Continental plus breakfast
2 rooms
Children, over 10
No pets
No smoking

1840 home overlooks picturesque Marblehead Harbor. Water views from living room with cozy fireplace, period dining room, and sunny breakfast porch. Near shops, restaurants, historic sites and beach. Hostess is professional dressmaker and nationally-ranked Masters swimmer.

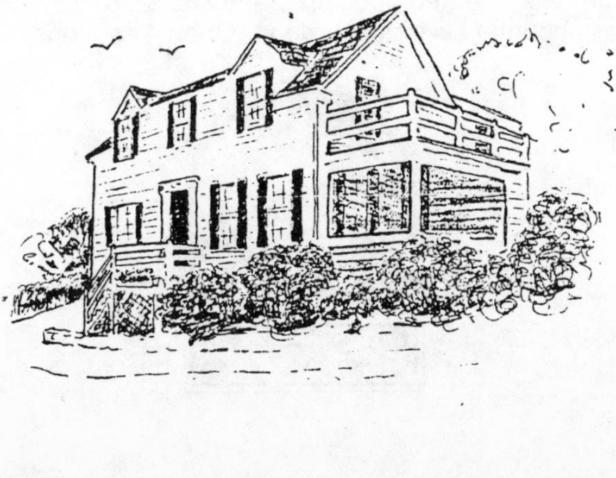

BANANA MUFFINS

1 cup whole wheat flour
3/4 cup white flour
1/2 cup rolled oats
1 cup sugar
1/2 teaspoon salt
3/4 teaspoon baking powder
1 teaspoon cinnamon
1 cup nuts (pecans or walnuts)
2 eggs
1 cup mashed ripe banana
1 teaspoon vanilla extract
1/4 cup milk, buttermilk, half & half, or cream
1 cup butter or margarine, melted

Combine all dry ingredients with a whisk. In separate bowl, beat eggs with whisk, then whisk in (in order) banana, vanilla, cream, and butter. Add this mixture to dry ingredients; stir to blend. Spoon into greased muffin tins. Sprinkle batter with a little granulated sugar. Bake 25 minutes at 375°. Makes 12 muffins.

Our breakfast cook says that this is an easy and very popular muffin at our inn.

Submitted by:

Wildflower Inn
Darling Hill Road
Lyndonville, Vermont 05851
(802) 626-8314
Jim & Mary O'Reilly
$75.00 to $150.00

Full breakfast
20 rooms, 16 private baths
Children allowed
No pets
No smoking
Mastercard & Visa

Family-oriented country inn set on a hilltop. Wonderful views in every direction. Afternoon "tea-time" with homemade specialties and gourmet dinners. Heated pool, spa, and sauna. Near Burke Mt. Ski Area. Cross-country ski from our door. Open 4 seasons.

BANANA ORANGE MUFFINS

1 1/2 cups flour
1/2 cup sugar
3 teaspoons baking powder
1/4 teaspoon salt
1 cup wheat germ
1 cup mashed bananas (2 small)
1/2 cup orange juice
1/4 cup vegetable oil
2 eggs

Sift together flour, sugar, baking powder and salt. Stir in wheat germ. Make a well in the center. In another bowl, combine banana, orange juice, oil and eggs. Add to flour mixture all at once. Stir enough to blend. Fill greased muffin tins 3/4 full. Bake at 400° for 20 - 25 minutes. Yield: 18 muffins.

A good-for-you breakfast muffin.

Submitted by:

The Inn At Woodchuck Hill Farm
Middletown Road
Grafton, Vermont 05146
(802) 843-2398
Anne & Frank Gabriel
$65.00 to $110.00

Continental breakfast
7 rooms, 5 private baths, plus barn dwelling
Children, over 10
No pets
Mastercard, Visa, Am Ex

Restored 1790 colonial farmhouse furnished in antiques. On hilltop with breathtaking view, swimming pond, fishing, walking trails, & 200 acres. Enjoy the peace and quiet of rural New England, and our own Antique Shop. Near tennis, bike rentals, galleries and unique shops.

BLUEBERRY LEMON YOGURT MUFFINS

2 cups all-purpose flour
1 teaspoon baking powder
1 teaspoon baking soda
1/4 teaspoon salt
1/4 cup sugar
1 1/4 cups plain yogurt
1/4 cup butter, melted
1 tablespoon lemon juice
1 tablespoon lemon peel, grated
1 cup blueberries

Crumb Topping:
Mix together 1/2 cup flour, 1/4 cup butter, & 1/4 cup sugar

Lemon Drizzle:
1/3 cup lemon juice
1/3 cup sugar
3 tablespoons water

Preheat oven to 375°. Butter muffin tins. In one bowl mix together the first four ingredients. In another bowl mix together the next five ingredients thoroughly. Add the dry ingredients and mix until just blended. Fold in blueberries. Spoon into muffin cups filling 3/4 full. Sprinkle with Crumb Topping. Bake 15 - 18 minutes. While muffins are baking, combine ingredients for Lemon Drizzle and heat to boil for one minute. Set aside. When muffins are done, remove from oven, pierce the top of each muffin, and, while still in the muffin tin, spoon about 2 teaspoonsful of Lemon Drizzle over each muffin. Let muffins absorb Drizzle a few minutes, then remove and serve warm. Makes 12 muffins.

Submitted by:

The Loom Room
RD 1, Box 1420
Leesport, Penn. 19533
(215) 926-3217
Gene & Mary Smith
$40.00 to $50.00

Full breakfast
3 rooms, 2 private baths
Children allowed
No pets
Restricted smoking

A restored 1812 farmhouse with 5 fireplaces and a 1760 log addition where Mary weaves custom clothing. The herb garden, shaded lawn and colonial gazebo create an atmosphere of relaxation. Near tennis, shopping outlets, great antiquing, golf, hiking, fishing and boating.

BUTTERMILK BRAN MUFFINS

3 cups 100% bran
1 cup boiling water
1 cup shortening
1 1/2 cups sugar
2 eggs
2 cups buttermilk
2 1/2 cups flour
2 1/2 teaspoons baking soda
2 1/2 teaspoons salt
3/4 cup raisins (if desired)

Pour boiling water over bran and set aside. Cream shortening & sugar. Add eggs, buttermilk, bran mixture, dry ingredients & raisins. Mix well. Bake in greased muffin tins at 375° for 20 minutes. Makes 3 dozen muffins. Batter keeps well in refrigerator up to 6 weeks.

Submitted by:

Longwood Inn
Route 9, Box 86
Marlboro, Vermont 05344
(802) 257-1545
Doug & Andrea Sauer
$85.00 to $135.00

Full breakfast
15 rooms, 13 private baths
Children, over 10
No pets
Restricted smoking
Mastercard, Visa, Am Ex

"An inn for all seasons," this 1790 colonial farmhouse offers it all -- the rainbow colors of Autumn, downhill or cross-country skiing in Winter, the freshness of Vermont in Spring, and the world famous Marlboro Music Festival in Summer. American cuisine rated 3-stars; or simply rest & relax.

CAPPUCCINO CHIP MUFFINS

- **2 cups all purpose flour**
- **1/2 cup sugar**
- **2 1/2 teaspoons baking powder**
- **2 teaspoons instant espresso coffee powder**
- **1/2 teaspoon ground cinnamon**
- **1/2 teaspoon salt**
- **1 cup milk (scalded and cooled)**
- **1/2 cup butter, melted and cooled**
- **1 egg, lightly beaten**
- **1 teaspoon vanilla**
- **3/4 cup semisweet chocolate mini-chips**

Preheat oven to 375°. Grease twelve 3" x 11/4" muffin cups. In large bowl, stir together flour, sugar, baking powder, espresso coffee powder, salt, and cinnamon. In another bowl, stir together milk, butter, egg, and vanilla until blended. Make a well in center of dry ingredients; add milk mixture and stir just to combine. Stir in chips. Spoon batter into prepared muffin cups, bake15 - 20 minutes or until cake tester inserted in center of one muffin comes out clean. These muffins freeze well. Makes 12 muffins.

Origin: Developed by Nadine for a special 20th Anniversary celebration for Ralph Lauren Polo Company.

Submitted by:

The Wedgwood Inn
111 W. Bridge Street
New Hope, Penn. 18938
(215) 862-2570
Nadine Silnutzer &
Carl Glassman

Continental plus breakfast
12 rooms, 10 private baths
Children, over 8
Pets allowed, with restrictions
No smoking

Voted 1989 "Inn of the Year" by inn guidebook readers. On 2 lovely landscaped acres; only steps from the village center. Complimentary horse-drawn carriage rides on Pennsylvania Dutch surries. Two gazebos, hammocks, croquet and a 3-sided Victorian veranda.

CARROT AND RAISIN MUFFINS

1 cup all-purpose flour
1 cup whole wheat flour
2 teaspoons baking powder
1/4 teaspoon salt
1/4 teaspoon pumpkin pie spice
1/4 cup finely shredded carrots
1/3 cup raisins
1 egg, beaten
1 cup skim milk
2 tablespoons vegetable oil
2 tablespoons molasses
Vegetable cooking spray

Combine first 5 ingredients in a large bowl, stir in carrots and raisins. Make a well in the center of mixture. Combine egg, milk, oil and molasses, stir well. Add to dry ingredients, stirring just until moistened. Spoon into muffin pans coated with spray, filling 3/4 full. Bake at 425° for 15 minutes. Makes 1 dozen.

Origin: An old family recipe.

Submitted by:

Pine Ridge Inn
2893 West Pine Street
Mount Airy, N.C. 27030
(919) 789-5034
Ellen & Manford Haxton
$50.00 to $85.00

Continental breakfast
6 rooms, 5 private baths
Children allowed
No pets
Restricted smoking
Mastercard, Visa, Am Ex

Pine Ridge Inn is a grand English-style mansion set on eight acres at the foot of the Blue Ridge Mountains. This 10,000 square foot inn prides itself on providing many amenities. Nautilus room with hot tub, outdoor swimming pool, gourmet dining in restaurant.

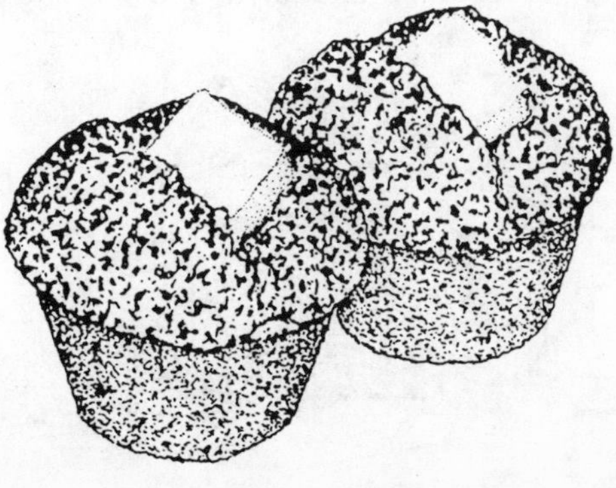

CHEESE-STUFFED PECAN PUMPKIN MUFFINS

2 cups flour
1/2 cup sugar
1/2 cup chopped pecans
1 1/2 teaspoons pumpkin pie spice
1 tablespoon baking powder
1/2 teaspoon salt
2 eggs slightly beaten
3/4 cup canned pumpkin
1/2 cup butter or margarine, melted
1/4 cup sour cream
1 package (3 ozs) cream cheese, cubed
Optional:
Cinnamon-sugar to taste
Wheat germ to taste

In large bowl mix flour, sugar, pecans, pumpkin pie spice, baking powder and salt. In small bowl mix eggs, pumpkin, butter and sour cream. Add to flour mixture; stir just until blended. Fill greased or paper lined pans 1/3 full; place cream cheese cube in the center of each and add more batter. Sprinkle top with cinnamon-sugar / wheat germ mixture if you wish. Bake at 400° for 25 minutes. Makes 12 muffins.

Submitted by:

BarnaGate Bed & Breakfast
637 Wesley Avenue
Ocean City, N. J. 08226
(609) 391-9366
Frank and Lois Barna
$50.00 to $70.00

Continental breakfast
5 rooms, 1 private bath
Children, over 10
No pets
Restricted smoking
Mastercard & Visa

A seashore country Victorian decorated in antiques, with paddle fans in each room as well as quilts on the beds. Near Atlantic City and Cape May. Centrally located within walking distance of beaches, downtown shopping, restaurants and various sporting activities.

CHEF ELMER'S BREAKFAST JELLY MUFFINS

2 cups flour
3 teaspoons baking powder
1/2 teaspoon salt
1 cup sugar
1/2 cup salad oil
1/2 teaspoon vanilla
1 cup half & half
Jam
Grape Nuts

Mix all ingredients except jam and Grape Nuts. Grease muffin tins and fill 1/4 full. Take 1 teaspoon of jam and spoon on top of batter. Cover with remaining batter. Sprinkle top with Grape Nuts. Bake at 400° for 25 minutes. Makes 12 large muffins.

Submitted by:

Red Hill Inn
RFD 1, Box 99M
Centre Harbor,
New Hampshire 03226
(603) 279-7001
Rick Miller & Don Leavitt
$65.00 to $125.00

Full breakfast
21 rooms, 21 private baths
Children allowed
No pets
Smoking allowed
Mastercard, Visa, Am Ex,
Diner's Club, Carte Blanche

Red Hill Inn is a restored, turn of the century mansion on 60 acres overlooking Squam Lake and the White Mountains. Gourmet restaurant, Runabout Lounge. Many rooms with fireplaces and some with jacuzzis. Cross-country ski trails. Open all year long.

CHERIE'S DOOR COUNTY CHERRY MUFFINS

- 4 cups flour
- 1 cup sugar
- 2 tablespoons baking powder
- 1 teaspoon cinnamon
- 3 cups frozen & rinsed Door County cherries
- 1 cup melted butter
- 1 cup milk
- 4 eggs
- 1 teaspoon vanilla

Topping:

- 1 cup flour
- 1/2 cup sugar
- 1/3 cup soft butter
- 1/2 teaspoon cinnamon

Preheat oven to 425°. Combine dry ingredients and blend. In separate bowl, toss 1 tablespoon of dry ingredients with cherries. Mix butter, milk, eggs and vanilla. Add to dry ingredients and stir until well moistened. Stir in cherries. Spoon batter into muffin tins to about 3/4 full. Blend topping ingredients together and sprinkle over batter. Bake for 15 - 20 minutes. Makes 2 dozen.

Submitted by:

White Lace Inn
16 N. Fifth Avenue
Sturgeon Bay, Wisconsin
54235
(414) 743-1105
Bonnie & Dennis Statz
$65.00 to $135.00

Continental breakfast
15 rooms, 15 private baths
Children, over 12
No pets
Restricted smoking
Mastercard, Visa, Am Ex

3 historic houses connected by a winding garden pathway. Each guest room decorated with fine antiques. Some with double whirlpool tubs or a fireplace, cozy down comforters and the hospitality to keep people coming back.

CRANBERRY-NUT MUFFINS

2 cups flour
3/4 cup sugar
3 teaspoons baking powder
1 teaspoon salt
3/4 teaspoon cinnamon
1/4 teaspoon nutmeg
1/4 cup chopped walnuts
2 well-beaten eggs
2/3 cup milk
1/3 cup vegetable oil
1 1/2 cups fresh cranberries, chopped & rinsed to remove seeds
1 cup whole wheat cereal flakes
2 tablespoons sugar
1/4 teaspoon cinnamon

In large bowl, stir together first seven ingredients. Set aside. In another bowl, combine eggs, milk and oil. Add to dry ingredients and stir until moistened. Fold in cranberries and cereal. Fill muffin cups. Combine sugar and cinnamon and sprinkle over batter. Bake at 400° for 20 - 25 minutes. Makes 12 muffins.

Submitted by:

Tiffany Inn
206 Algoma Boulevard
Oshkosh, Wisconsin 54901
(414) 231-0909
Mary & Tom Rossow
$55.00 to $109.00

Continental plus breakfast
11 rooms, 11 private baths
Children allowed
No pets
Restricted smoking
Mastercard, Visa,
Am Ex, Discover

Antique appointed rooms in turn of the century home. Queen-sized beds, remote-controlled color cable television, and phones. Located near downtown: fine dining, outlet shopping, & museums. Home of Experimental Aircraft Association. Near boating, fishing, & swimming.

DATE MUFFINS

1 pkg. dates (12 ounces)
1 1/2 cups boiling water
1/2 teaspoon baking soda
1/2 cup butter
1 1/2 cups sugar
2 eggs
2 cups sifted flour
1/2 teaspoon vanilla
1 cup broken nuts

Topping:
Glazed cherries, red and green

Combine dates and boiling water. Add soda, set aside. Cream butter and sugar. Add eggs, beating well. Add date mixture and flour, blend well. Add vanilla and nuts, mix. Pour into small, well-greased muffin pans. Top each muffin with 1/2 red and 1/2 green glazed cherries. Bake at 350° for 8 - 15 minutes until toothpick tests clean. Yields 18.

Origin: Brought from Chicago in l927 by Mrs. Harding's mother, Mary Armstrong Helm. This is now a Christmas tradition in our family.

Submitted by:

Harding House
Bed & Breakfast
219 North 20th Street
St. Joseph, Missouri 64501
(816) 232-7020
Glen & Mary Harding
$30.00 to $45.00

Full breakfast
4 rooms, 1 private bath
Children allowed
No pets
Restricted smoking
Mastercard, Visa, Am Ex

A renovated turn of the century home, with elegant oak woodwork and pocket doors, beveled glass windows and antiques collected for 40 years. Each bedroom is unique: the Blue Room has an iron baby bed; the Eastlake Room has a romantic working fireplace.

DORIS' DELICIOUS BRAN MUFFINS

2 cups Kellogg's Bran Buds
2 cups boiling water
1 1/2 cups margarine
3 cups sugar
4 eggs
1 quart buttermilk
5 cups flour
5 teaspoons soda
1 teaspoon salt
4 cups Kellogg's All Bran
2 cups raisins or dates, if desired

Mix & cool Bran Buds & boiling water. Cream margarine, sugar, eggs and buttermilk. Combine Bran Buds mixture and margarine mixture and add remaining ingredients. Stir and store in gallon jar in refrigerator overnight before baking. Bake at 400° for 20 - 25 minutes. Will last up to 4 weeks in refrigerator. Makes 36 muffins.

Origin: From Doris' daughter, Sue Mahoney.

Submitted by:

Hill Top Bed & Breakfast
5832 Church Road
Ferndale, Washington 98248
(206) 384-3619
Doris Matz
$39.00 to $49.00

Continental plus breakfast
3 rooms, 2 private baths
Children allowed
No pets
Restricted smoking
Mastercard & Visa

We overlook Mt. Baker and the Cascade Mountain Range, and are near state and local parks. An especially nice view from our patio. Large comfortable rooms in Early American decor, with sitting areas, 1 with fireplace, four-poster beds, and quilts made by your hostess.

DOUBLE CHOCOLATE CHIP MUFFINS

1 egg
1/4 cup vegetable oil
2 cups all-purpose flour
1 cup chocolate powder
1/2 cup sugar
2 teaspoons baking powder
1 teaspoon cinnamon
1 cup chocolate chips
1 cup milk

Mix together the egg and oil. Combine dry ingredients making sure the chocolate chips are well-coated. Add the egg mixture to the dry ingredients and slowly stir in the milk until the batter is moist. Do not overmix. Sprinkle the tops of muffins with sugar and bake in preheated 350° oven for 20 - 25 minutes. Serve warm with lots of butter. Makes 12 muffins.

These are an Old Cape House featured breakfast treat.

Submitted by:

Old Cape House
108 Old Main Street
Bass River (Cape Cod)
Massachusetts 02664
(508) 398-1068
George & Linda Arthur
$50.00 to $65.00

Continental plus breakfast
4 rooms, 4 private baths
Children, over 15
No pets
No smoking

Bed and breakfast in the English tradition, in an 1820 Greek Revival house with beamed ceilings and comfortable furnishings. Breakfast features homemade muffins, coffee cakes and fresh fruit. Close to beaches, restaurants, and all Cape attractions.

DR. FOWLER'S ORANGE MUFFINS

- **2 3/4 cups flour**
- **4 teaspoons baking powder**
- **1/4 teaspoon salt**
- **1 tablespoon grated orange rind**
- **3 eggs**
- **1/3 cup melted and cooled butter**
- **1 cup milk**
- **1/4 cup honey**
- **1/4 cup sugar (optional)**
- **Orange marmalade**
- **Ricotta**

Sift together the flour, baking powder, salt and orange rind. In a separate bowl, beat eggs. Add butter, milk, honey and sugar (if desired) to eggs. Mix wet and dry ingredients together, stir as little as possible. Fill greased muffin tins 1/2 full. Spoon 1/2 teaspoon each of ricotta & marmalade. Fill muffin tins with remaining batter. Bake at 400° for 10 minutes. Reduce temperature to 350° and bake for 10 minutes more. Yield: 1 dozen.

Submitted by:

The Fowler House
Bed & Breakfast
P.O. Box 432 Plains Road
Moodus, Connecticut 06469
(203) 873-8906
Barbara Ally & Paul Seals
$65.00 to $90.00

Continental plus breakfast
6 rooms, 4 private baths
Children, over 12
No pets
Restricted smoking
Mastercard & Visa

An 1890 Queen Anne Victorian with original stained glass windows, 8 working fireplaces, and ornately carved woodwork. Afternoon tea, concierge and turndown service. Featured in Better Homes & Gardens: 1001 Home Decorating Ideas, and selected as the Yankee Magazine Travel Guide favorite Connecticut B&B.

FORSYTH TROPICAL MUFFINS

2 1/2 cups unprocessed bran
1 1/3 cups flour
2 1/2 teaspoons baking soda
1/2 teaspoon salt
1 cup raisins
1 cup shredded coconut
2 eggs
1/2 cup buttermilk
1/2 cup vegetable oil
1 cup mashed ripe bananas
1/2 cup honey

In large bowl combine bran, flour, baking soda, salt, raisins and coconut. Mix to blend. In small bowl beat eggs. Add remaining ingredients to dry mixture. Mix just until blended. Bake in 375° oven 20 - 25 minutes. Yield: 18 - 24 muffins.

Submitted by:

The Forsyth Park Inn
102 West Hall Street
Savannah, Georgia 31401
(912) 233-6800
Hal and Virginia Sullivan
$60.00 to $145.00

Continental breakfast
10 rooms, 10 private baths
Children allowed
No pets
Smoking allowed
Mastercard, Visa, Am Ex

1893 Queen Anne Victorian in country's largest historic district. King & queen four poster beds, fireplaces, antiques, whirlpool tubs, 16' ceilings, 14' oak-carved doors, & beautiful detailing. Near a 23-acre park, museums, forts, beach, golf, tennis, fine restaurants & shops.

FRESH BLACKBERRY MUFFINS

1/2 cup unsalted butter, room temperature
1 1/4 cups sugar
2 large eggs, room temperature
2 cups all purpose flour
1/2 teaspoon salt
2 teaspoons baking powder
1/2 cup milk
2 cups fresh or frozen blackberries, thawed and drained
4 teaspoons sugar

Preheat oven to 375°. Grease 18 - 1/2 cup muffin cups. Using electric mixer, cream 1/2 cup butter and 1 1/4 cups sugar in large bowl until light. Add eggs 1 at a time, beating well after each addition. Sift flour, salt and baking powder into small bowl. Mix dry ingredients into butter mixture alternately with milk. Fold in berries. Divide batter among prepared cups. Sprinkle with 4 teaspoons sugar. Bake about 30 minutes, or until tester comes out clean. Serve warm or at room temperature. Makes 18 muffins.

Origin: My mother's Boston Blueberry Muffin recipe, modified for Northwest berries.

Submitted by:

White Swan Guest House
1388 Moore Road
Mt. Vernon, Wash. 98273
(206) 445-6805
Peter Goldfarb
$55.00 to $85.00

Continental breakfast
4 rooms, 1 private bath
Children allowed
No pets
No smoking
Mastercard & Visa

A storybook Victorian farmhouse, 6 miles from the fishing village and historic town of La Conner. Surounded by English style flower gardens, quilts and samplers fill the recently restored 1898 home. Peace and quiet and a country road.

FRESH GINGER MUFFINS

3 ounces unpeeled ginger root
1/4 cup sugar
1 cup sugar
2 tablespoons lemon zest
1 stick margarine
2 eggs
3/4 cup buttermilk
2 cups flour
1/2 teaspoon salt
3/4 teaspoon baking soda

Process ginger root fine and mix with 1/4 cup sugar. Cook slowly together until all the sugar is melted and then 1 minute more. Stir. Do not leave it; it burns easily. Set aside. Process together 1 cup sugar, lemon zest, margarine, and eggs. Mix in buttermilk, but do not process. In another bowl, sift together flour, salt and baking soda. Add processed mixture and cooked ginger mix to the dry. Stir until well mixed. Bake at 375° for 18 minutes, or until done. For an added treat, fold in 1 cup fresh blueberries that have been rolled in 2 tablespoons sugar. Makes 12 - 14 muffins.

Origin: This recipe was born from my mother's love of ginger.

Submitted by:

Nauset House Inn
Box 774, 143 Beach Road
East Orleans, Mass. 02643
(508) 255-2195
Diane & Al Johnson
$55.00 to $90.00

Full or continental breakfast
14 rooms, 9 private baths
Children, over 12
No pets
Restricted smoking
Mastercard & Visa

A place where the gentle amenities of life are still observed. On Cape Cod, within walking distance of wonderful beach. Old-fashioned country breakfast; our unique turn-of-the-century conservatory, filled with plants and wicker furniture, helps to make your visit memorable.

FRESH GINGER PEACHY MUFFINS

- 1 cup all-purpose flour
- 3/4 cup whole wheat flour
- 1/4 cup oat bran
- 1 1/2 teaspoons baking powder
- 1/2 teaspoon baking soda
- 1 teaspoon ground ginger
- 1 egg
- 2/3 cup brown sugar, lightly packed
- 3/4 cup buttermilk
- 1/4 cup corn oil
- 1/2 teaspoon almond extract
- 1 cup diced fresh peaches
- Cinnamon-sugar mixture

Heat oven to 375°. Spray a muffin pan with non-stick spray. Set aside. In a medium bowl, combine the flours, oat bran, baking powder, soda and ginger. Mix well. In another bowl, beat egg lightly; stir in sugar, buttermilk, oil, and almond extract. Blend well. Add flour mixture and gently fold until moistened. Fold in peaches. Fill muffin cups 3/4 full. Sprinkle with cinnamon sugar and garnish with pecan half. Bake 20 - 25 minutes or until toothpick comes out clean. Makes 1 dozen large or 30 mini-muffins.

Origin: Missouri produces many delicious peach varieties. This is our concoction to take advantage of the prodigious crop!

Submitted by:

The Admiral Coontz House
303 N. Sixth Street
Hannibal, Missouri 63401
(314) 221-7244 or 221-3544
Toto & Charles Rendlen
$45.00

Continental plus breakfast
2 rooms, 2 private baths
Children allowed
Pets allowed
Restricted smoking
Personal checks accepted

A lovely pre-Civil War brick Neo-classic house on the National Register. Flower-filled porches, antiques, central air-conditioning, common room with television, games & books. We serve delicious breakfasts. Walk to Mark Twain boyhood home and Riverfront.

FRESH PEACH MUFFINS

2 cups white all purpose flour
1 cup whole wheat flour
1/2 teaspoon salt
Pinch of baking soda
1 tablespoon baking powder
1 stick unsalted butter softened
1 1/8 cups sugar
1 teaspoon vanilla
2 eggs
2 cups fresh peaches, skinned and cut in small pieces
1/2 cup milk & 1/2 cup peach or apricot nectar, mixed (or all milk)

In medium bowl mix together flours, salt, baking soda and baking powder. In large bowl cream butter and sugar. Add vanilla and eggs and mix until smooth. Alternately add flour mixture and milk (or milk mixture) to butter mixture, mixing just until moistened. Do not overmix. Stir in peaches. (Note: Place skinned, cut-up peaches on cookie sheet and freeze for about 1 hour. They will not brown and will bake better.) Bake at 400° for 18 - 23 minutes. Makes 14 large muffins, 18 medium muffins.

Submitted by:

The Barrington Inn
P.O. Box 397, Beach Avenue
Block Island, Rhode Island
49858
(401) 466-5510
Joan & Howard Ballard
$85.00 to $125.00

Continental breakfast
6 rooms, 6 private baths
Children, over 12
No pets
Smoking allowed
Mastercard & Visa

A century-old, recently renovated Victorian farmhouse on Block Island. Guest rooms offer spectacular water and sunset views. Open April through November, reasonable off-season rates. Block Island is sometimes referred to as "The Bermuda of the North."

GIANT CRANBERRY ORANGE MUFFINS

1 cup chopped fresh or frozen cranberries
1/4 cup sugar
2 teaspoons freshly grated orange peel
2 cups flour
1/2 cup sugar
2 teaspoons baking powder
1/2 teaspoon salt
1/2 cup oil
1/2 cup orange juice
2 eggs
1/2 cup chopped nuts

Preheat oven to 375°. Grease giant muffin tin. Mix cranberries, 1/4 cup sugar and orange peel; set aside. Combine all dry ingredients except nuts. In separate bowl, mix oil, juice, and eggs. Pour liquid mix all at once into dry ingredients and stir just until moistened. Fold in cranberry mix and nuts. Put into muffin tin. Bake 25 minutes. Cool in pan 5 minutes. Makes 6 giant muffins.

This recipe's a natural for Cape Cod!

Submitted by:

Four Winds
345 High Bank Road
South Yarmouth, Mass. 02664
(508) 394-4182
Mary & Walt Crowell
$50.00 to $100.00

Continental breakfast
1 room with private bath, plus cottage & carriage house
Children allowed
No pets
Smoking allowed

A charming 1712 sea captain's homestead. Enjoy beaches, bicycle & nature trails, quaint antique, craft & gift shops, river & ocean fishing, swimming, golfing, tennis, museums & art galleries, and many fine restaurants and pubs, with an abundance of peace and quiet.

GRAPE NUT MUFFINS

2 cups Grape Nuts with
3 cups boiling water
4 eggs, beaten
3 cups sugar
1 quart buttermilk
1 cup oil
3 cups Grape Nuts
5 cups flour
5 teaspoons soda
2 teaspoons salt
1 1/2 cups raisins

Let 2 cups Grape Nuts with 3 cups boiling water soak while mixing other ingredients. Beat eggs, sugar, buttermilk, oil and Grape Nuts. Mix flour, soda and salt, and add to other ingredients. Stir until flour mixture is mixed well. Add Grape Nuts and boiling water. Mix well. Add raisins. Bake at 400° for 20 minutes. Will keep for 6 weeks in refrigerator. Makes 4 to 6 dozen muffins.

Origin: We created this very favorite recipe of our guests. Originally used Raisin Bran, but we like Grape Nuts instead.

Submitted by:

Swedish Country Inn
112 W. Lincoln
Lindsborg, Kansas 67456
(913) 227-2985
Virginia Brunsell
$40.00 to $70.00

Full breakfast
19 rooms, 19 private baths
Children allowed
No pets
No smoking
Mastercard & Visa

A restored hotel with imported Swedish pine furniture throughout and hand-quilted quilts on the beds. Sauna and tandem or regular bicycles for guests to ride. Telephones available in the lobby only. Nearby are art galleries, shops, museum, tennis, swimming & parks.

HIGH-TOP MUFFINS

1 3/4 cups flour
1/4 cup sugar
2 teaspoons baking powder
1/2 teaspoon baking soda
1/2 teaspoon salt
3/4 cup buttermilk
1/3 cup vegetable oil
1 egg
1/2 cup any dried or fresh fruit

Combine dry ingredients. Combine wet ingredients, mix together well. Fold in fruit. Bake at 425° for 20 - 25 minutes. Makes approximately 12 muffins.

Submitted by:

Crook' Jaw Inn
186 Main St. Route 6A
Yarmouth Port, Mass. 02675
(508) 362-6111
Don Spagnolia & Ed Shedlock
$85.00 to $99.00

Full breakfast
7 rooms, 7 private baths
Children allowed
No pets
Smoking allowed
Mastercard, Visa, Am Ex

Crook' Jaw Inn is listed in the National Register of Historic Places. Choice of dinner menu and full breakfast are included in the nightly rate, which may be enjoyed in our intimate dining room or on the patio of our English country garden. Picnic baskets available for day trips.

JOAN'S OAT BRAN MUFFINS

1 cup flour
1 cup oat bran
2 teaspoons baking soda
1 teaspoon baking powder
1/2 teaspoon salt
2 teaspoons cinnamon
1 cup brown sugar
1 1/2 cups shredded carrots
1/2 cup raisins
2 large apples, shredded
1 cup chopped nuts
1/4 cup oil
1/2 cup skim milk
2 eggs or 4 egg whites
1 teaspoon vanilla

Combine flour, oat bran, baking soda, baking powder, salt, cinnamon and brown sugar. Then add carrots, raisins, apples and nuts to dry ingredients and make a well in the center. Add the remaining ingredients (oil, skim milk, eggs or whites and vanilla) and mix until blended. Bake at 375° for 18 - 20 minutes in muffin tins.

Origin: In Joan's family for many years; our guests' favorite muffin. We served them 3 times before there was one leftover for us to taste.

Submitted by:

The Westchester House
P.O. Box 944
102 Lincoln Avenue
Saratoga Springs, N.Y. 12866
(518) 587-7613
Bob & Stephanie Melvin
$55.00 to $90.00

Continental plus breakfast
7 rooms, 5 private baths
Children, over 12
No pets
Restricted smoking
Mastercard, Visa, Am Ex

1885 Queen Anne Victorian built by master carpenter Almeron King. Savor the serenity of a bygone era, part of Saratoga's gilded past and glittering present. Walk to museums, restaurants and shops. Nearby are Spa State Park, concerts, tennis, golf, boating, and antiquing.

LEMON GINGER MUFFINS

- **1 large lemon**
- **1 section ginger root (3")**
- **1 cup plus 3 tablespoons sugar**
- **1 stick butter**
- **2 large eggs**
- **2 cups flour**
- **1 1/2 teaspoons baking soda**
- **1 cup plain yogurt**

Carefully peel the lemon and the ginger root and cut into several pieces. Place in food processor with steel blade. Add 1/2 cup sugar and process. In a large bowl, beat softened butter and 1/2 cup sugar. Beat in eggs. Add processed ginger root and lemon peel mixture. In another bowl, mix flour and baking soda. Fold flour and yogurt into lemon-egg mixture. Spoon into greased muffin pan. Bake in 375° oven about 20 minutes. Squeeze the lemon juice from the peeled lemon. Brush onto muffin tops after they are baked. Sprinkle remaining sugar on each muffin. Makes 12 medium muffins.

Submitted by:

Durham House
Bed & Breakfast
921 Heights Boulevard
Houston, Texas 77008
(713) 868-4654
Marguerite Swanson
$40.00 to $60.00

Full breakfast
5 rooms, 3 1/2 private baths
Children, over 12
No pets
No smoking
Mastercard & Visa

Queen Anne style Victorian on National Register of Historic Places, just 10 minutes from downtown Houston. Bicycle-built-for-two, parlor player piano, screened-in back porch and garden gazebo. We also host weddings, receptions, parties, and murder mystery dinners.

MINCEMEAT APPLE MUFFINS

2 cups flour
2 teaspoons baking powder
1/2 teaspoon soda
1 teaspoon salt
1 teaspoon cinnamon
1/2 teaspoon nutmeg
1/4 teaspoon ginger
1 cup sugar
1 cup mincemeat
1/2 cup milk
2 eggs
1 cup oil
1 medium apple, peeled, cored and diced

Combine dry ingredients and mix well. Add the rest of the ingredients and mix just until blended. Pour into greased muffin tin, bake at 350° for 20 - 25 minutes. Yield: 1 dozen muffins.

Submitted by:

Seven Gables Inn
555 Ocean View Boulevard
Pacific Grove, California 93950
(408) 372-4341
The Flatley Family
$85.00 to $165.00

Continental plus breakfast
14 rooms, 14 private baths
Children, over 12 preferred
No pets
No smoking
Mastercard & Visa

Century-old Victorian home built at the edge of Monterey Bay. Victorian-era antiques provide an air of comfortable elegance. Sit-down breakfast in dining room; 4:00 tea served on sunporch with sweeping views of the Pacific. Near Cannery Row, Big Sur, golfing, bicycling and sailing.

MORNING GLORY MUFFINS

3 eggs
1 cup vegetable oil
1/2 teaspoon vanilla
1 1/4 cups sugar
2 cups flour
2 teaspoons soda
1/2 teaspoon salt
2 teaspoons cinnamon
1 1/2 cups shredded carrots
2 large apples, chopped
3/4 cup shredded coconut
1/2 cup raisins
1/2 cup pecans

Cream eggs, add oil and vanilla, beat until well blended. Add sugar. Add sifted flour with soda, salt, cinnamon. Beat well and add carrots, apples, coconut, raisins, & pecans. Pour into greased muffin tins and bake at 375° for 18 - 20 minutes. Makes 10 medium muffins.

Origin: My son's college friend told me it was one of Tennessee's favorites, and now it's one of mine.

Submitted by:

Middlefield Guest House
R.D. #3, Box 614, Rte. 166N
Cooperstown, N.Y. 13326
(607) 286-7056 or
(201) 670-8587
Jacqueline Dann
$40.00 to $55.00

Full breakfast
4 rooms
Children, over 6 (able to sleep in separate rooms)
Restricted smoking

1823 farmhouse, 6 miles from Baseball Hall of Fame. Clean air, comfortable, cozy. We are near riding, an airport for glider and plane rides, and feature good foods, and a friendly atmosphere. We are in our second year of operation, and establishing a return clientele.

MRS. C'S LEMON MUFFINS

1/2 cup butter
2/3 cup sugar
2 eggs
1/2 cup milk
1/2 cup sour cream
2 cups flour
2 teaspoons baking powder
1/4 teaspoon salt
1/2 cup lemon curd

Cream together butter and sugar until light and fluffy. Add eggs and beat well. Add milk and sour cream and mix well. Combine dry ingredients and add to above mixture. Fold in lemon curd. Spoon batter into greased muffin cups until 2/3 full. Bake at 350° for 20 minutes. Yield: 12 muffins.

Origin: My mother, "Mrs. C.", has been baking these muffins here in sunny San Diego since the 1950's. All of her friends and our guests love them, as they're light, tart, and delicious.

Submitted by:

Heritage Park
Bed & Breakfast Inn
2470 Heritage Park Row
San Diego, California 92110
(619) 295-7088
Lori Chandler
$75.00 to $115.00

Full breakfast
9 rooms, 7 private baths
Children, over 12
No pets
Restricted smoking
Mastercard & Visa

1889 Queen Anne mansion, restored to its original splendor. On a 7-acre Victorian park in historic Old Town, with antiques, and exquisite candlelight dinners. 10 minutes from International Airport, San Diego Zoo, and Sea World. Plenty of free, off-street parking.

OATMEAL BLUEBERRY MUFFINS

- 1 cup quick oats
- 1 cup sour milk
- 1 cup flour
- 1 teaspoon baking powder
- 1/2 teaspoon salt
- 1/2 teaspoon baking soda
- 3/4 cup brown sugar
- 1 egg, beaten
- 1/4 cup melted butter
- 1 cup blueberries

Combine oats and sour milk, let stand. Combine flour, baking powder, salt, soda, and brown sugar. Stir well to blend. Add egg and melted butter, mix well. Add oats to mixture all at once. Stir just until moistened. Fold in blueberries. Fill well-greased muffin tins 3/4 full. Bake at 400° for 15 - 22 minutes. Makes approximately 12 large muffins.

Submitted by:

Clown 'N Country
Bed & Breakfast
Rural Route, Box 115
Madrid, Nebraska 69150
(308) 326-4378
Ford & Lou Cornelius
$25.00 to $35.00

Full & continental breakfast
2 rooms, 1 private bath
Children allowed
No pets
Restricted smoking

Clown 'N Country is located on a quiet, working farm in western Nebraska. We offer breakfast of your choice, indoor swimming, hot tub, croquet court and horseshoes, along with our clown collection. A warm welcome is our specialty.

OLD-FASHIONED MOLASSES MUFFINS

4 cups flour
2 cups sugar
1 cup Crisco
2 cups boiling water
1 cup baking molasses
2 teaspoons baking soda

Mix flour, sugar and Crisco together. Set aside 1 cup for crumbs for topping. Add to flour mixture the remaining ingredients. Mix by hand or electric mixer. Spray Pam in muffin tins, add batter and finally, crumbs on top. Bake at 350° for 25 - 30 minutes. Makes 36 medium muffins, or can also be baked as a cake.

Origin: This was my great-grandmother's recipe. Very moist.

Submitted by:

200 South Street Inn
200 South Street
Charlottesville, Virginia 22901
(804) 979-0200
Donna Deibert
$85.00 to $160.00

Continental breakfast
20 rooms, 20 private baths
Children allowed
No pets
Smoking allowed
Mastercard, Visa, Am Ex

Two restored houses built in the 1800's. We feature English and Belgian antiques throughout, with whirlpool tubs, fireplaces, canopy beds and private living room suites. Located in Historic District, just 4 miles to Monticello. Afternoon tea.

PEANUT BUTTER & CHOCOLATE CHIP MUFFINS

1/4 pound butter
1/3 cup sugar
1 egg
1 1/2 cups all-purpose flour
2 tablespoons baking powder
1 teaspoon baking soda
2 tablespoons creamy peanut butter
1/2 - 3/4 cup milk
1/2 cup semi-sweet chocolate chips

Preheat oven to 400°. Soften butter and blend with sugar until smooth, then beat in egg. Set aside. Mix flour, baking powder, and baking soda. Add peanut butter to butter, sugar, egg mixture and blend until smooth. Add this to flour mixture, and slowly add the milk, stirring to make sure all the flour becomes a creamy texture. Add chocolate chips and stir. Put into greased muffin tins and bake 20 - 30 minutes until toothpick comes out dry and muffins begin to brown. Makes 8 - 12 muffins.

Origin: Max Comins, innkeeper, created it for his 5 year old son.

Submitted by:

Kedron Valley Inn
Route 106
South Woodstock, Vermont 05071
(802) 457-1473
Max & Merrily Comins
$98.00 to $159.00

Full breakfast
28 rooms, 28 private baths
Children allowed
Pets allowed
Smoking allowed
Mastercard, Visa, Am Ex

In continuous operation since 1828. Individually appointed guest rooms, with antique quilts, 14 queen size canopy beds and 7 working fireplaces. Nestled in the foothills of the Green Mountains, with a 1-1/2 acre spring-fed swimming pond & beach! French cuisine nightly.

PIONEER APPLE MUFFINS

2 cups sifted flour
1/2 cup sugar
Pinch of salt
4 teaspoons baking powder
1/2 teaspoon cinnamon
1 cup peeled, chopped apples
1 well-beaten egg
1 cup tepid milk
1/4 cup butter
Cinnamon-sugar mixture

Sift flour, sugar, salt, baking powder and cinnamon. Combine with apples. Make a deep well in center of dry ingredients. Combine egg, milk and melted butter. Mix well with fork until ingredients are barely mixed. Do not beat. Batter will be lumpy. Drop batter by tablespoons into greased muffin tin (or paper cups). Mix together 2 tablespoons sugar and 1/2 teaspoon cinnamon. Sprinkle over muffins. Bake at 400° for 20 minutes or until done. Makes about 18 medium size muffins.

Origin: From a very old cookbook in the late 1800's.

Submitted by:

Peterson's Bed & Breakfast
95 North, 300 West
P.O. Box 142
Monroe, Utah 84754
(801) 527-4830
Mary Ann Peterson
$40.00 to $55.00
Children, $10.00 each extra

Full breakfast
3 rooms, 2 private baths
Children allowed, well-behaved only
No pets
No smoking

Over 100 years old, but now modernized, with country decor. Main suite: king size featherbed, refrigerator, English toiletries, in-room coffee, tea and cocoa. Adjoins Mural room with twin beds. Third bedroom has double canopy bed & refrigerator; television in rooms.

PUMPKIN CHOCOLATE CHIP MUFFINS

- **1 2/3 cups all purpose flour**
- **1 cup granulated sugar**
- **1 tablespoon pumpkin pie spice**
- **1/4 teaspoon baking powder**
- **1 teaspoon baking soda**
- **1/4 teaspoon salt**
- **2 large eggs**
- **1 cup plain pumpkin (1/2 of 1 lb. can)**
- **1/2 cup butter, melted**
- **1 cup chocolate chips (6 ounces)**

Preheat oven to 350°. Grease muffin cups or use foil or paper baking cups. Thoroughly mix flour, sugar, pie spice, baking powder, baking soda and salt in large bowl. Break eggs into another bowl. Add pumpkin and butter and whisk until well blended. Stir in chocolate chips. Pour over dry ingredients and fold in until dry ingredients are just moistened. Bake 20 - 25 minutes. Makes 12 large muffins.

These can be made without the chocolate if you like.

Submitted by:

Hacienda del Sol
P.O. Box 177
109 Mabel Dodge Lane
Taos, New Mexico 87571
(505) 758-0287
Carol & Randy Pelton
$45.00 to $100.00

Continental breakfast
7 rooms, 5 private baths
Children allowed
No pets
No smoking
Mastercard & Visa

Once part of the Mabel Dodge Luhan estate, parts of this historic inn date back 180 years. Adjoining the 95,000 acre Taos Pueblo Land; the yard & most rooms feature unobstructed views of Taos Mountain.

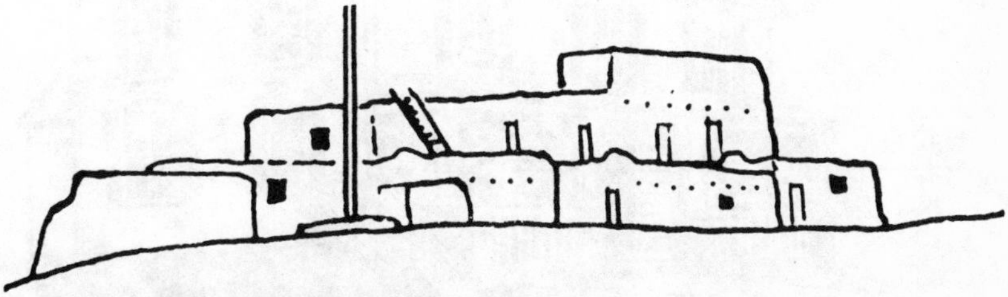

PUMPKIN MUFFINS

3 cups sugar
1 cup salad oil
2/3 cup water
2 cups pumpkin
4 eggs
3 1/2 cups flour
1 1/2 teaspoons salt
1 teaspoon cinnamon
1/2 teaspoon nutmeg
2 teaspoons soda
Optional:
2 cups raisins or
1 cup chopped walnuts

Dissolve sugar in liquids before adding dry ingredients. Pour into greased and floured pans. Bake at 350° approximately 20 minutes. Makes 3 - 4 dozen muffins.

Submitted by:

Dry Ridge Inn
26 Brown Street
Weaverville, N.C. 28787
(704) 658-3899
John & Karen Vander Elzen
$45.00 to $50.00

Full breakfast
6 rooms, 6 private baths
Children allowed
No pets
Restricted smoking
Mastercard & Visa

Originally two rooms built in 1849 as a parsonage for Salem Campground. Used as a hospital during the Civil War, & farmed until late 1950's. Very large guest rooms, antiques and handmade quilts. Gift shop featuring crafts indigenous to the Blue Ridge Mountains.

RHUBARB MUFFINS

1 stick butter
1 cup light brown sugar
1/4 teaspoon vanilla
1 egg
2 cups flour
4 teaspoons baking powder
1/4 teaspoon salt
1 cup milk
2 cups diced rhubarb

Cream butter and sugar. Beat in vanilla, add egg, beat 1 minute. Sift flour and dry ingredients. Mix 1/2 of dry, 1/2 milk. Add rest of dry ingredients and milk, do not overbeat - batter should be lumpy. Fold in rhubarb. Bake in paper lined muffin tins, 25 minutes. Also can be made in greased and floured small loaf pans. Bake 35 minutes at 400°. Makes 12 - 14 muffins.

Submitted by:

The Bird & Bottle Inn
Old Albany Post Road
Garrison, New York 10524
(914) 424-3000
Ira Boyar

Full & continental breakfast
4 rooms, 4 private baths
Children, over 12
No pets
Smoking allowed
Mastercard, Visa, Am Ex

From 1761, known as Warren's Tavern, we have had a colorful and romantic history. Our guest book has the names of satisfied patrons from the U.S. & over 30 foreign countries. Each room has a fireplace, and is furnished with period furniture & four-poster or canopied beds.

SESAME CORN MUFFINS

1 1/2 cups unsifted flour (3/4 cup white & 3/4 cup whole wheat)
1/2 cup sugar
1 1/2 teaspoons salt
1 1/4 teaspoons soda
2 cups cornmeal
1 cup wheat germ
1/2 cup toasted sesame seeds
2 cups buttermilk
3/4 cup melted butter
2 eggs, slightly beaten

Sift together flour, sugar, salt and soda. Blend in cornmeal, wheat germ and sesame seeds. In separate bowl, mix buttermilk, butter and eggs. Blend in dry ingredients and mix just until moistened. Do not overmix. Pour into prepared muffin tins (surface coated with a mixture of 1 cup flour, 1 cup Crisco and 1 cup oil blended in food processor and saved in a jar in refrigerator). Bake at 350° about 30 minutes. Makes 18 muffins.

Submitted by:

Turtleback Farm Inn
Route 1, Box 650
Eastsound, Orcas Island,
Washington 98245
(206) 376-4914
William & Susan Fletcher
$65.00 to $130.00

Full breakfast
7 rooms, 7 private baths
Children, over 8
No pets
No smoking
Mastercard & Visa

We overlook 80 acres of forest and farmland in the shadow of Turtleback Mountain with Mt. Constitution to the east. Rumford fireplace, game table, fine antiques and contemporary furnishings. Step back in time and recapture moments of good fellowship.

THE BEST BLUEBERRY MUFFINS

1/2 cup margarine
1 1/4 cups sugar
2 eggs
2 cups flour
2 teaspoons baking powder
1/2 cup milk
2 cups fresh or frozen blueberries (cranberries can be used)

Cream margarine and sugar, add eggs. Add dry ingredients alternately with milk. Fold in 2 cups whole berries. Fill muffin tins with batter. Sprinkle tops with granulated sugar. Bake at 375° for 30 minutes. Makes 1 dozen muffins.

Submitted by:

The Raspberry Patch
R.R. #2, Box 1915
Randolph Road
Stowe, Vermont 05672
(802) 253-4145
Linda Jones
$55.00 to $60.00

Full breakfast
4 rooms, 3 1/2 private baths
Children allowed
Pets allowed
Restricted smoking
Mastercard & Visa

Homey comfort, peace and quiet; cozy rooms with antiques & down comforters. A Vermont breakfast is served by the fire in winter, overlooking beautiful Mt. Mansfield. Only 5 minutes from fine restaurants, shops, and activities. Multi-day packages are available.

WILLIE'S PINEAPPLE BRAN MUFFINS

2 1/2 cups whole wheat flour
2 1/2 cups white flour
5 teaspoons soda
2 teaspoons salt
3 cups sugar
4 beaten eggs
1 cup melted shortening
1 quart buttermilk
2 - 20 oz. cans drained, crushed pineapple
2 cups walnuts
1 - 15 oz. box Raisin Bran
Topping:
Melted butter
3/4 cup sugar
1/4 cup cinnamon

Mix flours, soda, salt and sugar. In separate bowl mix eggs, shortening and buttermilk. Combine flour mixture and egg mixture. Add pineapple and walnuts, mix well. Add Raisin Bran and mix. Pour into greased muffin tins 2/3 full. Put 1 teaspoon of melted butter on top of each muffin, then sprinkle 3/4 teaspoon of sugar-cinnamon on top of butter. Bake at 400° for 20 minutes. Makes 4 dozen.

Submitted by:

Victorian Inn on the Park
301 Lyon Street
San Francisco, Calif. 94117
(415) 931-1830
Lisa & William Benau
$81.00 to $138.00

Continental breakfast
12 rooms, 12 private baths
Children allowed
No pets
Restricted smoking
Mastercard, Visa, Am Ex

1897 Queen Anne Victorian adjacent to Golden Gate Park. Belvedere Room has marble fireplace, balcony overlooking the park, and stained glass French doors leading to Roman tub for two. Family-owned and operated; each guest is personally welcomed.

COFFEE CAKES & OTHER CAKES

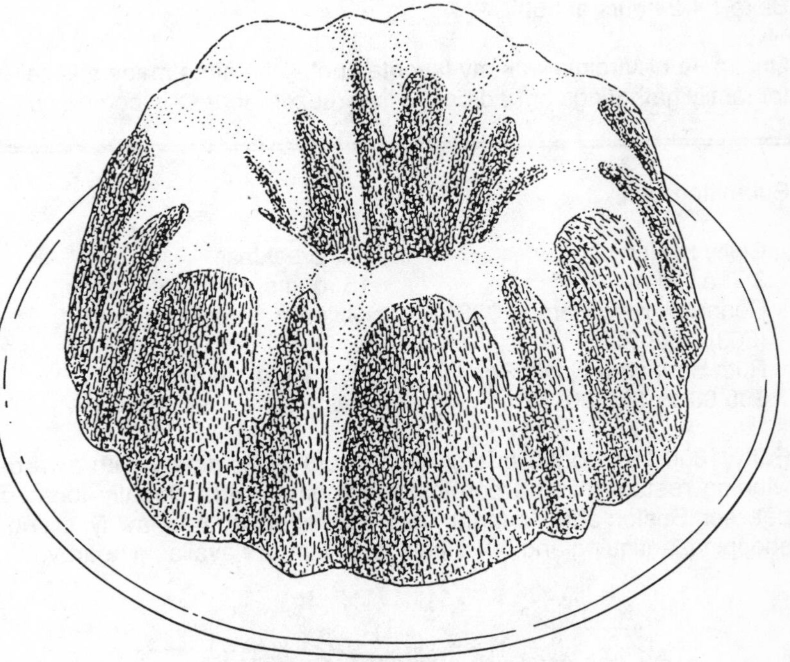

AUNT VIRGINIA'S APPLE CAKE

3 large apples
Cinnamon & sugar
3 cups flour
3 teaspoons baking powder
1/2 teaspoon salt
4 eggs, slightly beaten
2 cups sugar
1 cup oil
1/2 cup orange juice
3 teaspoons vanilla

Peel and slice apples, sprinkle with cinnamon & sugar, let stand while mixing other ingredients. Do not beat! Mix well together flour, baking powder, salt, eggs, sugar, oil, orange juice, and vanilla. Pour 1/2 of batter in a well-greased tube pan, sprinkled with flour. Put a layer of apples over batter, add remaining batter, then remaining apples. Bake 1 1/2 hours at 350°

Origin: Aunt Virginia was my favorite aunt. She often made this cake for family gatherings or had one in the freezer for drop-in company.

Submitted by:

Colby Hill Inn
3 The Oaks
Henniker, New Hamp. 03242
(603) 428-3281
Ruth Hannah & David Romin
$65.00 to $85.00

Full breakfast
15 rooms, 15 private baths
Children, over 6
No pets
Restricted smoking
Mastercard, Visa, Am Ex

Early 1800 farmhouse offers refuge from the ordinary with award-winning restaurant and comfortable rooms. Strategically located between Boston and Vermont, each only about an hour away; skiing, shopping, antiquing and other traditional fare are available nearby.

BEACH HOUSE INN CRANBERRY COFFEE CAKE

1/2 cup softened butter
1 cup sugar
2 eggs
2 cups all-purpose flour
1 teaspoon baking powder
1 teaspoon baking soda
1/2 teaspoon salt
8 oz. sour cream
1 teaspoon vanilla
1 can whole-berry cranberry sauce
Glaze:
3/4 cup powdered sugar
1/2 teaspoon vanilla
1 tablespoon warm water

Cream butter, gradually add sugar, beating until light and fluffy. Add eggs one at a time, beating well after each addition. Combine dry ingredients, add to creamed mixture alternately with sour cream, beating well after each addition. Add vanilla, mix well. Spoon 1/3 mixture into greased and floured 10" tube pan or bundt pan. Spread 1/3 cranberry sauce over batter. Repeat layers twice more, ending with cranberry sauce. Bake at 350° for 1 hour or until cake tests done. Let cool 5 minutes before removing from pan. Combine all ingredients for glaze, stir well, and drizzle over top of cake.

Submitted by:

Beach House Inn
4 Braddock Lane
Harwich Port, Mass. 02646
(508) 432-4444
Gregory Y. Winston
$95.00 to $130.00

Continental plus breakfast
10 rooms, 10 private baths
Children allowed
No pets
Smoking allowed
Mastercard, Visa, Am Ex

Beach House Inn: Outstanding ocean views across our large private beach, spacious rooms with efficiency refrigerator, color television, air conditioning, gourmet continental breakfast. Charming Harwich Port location near shops and restaurants. Our appeal is seasonless.

BLUEBERRY COFFEE CAKE

4 cups flour (can use 2 cups all-purpose & 2 cups whole wheat)
1 1/2 cups granulated sugar
2 teaspoons & 1 tablespoon baking powder
1 1/2 teaspoons salt
1/2 cup shortening
1 1/2 cups milk
2 eggs
4 cups fresh or frozen blueberries

Topping:
1 cup granulated sugar
2/3 cup flour
1 teaspoon cinnamon
1/2 cup soft butter

Preheat oven to 375°. Grease 2 - 9" square or round baking pans. Mix all ingredients except blueberries until moistened; beat vigorously 1/2 minute. Carefully stir in blueberries. Spread 1/2 of batter in each pan; sprinkle 1/2 of topping on each pan of batter. Bake 45 - 50 minutes until wooden pick inserted comes out clean. Serve warm. To freeze second cake: Cool thoroughly, wrap, label and freeze. 50 minutes before serving, remove from freezer and unwrap. Heat uncovered at 350° until warm, about 45 minutes.

Submitted by:

The Inn at Narrow Passage
U.S. 11 South (Int. 81, Exit 72)
Woodstock, Virginia 22664
(703) 459-8000
Ed & Ellen Markel
$55.00 to $80.00

Full breakfast
12 rooms, 8 private baths
Children allowed
No pets
Restricted smoking
Mastercard & Visa

Log inn on 5 acres on the Shenandoah River has welcomed travelers for over 200 years. Stonewall Jackson's headquarters in 1862. Early American decor with wing chairs, fireplaces, and queen-sized canopy beds. Near fishing, rafting, historic sites, caverns and antiquing.

BLUEBERRY OVERNIGHT COFFEE CAKE

Coffee Cake:
3/4 cup softened butter
1 cup sugar
2 eggs
1 cup sour cream
2 cups flour
1 teaspoon baking powder
1 teaspoon baking soda
1/2 teaspoon salt
1/2 teaspoon nutmeg

Topping:

2/3 cup flour
1 cup sugar
1 teaspoon cinnamon
1/2 teaspoon nutmeg
1/2 cup butter
2 - 3 cups blueberries, fresh or frozen

Butter 9" x 13" baking pan and dust with flour. Coffee Cake: Cream butter and sugar, add eggs and sour cream. Mix well. Combine dry ingredients, add to batter and mix well. Pour into pan, cover and refrigerate overnight. Topping: Combine dry ingredients, mix well. Cut in butter. Using pastry blender, two knives or your fingers, mix until crumbly. When ready to bake, preheat oven to 350°. Sprinkle berries on top of coffee cake and then sprinkle topping on top of blueberries. Caution: Dry frozen berries as much as possible or you may be serving "Blueberry Crumble", equally good, but requires bowls! Bake 50 - 60 minutes. Serves 12 - 15.

Submitted by:

Inn on Carleton
46 Carleton Street
Portland, Maine 04102
(207) 775-1910
Susan Holland
$50.00 to $80.00

Continental breakfast
7 rooms, 3 private baths
Children allowed
No pets
No smoking
Mastercard & Visa

We are a graciously restored 19th century Victorian townhouse located in Portland's historic West End. Close to downtown, art museum, performing arts center and Old Port District. A custom bookbindery operated on the premises.

BOHEMIAN ROLLED COFFEE CAKE

2 sticks margarine
4 cups flour
1 unit yeast
1 tablespoon sugar
1/4 cup warm water
2 eggs
1 cup cold milk
1/4 teaspoon salt
Commercial filling or your own choice of nuts and fruit

Use pastry blender to work margarine sticks into flour. Add 1 tablespoon sugar to 1 unit yeast in 1/4 cup warm water. Beat 2 eggs in 1 cup cold milk. Combine egg-milk mixture with yeast, sprinkle in salt. Add first mix of margarine-flour to milk mix. Add flour as necessary to work into a ball. Chill at least 4 hours. Roll dough thin, fill, and roll-up, sealing ends. Let stand 1 hour. Bake on unbuttered cookie sheet for 40 minutes at 350°.

Origin: From mother-in-law's recipe file, received from unnamed Czech neighbor in Chicago, circa 1925.

Submitted by:

Trout City Inn
P.O. Box 431
Buena Vista, Colorado 81211
(719) 495-0348
Juel & Irene Kjeldsen
$30.00 to $40.00

Full breakfast
5 rooms, 4 private baths
Children, over 10
No pets
Restricted smoking
Mastercard & Visa

Historic railway station on Trout Creek Pass in National Forest. Victorian decor and antiques in depot rooms plus private Pullman car and caboose. Railroad, trout stream, beaver ponds & gold mine with grand view of canyon and collegiate peaks along Continental Divide.

TROUT CITY INN

ON THE SOUTH PARK LINE

CHEESE-APPLE-PUMPKIN CAKE

1/2 cup butter (1 stick)
1 1/2 cups firmly-packed brown sugar
2 eggs
1 cup canned pumpkin
2 cups loosely-packed, unpeeled & shredded cooking apples (2 large)
1 cup (4 oz.) shredded Cheddar cheese
2 cups all-purpose flour
1 tablespoon baking powder
1/2 teaspoon baking soda
1/2 teaspoon salt
1/2 teaspoon cinnamon
1/2 teaspoon ginger

Topping:
Confectioners sugar

Preheat oven to 350°. Cream butter in large mixer bowl. Add sugar and beat until light and fluffy. Beat in eggs, pumpkin, apples and cheese. Combine dry ingredients, gradually stir into butter mixture. Pour into buttered and floured 12 cup bundt cake pan. Bake 55 - 60 minutes, or until wooden pick inserted comes out clean. Let cool in pan 15 minutes before removing. Cool completely on wire rack; wrap in plastic wrap and let rest 24 hours before serving. Dust lightly with confectioners sugar. Serve with unsweetened whipped cream. Makes 1 - 10" bundt cake.

Submitted by:

Pleasant Grove Farm
368 Pilottown Road
Peach Bottom, Penn. 17563
(717) 548-3100
Charles & Labertha Tindall
$40.00 to $45.00

Full breakfast
4 rooms
Children allowed
No pets
Restricted smoking

Located in beautiful, historic Lancaster County, this 160 acre dairy farm has been family-run for 108 years, earning it the title of "Century Farm". As a working farm, it lets guests experience daily life in a rural setting. 176 years ago, our home was a country store & post office.

CINNAMON-BUTTERMILK COFFEE CAKE

2 1/4 cups flour
1 cup light brown sugar
3/4 cup granulated sugar
2 teaspoons cinnamon
1/2 teaspoon salt
1/4 teaspoon ginger
3/4 cup corn oil
1 cup sliced almonds
1 teaspoon baking powder
1 teaspoon baking soda
1 egg
1 cup buttermilk

Mix flour, light brown sugar, sugar, 1 teaspoon cinnamon, salt and ginger. Mix in oil until smooth. Remove 3/4 cup mixture and combine with almonds and remaining 1 teaspoon cinnamon. Mix and set aside for topping. To remaining flour mixture, add baking powder and baking soda, egg and buttermilk. Blend until smooth. Pour into greased 9" x 13" pan. Sprinkle nut mixture over batter. Bake at 350° for 35 - 40 minutes.

Submitted by:

The Lamplight Inn
2129 Lake Avenue
P.O. Box 70
Lake Luzerne, N.Y. 12846
(518) 696-5294
Eugene & Linda Merlino
$60.00 to $125.00

Full breakfast
10 rooms, 10 private baths
Children, over 12
No pets
Restricted smoking
Am Ex

1890 Victorian with 5 fireplaces. Full breakfast served on spacious sunporch with mountain view. Antiques, fluffy comforters, porch swing on wraparound porch. 1 block from Lake Luzerne, near Lake George and Saratoga Springs.

COFFEE CAKE SUPREME

Batter:
1/2 cup butter
1/2 cup sugar
1/2 teaspoon vanilla
1 egg
1 1/2 cups enriched flour
1/2 teaspoon salt
1 1/2 teaspoons baking powder
1/2 cup milk

Filling:
1/4 cup melted butter
1/2 cup brown sugar
1 tablespoon flour
1 tablespoon cinnamon
1/4 cup chopped walnuts
1/4 cup chopped date nuggets
Topping: 1/4 cup chopped walnuts

Blend filling ingredients together and set aside. For cake: thoroughly cream butter, sugar & vanilla. Add egg. Beat thoroughly. Add sifted dry ingredients alternately with milk. Spread half the batter in greased 8" square pan or 8" tart pan. Cover with filling. Add remaining batter over filling, spreading it evenly to edge of pan. Top with walnuts. Bake in moderate oven at 350° for about 45 minutes. Dust lightly with sifted powdered sugar, if desired.

Submitted by:

The Hope-Merrill and
Hope-Bosworth House
P.O. Box 42
Geyserville, California 95441
(707) 857-3356
Bob & Rosalie Hope
$60.00 to $115.00

Full breakfast
12 rooms, 10 private baths
Children allowed
No pets
No smoking
Mastercard, Visa, Am Ex

Vintage Victorians welcome travelers in grand style. Whirlpool jacuzzis, beautiful Victorian gardens, gazebo, and heated swimming pool. Featured in Country Homes, Sunset, and House Beautiful. Country breakfast with Rosalie Hope's prize-winning recipes.

COFFEE COFFEE CAKE

3/4 cup soft butter
1 cup sugar
2 eggs
2 teaspoons vanilla
2 cups flour
1/2 teaspoon baking soda
1/4 teaspoon salt
1 teaspoon baking powder
1 cup sour cream
2 tablespoons instant espresso dissolved in 1 tablespoon hot water

Glaze:
2 - 3 tablespoons strong coffee
1/2 teaspoon instant espresso mixed with 3/4 cup confectioners sugar

Cream butter and sugar, add eggs one at a time. Add vanilla. In separate bowl mix dry ingredients and add alternately with sour cream to the butter mixture. Remove 1/3 of batter and add dissolved espresso. Spoon 1/2 of remaining batter into greased and floured bundt pan. Cover with coffee batter and top with remaining plain batter. Bake at 350° for 50 - 60 minutes. Cool on cake rack, invert and cool completely. Pour glaze over cake and let stand 10 minutes. Double recipe to fit a 10" angel food pan.

Submitted by:

Inn at Manchester
Box 41
Manchester Village, Vermont 05254
(802) 362-1793
Stan & Harriet Rosenberg
$60.00 to $100.00

Full breakfast
21 rooms, 11 private baths
Children, over 8
No pets
Restricted smoking
Mastercard, Visa & Am Ex

Colonial inn in a meadow amidst huge pines, spruces, maples and birches, and ringed by the Green Mountains. Country antiques, and collections of paintings and posters. Great front porch, secluded pool, with skiing nearby.

DATE BREAKFAST CAKE

1 cup sugar
1 cup brown sugar
3 cups flour
1/2 teaspoon salt
3/4 cup shortening
1 cup pitted, cut-up dates
3/4 cup chopped walnuts
1 cup soured milk with 1 teaspoon soda added

Combine first four ingredients. Cut in shortening. Reserve 1 cup of this mixture for topping. Add remaining ingredients. Mix well. Spread in 2 - 8" x 9" greased cake pans. Cover with reserved topping. Bake at 350° for 25 minutes. Freezes well. Makes 16 servings.

Origin: A family favorite.

Submitted by:

Serenity, a
Bed & Breakfast Inn
15305 Bear Cub Drive
Sonora, California 95370
(209) 533-1441
Fred & Charlotte Hoover
$75.00

Full breakfast
4 rooms, 4 private baths
No children
No pets
Restricted smoking
Mastercard, Visa, Am Ex

Listen to the wind in the pines, relax on the veranda, browse in the library, or dream by the fire. Luxuriate in your beautifully decorated room, and appreciate the nicety of ironed, lace-trimmed linens. Waken to enticing aromas. Most importantly, find complete serenity.

EASTER POUND CAKE

- 1 lb. sweet butter
- 2 cups sugar
- 4 eggs
- 3 cups flour
- 3 teaspoons baking powder
- 1 teaspoon baking soda
- 1/2 teaspoon salt
- 1 pint sour cream
- 1 teaspoon vanilla
- 1/2 cup sugar combined with 1/2 teaspoon cinnamon

Cream butter and sugar together, add eggs one at a time. Combine dry ingredients. Add dry ingredients and sour cream alternately, beginning and ending with dry. Add vanilla. Put in 2 greased loaf pans and sprinkle with sugar-cinnamon. Bake at 350° for 50 - 60 minutes.

Origin: Traditionally served at Easter open house buffet at our home in Pittsburgh, Pennsylvania.

Submitted by:

Ashling Cottage
106 Sussex Avenue
Spring Lake, N.J. 07762
(201) 449-3553
Goodi & Jack Stewart
$50.00 to $115.00

Continental plus breakfast
10 rooms, 8 private baths
Children, over 12
No pets
Restricted smoking

Under sentinel sycamores for 100 years, Ashling Cottage has served for a select few as a portal to the genteel lifestyle of the 19th century. Escape from today's pace into the romantic style of years past, and discover a new meaning for the word "vacation".

EASY COFFEE CAKE

2 cups flour
1/2 cup granola
3/4 cup white sugar
1 cup brown sugar
1 teaspoon cinnamon
1/2 teaspoon salt
3/4 cup vegetable oil
1/2 cup nuts
1 teaspoon soda
1 teaspoon baking powder
1 cup buttermilk or 1 cup milk soured with 1 tablespoon vinegar
1 egg
1 teaspoon vanilla

Mix flour, granola, sugars, cinnamon, salt and vegetable oil. Remove 1/2 cup for topping. Add nuts, soda, baking powder, buttermilk, egg and vanilla. Pour in Pam-sprayed 9" x 13" pan. Sprinkle topping over batter. May add more nuts to topping if desired. Bake for 30 minutes at 350°.

Submitted by:

Davidson's Country Inn
Box 87
Pagosa Springs, Colo. 81147
(303) 264-5863
Gilbert & Evelyn Davidson
$36.00 to $55.00

Full breakfast
7 rooms, 4 private baths
Children allowed
Pets allowed
No smoking
Mastercard & Visa

A 3-story log home with heirlooms and antiques in a "homey" decor, surrounded by beautiful mountains. Library and game area, game room, children's room, outside activities, & hiking area provided. Near skiing, fishing, backpacking, horseback riding and swimming.

EGGNOG COFFEE CAKE

1/2 cup softened butter
1 1/3 cups sugar
2 eggs
3 cups flour
1 1/2 teaspoons nutmeg
1 tablespoon baking powder
2 cups eggnog
1 cup chopped nuts

Cream together butter and sugar. Beat in eggs. Stir together flour, nutmeg, and baking powder. Stir flour mixture and eggnog into butter mixture alternately. Add chopped nuts. Pour into greased 2 1/2" fluted cake pans or muffin pans. We use "Christmas-shaped" miniature pans: Christmas trees, wreaths, etc. Bake at 325° for 30 minutes. To serve, drizzle or pour a raspberry puree over the cake and garnish with holly sprigs.

Submitted by:

Christmas House
Bed & Breakfast Inn
9240 Archibald Avenue
Rancho Cucamonga,
California 91730
(714) 980-6450
Janice Ilsley
$55.00 to $115.00

Full breakfast
5 rooms, 2 private baths
Children, over 12
No pets
Restricted smoking

1904 Victorian has 7 fireplaces, intricate woodwork, & stained glass. Located 40 miles east of Los Angeles, near Ontario International Airport, the freeway, and southern California's attractions. Gracious turn-of-the-century hospitality, and "Norman Rockwell" Christmases!

MASON COTTAGE APPLE BRUNCHCAKE

1/2 cup butter
8 oz. cream cheese
1 cup sugar
2 eggs
1/2 teaspoon vanilla
2 cups flour
1/4 teaspoon salt
1 teaspoon baking powder
1/2 teaspoon baking soda
1/4 cup milk
3 Granny Smith apples, diced

Topping:
1 cup flour
1/2 cup sugar
1/4 cup butter
1/4 teaspoon cinnamon (optional)

Cream butter and cream cheese. Add sugar and eggs, beat well. Add vanilla. Sift flour, salt, baking powder and baking soda together; add to batter alternately with milk. Stir in apple pieces. Pour into greased and floured 9" x 9" pan. Mix topping ingredients, sprinkle on top of batter, bake at 350° for 30 - 35 minutes.

Submitted by:

The Mason Cottage
625 Columbia Avenue
Cape May, New Jersey 08204
(609) 884-3358
Dave & Joan Mason
$70.00 to $120.00

Continental plus breakfast
5 rooms, 4 private baths
Children, over 12
No pets
Restricted smoking
Mastercard & Visa

Built in 1871, our inn is French Second Empire. Elegantly restored parlor and guest rooms. Most of the furniture is original to the house. Centrally located in primary historic district one block from the ocean and near the Victorian Shopping Mall.

MOLASSES-SOUR CREAM COFFEE CAKE

1 cup sugar
1/2 cup light molasses
3/4 cup softened butter
3 eggs
1 1/2 teaspoons vanilla
3 cups flour
1 1/2 teaspoons baking powder
2 teaspoons baking soda
3/4 teaspoon salt
1 1/3 cups sour cream

Filling:
1/2 cup packed brown sugar
1/2 cup chopped nuts
1 1/2 teaspoons ground cinnamon

Preheat oven to 350°. Grease 2 loaf pans or 12-cup bundt pan. Beat sugar, molasses, butter, eggs and vanilla in large bowl on medium speed, 2 minutes. Beat in flour, baking powder, baking soda and salt alternately with sour cream on low speed. Prepare filling. For bundt cake, spread 1/3 of batter in pan and sprinkle with 1/3 of filling, repeat 2 times. For loaves, spread 1/4 of batter in each pan and sprinkle each with 1/4 filling, repeat. Bake 55 - 60 minutes, until wooden pick inserted comes out clean. Cool slightly, remove from pan. Cool 10 minutes.

Submitted by:

Kincraft Inn
Route 100, P.O. Box 96
Hancock, Vermont 05748
(802) 767-3734
Irene & Ken Neitzel
$22.00 to $32.00

Full breakfast
6 rooms
Children allowed
No pets
No smoking
Mastercard, Visa, Am Ex

1820's refurbished farmhouse with handmade quilts and Shaker style furniture in guest bedrooms, made by hosts. Homemade breads, muffins, jams. Near 5 major ski areas with cross-country skiing, hiking, fishing & hunting nearby. Craft shop across street.

MORAVIAN SUGAR CAKE

1 env. or cake of yeast
1 cup lukewarm milk
1/2 cup sugar
1/2 cup butter, softened (not margarine)
1 cup mashed potatoes & potato water
2 eggs, slightly beaten
2 teaspoons salt
Flour, enough to make heavy batter

Topping: Butter, brown sugar & cinnamon

Add yeast to milk, set aside. In large bowl, cream sugar and softened butter. Add potatoes mashed with potato water instead of milk, eggs and dissolved yeast. Mix well. Add salt and flour to make heavy batter. Let rise until double in bulk. Spread into two large greased pans. Let rise in pans until very light. Make indentations with thumb and fill with pieces of butter. Cover generously with brown sugar and dust with cinnamon. Bake in 350° oven for 15 - 20 minutes or until brown.

Submitted by:

The Waverly Inn
783 N. Main Street
Hendersonville, North Carolina 28792
(800) 537-8195 or
(704) 692-1090
John & Diane Sheiry

Full breakfast
17 rooms
Children allowed
No pets
Smoking allowed
Mastercard, Visa, Am Ex, Discover

Listed in The National Register and open all year, we have something for everyone, including clawfoot tubs, king & queen four poster canopy beds, and private baths. Convenient to Biltmore Estate, Carl Sandburg Home, Blue Ridge Parkway, and Flatrock Playhouse.

OATMEAL COFFEE CAKE

1 1/4 cups boiling water
1 stick margarine
1 cup quick cooking oatmeal
2 eggs
1/2 teaspoon salt
1 cup sugar
1 cup brown sugar
1 teaspoon vanilla
1 teaspoon baking soda
1 1/2 cups flour

Topping:
2 tablespoons butter
2 tablespoons flour
1 cup brown sugar
1 teaspoon cinnamon

Mix boiling water, margarine and oatmeal, and let set 20 minutes. Mix remaining ingredients and add to oatmeal mixture. Pour into greased and floured 9" x 13" pan or bundt cake pan and bake at 350° for 25 minutes. Remove from oven and put on topping. Crumble topping ingredients with hands and add to top of cake, return to oven to brown.

Submitted by:

The Cliff House
122 Fairmount Drive
Madison, Indiana 47250
(812) 265-5272
Jae Breitweiser
$75.00

Continental plus breakfast
6 rooms, 6 private baths
Children allowed
No pets
Restricted smoking

1885 Victorian home overlooks the Ohio River. Candlelit breakfast, a tour of the home, & a breathtaking view from the widow's walk. Near historic museums, antique shops, specialty shops, state parks, tennis, golfing, boating, fishing & swimming. Handicapped facilities.

OVERNIGHT COFFEE CAKE

2/3 cup butter or margarine
1 cup sugar
1/2 cup brown sugar
2 eggs
1 cup buttermilk
1 teaspoon soda
1/2 teaspoon salt
1 teaspoon cinnamon
1 teaspoon baking powder
2 cups flour

Topping:
1/2 cup brown sugar
1/2 teaspoon cinnamon
1/2 cup macadamia nuts

Mix all ingredients (except topping) together. Put into greased 9" x 13" cake pan. Mix topping ingredients and sprinkle over cake. Cover, and refrigerate overnight. Bake uncovered at 350° for 30 - 35 minutes.

Submitted by:

Haikuleana Bed & Breakfast
69 Haiku Road
Haiku, Maui, Hawaii 96708
(808) 575-2890
Clark & Denise Champion
$65.00

Continental breakfast
2 rooms
Children allowed
Restricted smoking

House built about 1850, among pineapple fields and pine trees, for the plantation doctor. Warm tropical days and cool nights make it the perfect vacation spot. Close to great beaches and dreamy freshwater swimming. Superior restaurants, shopping, and golf all nearby.

PEACH-RASPBERRY BREAKFAST CAKE

Batter:
2 cups all purpose flour
1 tablespoon baking powder
1/2 teaspoon salt
2 tablespoons sugar
1/3 cup shortening
1 egg
1 cup milk

Filling:
1/4 cup melted butter
1/4 cup brown sugar, firmly packed
1/4 teaspoon cinnamon
1/4 teaspoon nutmeg
2 cups fresh, frozen or canned peaches, thinly sliced
1/3 cup sour cream
1/2 cup red raspberry preserves

Batter: Sift first four ingredients. Cut in shortening. Beat egg with milk, add to flour mixture. Stir lightly until just mixed. Set aside. Filling: Combine melted butter, brown sugar, cinnamon and nutmeg. Spread over bottom of a 9" square pan. Arrange peach slices in four rows. Spoon half the batter over peaches and smooth. Combine sour cream and red raspberry preserves. Pour over batter. Drop spoonfuls of remaining batter over preserves mixture. Bake in preheated 350° oven for about 45 minutes. Cool. Invert cake over plate and remove pan. Serve warm.

Submitted by:

The Inn at Mitchell House
Box 329, RD 2
Chestertown, Maryland 21620
(301) 778-6500
Jim & Tracy Stone
$75.00 to $90.00

Full breakfast
6 rooms, 5 private baths
Children allowed
No pets
Smoking allowed
Mastercard & Visa

Nestled on ten rolling, wooded acres, this 18th century manor home greets you with warmth and a touch of tranquility. Awake to birdsong or migrating geese. See deer, fox or an eagle at sunset. A mere 1/2 mile from the Chesapeake Bay. A true nature lover's paradise.

PECAN PRALINE COFFEE CAKE

1/2 cup butter
3/4 cup sugar
1 teaspoon vanilla
3 eggs
1 cup raisins
2 cups flour
1 teaspoon baking powder
1 teaspoon baking soda
1/2 teaspoon salt
1 cup sour cream

Praline Filling:
1 cup firmly packed brown sugar
2 teaspoons cinnamon
1/3 cup butter
3/4 cup coarsely chopped pecans

Cake: Beat butter, sugar, and vanilla until fluffy. Blend in eggs 1 at a time, then add raisins. Add flour sifted with baking powder, baking soda and salt, alternately with sour cream. Mix until smooth. Spread half of batter in greased and floured tube pan (10"). Filling: Mix brown sugar and cinnamon. Cut in butter, add pecans. Sprinkle Pecan Praline mix over cake and repeat layers. Bake at 350° for 50 minutes or until done. Cool 10 minutes in pan, then turn out onto wire rack.

Submitted by:

The Sand Castle
829 Stockton Avenue
Cape May, New Jersey 08204
(609) 884-5451
Pat Fitzmorris
$65.00 to $120.00

Continental breakfast
10 rooms, 4 private baths
Children allowed
No pets
Restricted smoking
Mastercard & Visa

Experience the charm and atmosphere of the Victorian era in a gothic cottage built in 1873. Wraparound veranda is inviting for an ocean view while being enticed with homebaked muffins, breads and cakes. Open year round. Near many fine restaurants & recreational facilities.

PENNSYLVANIA DUTCH CRUMB COFFEE CAKE

4 cups unsifted flour
1 teaspoon baking powder
2/3 cup shortening
1/2 teaspoon salt
2 1/2 cups granulated sugar
2 eggs, prebeaten
1 1/2 cups buttermilk
1 teaspoon baking soda
1 cup brown sugar
1/2 cup coconut
1 teaspoon cinnamon

Blend first five ingredients together, and set aside 1 cup of this mixture as a topping base for use later. In separate bowl, mix the eggs, buttermilk and baking soda together. Then blend the remaining portion of the original crumb mixture, stirring thoroughly. There will be some small lumps in batter. Add 1 cup brown sugar, 1/2 cup coconut and 1 teaspoon cinnamon to the cup of original crumb topping mixture set aside earlier. Pour coffee cake batter mixture into 3 greased and floured 8" cake pans. Sprinkle topping equally on top of batter in all 3 pans. Bake at 350° for 35 minutes.

Submitted by:

Bechtel Mansion Inn
400 W. King Street
East Berlin, Penn. 17316
(717) 259-7760
Ruth Spangler, Charles & Mariam Bechtel
$72.50 to $130.00

Continental plus breakfast
8 rooms, 7 private baths
Children allowed
No pets
Restricted smoking
Mastercard, Visa, Am Ex

A gracious restored Queen Anne style mansion in Pennsylvania Dutch country, on the National Register. Air-conditioned & tastefully furnished with antiques, Mennonite quilts & period items. Popular with Civil War, history, antique & architecture buffs & honeymooners.

RASPBERRY CREAM CHEESE COFFEE CAKE

2 1/4 cups flour
3/4 cup sugar
3/4 cup butter
1/2 teaspoon baking powder
1/2 teaspoon baking soda
1/4 teaspoon salt
3/4 cup sour cream
1 egg
1 teaspoon almond extract
8 oz. softened cream cheese
1/4 cup sugar
1 egg
1/2 cup raspberry preserves
1/2 cup sliced almonds

In large bowl, combine flour and 3/4 cup sugar. Using pastry blender, cut in butter until like coarse crumbs. Reserve 1 cup of crumb mixture. Add baking powder, baking soda, salt, sour cream, 1 egg and almond extract. Blend well. Spread batter over bottom and 2" up sides of greased & floured 10" springform pan. In small bowl, combine cream cheese, 1/4 cup sugar and 1 egg. Blend well. Spread over batter in pan. Spoon preserves evenly over cheese filling. In small bowl, combine 1 cup of crumb mixture and sliced almonds. Sprinkle over top. Bake at 350° for 45 - 55 minutes. Serves 8.

Submitted by:

Harbour Carriage House
420 West Montecito Street
Santa Barbara, Calif. 93101
(805) 962-8447
Vida McIssac & Sue Occhiuto
$85.00 to $175.00

Full breakfast
9 rooms, 9 private baths
Children allowed
No pets
Restricted smoking
Mastercard & Visa

A renovated 1895 house tastefully decorated with French and English antiques. Fireplaces & spas in six rooms. Breakfast is served in the sunny solarium, and evening refreshments are served fireside. 3 blocks from the harbor; adjoins the gardens of 2 historic houses.

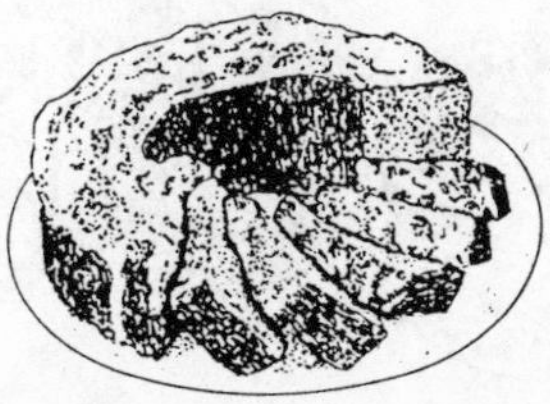

SOUR CREAM & APPLE COFFEE CAKE

1/2 cup shortening
1 cup sugar
1 teaspoon salt
1 teaspoon vanilla
2 eggs
2 1/2 cups flour
1 teaspoon baking soda
1 teaspoon baking powder
1 cup sour cream
2 cups chopped apples

Topping:
1 cup brown sugar
2 teaspoons cinnamon
1/2 cup melted butter
1 cup chopped pecans

Preheat oven to 350°. Cream together shortening and sugar. Add salt, vanilla and eggs, mixing well. Combine dry ingredients in separate bowl. Add dry ingredients alternately with the sour cream to the creamed mixture. Stir in apples. Pour batter into greased 9" x 13" pan. Combine brown sugar, cinnamon, butter and pecans. Pour over the top of the coffee cake. Bake for 25 minutes, or until toothpick inserted into center comes out clean.

Submitted by:

Big Moose Inn
On Big Moose Lake
Eagle Bay, New York 13331
(315) 357-2042
Doug & Bonnie Bennett
$42.00 to $85.00

Full & continental breakfast
14 rooms, 5 private baths
Children allowed
No pets
Smoking allowed
Mastercard, Visa, Am Ex

Located in the warmth of the Central Adirondack Mts., with lakeside dining and lounging by the fire. Big Moose Lake has its own unique charm and awesome natural beauty. Hiking, skiing, snowmobiling, and canoeing are available. Good food and an informal atmosphere.

STRAWBERRY SWIRL COFFEE CAKE

3/4 cup softened butter or margarine
1 1/2 cups sugar
3 eggs
1 1/2 teaspoons vanilla
3 cups Gold Medal flour
1/4 teaspoon salt
1 1/2 teaspoons baking powder
1 1/2 teaspoons baking soda
1 1/2 cups dairy sour cream
Strawberry preserves

Heat oven to 350°. Grease 2 loaf pans, 9" x 5" x 3". Combine butter, sugar, eggs and vanilla in large mixer bowl. Beat on medium speed 2 minutes or 300 vigorous strokes by hand. Mix in flour, salt, baking powder, and soda alternately with sour cream. (If using self-rising flour, omit baking powder, soda and salt). Spoon batter into each pan, reserving enough to cover the tops. Spread thin layer of preserves onto batter and swirl with a fork. Do not blend into batter. Cover with reserved batter and dust tops lightly with sugar. Bake about 1 hour or until wooden pick comes out clean. Cool slightly in pans before removing. Makes 14 - 16 servings.

Submitted by:

Silver Maple Lodge
R.R. #1, Box 8
Fairlee, Vermont 05045
(802) 333-4326
Scott & Sharon Wright
$38.00 to $58.00

Continental breakfast
14 rooms, 12 private baths
Children allowed
No pets
Restricted smoking
Mastercard, Visa, Am Ex

Historic inn located in scenic four-season recreational area. Enjoy boating, fishing, golfing, hiking, tennis and hot air balloon rides. Cozy rooms with private baths in an antique farmhouse or handsome knotty pine cottage rooms. Just 17 miles to Dartmouth College.

SWEDISH APPLE CAKE

10 apples
1 cup butter (2 sticks)
1 - 16 oz. pkg. brown sugar
2 cups flour
2 teaspoons nutmeg

Peel apples and slice into an 8" x 10" pan. Mix butter, sugar, flour and nutmeg together. Pour mixture over apples (batter may be stiff). Bake at 375° for 45 minutes. Very simple and good.

Submitted by:

The Inn on Providence
6700 Providence Road
Charlotte, N.C. 28226
(704) 366-6700
Daniel & Darlene McNeill
$55.00 to $75.00

Full breakfast
5 rooms, 3 private baths
Children, over 12
No pets
Restricted smoking
Mastercard & Visa

A 3-story colonial nestled on 2 acres amidst gardens and an outdoor swimming pool. Early American antiques, quilts and family heirlooms. Breakfast features special egg dishes, apple pannekoeken, home-made breads & muffins; served on our veranda, weather permitting.

QUICK & YEAST BREADS

ANGEL BISCUITS

5 cups flour
1 teaspoon baking soda
1 teaspoon salt
1 tablespoon baking powder
3 tablespoons sugar
1/2 cup buttermilk powder
3/4 cup shortening
1 envelope dry yeast
1/2 cup warm water
2 cups warm water

Sift together flour, soda, salt, baking powder, sugar and buttermilk powder. Cut in shortening until texture of cornmeal. Dissolve yeast in 1/2 cup of warm water. Add yeast water and 2 cups warm water to dry ingredients, mixing well. Place dough in covered container and refrigerate at least 2 hours before baking. Roll on floured board to 1/2" thick. Bake on ungreased baking sheet at 400° for 10 - 12 minutes. Makes 5 dozen.

Submitted by:

Merlinn Guesthouse
811 Simonton Street
Key West, Florida 33040
(305) 296-3336
Pat Hoffman
$49.00 to $110.00

Full breakfast
18 rooms, 18 private baths
Children allowed
Pets allowed
Smoking allowed
Mastercard, Visa, Am Ex

A magically romantic world in the heart of Historic Old Town Key West. Freshly baked breakfast served among exotic birds in a secluded garden of huge flowering trees, colorful hibiscus and rare orchids. Relax in our tropical pool/jacuzzi.

APPLEBUTTER SWEET ROLLS

1 pkg. dry yeast
1/4 cup warm water
1 tablespoon sugar
1 3/4 cups scalded milk
1/4 cup sugar
1 teaspoon salt
1 egg, beaten
7 cups flour
3 teaspoons melted shortening
Applebutter for filling

Glaze:
2 cups powdered sugar
4 tablespoons milk
1 teaspoon vanilla

Dissolve yeast in 1/4 cup warm water with 1 tablespoon sugar, let stand 5 minutes. Let milk cool in mixing bowl. Add sugar, salt and yeast mixture, add well-beaten egg. Sift flour and add 1/2 of it, beating well. Add melted shortening and mix in remaining flour. Let rise until double in size. Divide dough in half and roll on floured surface into large rectangle 1/2" thick. Spread with applebutter. Roll up and cut in 1" slices. Spacing about 2" apart on baking pan, refrigerate overnight. Remove from refrigerator, let rise 1 hour and bake at 350° for 25 minutes. Glaze. Makes 2 dozen rolls.

Origin: Developed by our chef, Lynda Moore, due to our inn's name.

Submitted by:

Applebutter Inn
152 Applewood Lane
Slippery Rock, Penn. 16057
(412) 794-1844
Sandra & Gary McKnight
$79.00 to $115.00

Full breakfast
11 rooms, 11 private baths
Children allowed
No pets
No smoking
Mastercard & Visa

A charming solid brick 1844 farmhouse, restored and added-to in 1987, retaining its original woodwork, chestnut and poplar flooring and 5 fireplaces. Lovely period antiques, including canopied rope beds are accented by decorator fabrics, wallcoverings and stenciling.

APPLESAUCE-SOUR CREAM GINGERBREAD

6 tablespoons shortening
1/3 cup sugar
1 egg
1/2 cup molasses
1/3 cup applesauce
1/3 cup sour cream
1 3/4 cup flour
1 teaspoon baking soda
1 teaspoon cinnamon
1/2 teaspoon ginger
1/2 teaspoon salt

Cream shortening and sugar, beat in egg, molasses, applesauce and sour cream. Sift flour, soda, spices and salt. Mix with liquids quickly. (Can be stored overnight at this point and baked later.) Bake in wax paper-lined 9" x 9" pan at 350° for 30 minutes. Cut in squares, serve warm as is or with a hard sauce.

Origin: From my grandmother's cookbook of her favorite "receipts".

Submitted by:

Mira Monte Inn
69 Mt. Desert Street
Bar Harbor, Maine 04609
(207) 288-4263
Marian Burns
$75.00 to $135.00

Continental breakfast
11 rooms, 11 private baths
Children allowed in some rooms
No pets
Restricted smoking
Mastercard, Visa, Am Ex

Former Bar Harbor summer estate, on 1 1/2 acres of landscaped grounds in town. Simple elegance, balconies, fireplaces, library, piano, dining room where breakfast buffet is served. Picked as a "Best Choice" in Bar Harbor.

BANANA LEMON LOAF

1/2 cup shortening
1 cup sugar
2 eggs, beaten
1 1/2 cups mashed ripe bananas
6 tablespoons lemon juice
2 cups flour
1 teaspoon baking soda
2 - 3 tablespoons grated lemon peel

Preheat oven to 350° and grease pans. Cream shortening and sugar, blend in eggs, bananas and juice and stir in sifted dry ingredients. Add grated lemon peel. Pour into two greased loaf pans or one bundt pan and bake 1 hour.

Origin: A Garden Island recipe.

Submitted by:

Victoria Place
P.O. Box 930
Lawai, Kauai, Hawaii 96765
(808) 332-9300
Edee Seymour
$45.00 to $95.00

Continental plus breakfast
4 rooms, 4 private baths
No children
No pets
Restricted smoking

High in the hills of southern Kauai, two minutes from Highway 50. Spacious & skylit with jungle & ocean views. Guest rooms open onto pool in tropical garden. Near beaches, boutiques & golf. Island fruits, homemade muffins, handicapped access, and "Aloha." We pamper!

BANANA NUT BREAD

1/2 cup butter or oleo
1 cup sugar
2 well-beaten eggs
2 cups flour
1 teaspoon baking soda
1 teaspoon baking powder
3 ripe bananas, mashed
1 cup chopped pecans

Cream butter, sugar and eggs. Add flour, baking soda and baking powder, sifted together. Mix in bananas and nuts. Pour into greased loaf pan. Bake at 300° for one hour.

Submitted by:

Anchuca
1010 First East
Vicksburg, Mississippi 39180
(601) 636-4931 or
(800) 262-4822 (outside MS)
May White
$75.00 to $115.00

Full breakfast
9 rooms, 9 private baths
Children allowed
Small pets allowed
Smoking allowed
Mastercard, Visa,
Am Ex, Discover

Beautiful 1830 Greek Revival antebellum mansion. Decorated with 18th and 19th century antiques, and gas-lighted chandeliers. Guest rooms are furnished with period antiques. Included in rates are a Southern breakfast, a tour of the home, & use of the pool & hot tub.

BLUEBERRY LEMON LOAF

2 1/2 cups flour
1 1/2 teaspoons baking powder
1/2 teaspoon baking soda
1 teaspoon salt
1/2 cup butter
1 cup sugar
2 eggs
1 cup sour cream
2 tablespoons lemon peel
1 teaspoon vanilla
1/4 teaspoon nutmeg
1 cup walnuts
1 cup fresh or frozen blueberries

Preheat oven to 350°. Grease a 9" x 5" pan. Sift together flour, baking powder, soda and salt. Beat butter and sugar until light and fluffy. Add eggs, sour cream, lemon peel, vanilla and nutmeg. Beat till smooth. Gradually beat in dry ingredients until blended. Stir in walnuts. Fold in blueberries tossed in 1 tablespoon flour. Using spatula, gently spread batter into pan. Bake 1 hour, 30 minutes. If top gets too brown, cover with foil last 20 minutes or so of baking time. Cool in pan or on rack 15 minutes before removing.

Submitted by:

Sally Webster Inn
34 Mount Pleasant Street
Rockport, Mass. 01966
(508) 546-9251
The Webster Family
$62.00 to $72.00

Continental breakfast
6 rooms, 6 private baths
Children, over 16
No pets
Smoking allowed

An historic home built in 1832. Period decor. Walking distance to beaches and village. Flowers, candles and lots of personal attention. A must-do is whale watching! Welcome to the charm of yesteryear.

BLUEBERRY-ORANGE NUT BREAD

3 eggs
1 tablespoon grated orange rind
2/3 cup orange juice
1/2 cup milk
1/2 cup melted butter or margarine
3 cups all-purpose flour
3/4 cup sugar
1 tablespoon baking powder
1/4 teaspoon baking soda
1/2 teaspoon salt
1 cup fresh blueberries
1/2 cup chopped walnuts

Combine first 5 ingredients, beat on medium speed of electric mixer 30 seconds. Combine flour, sugar, baking powder, soda, and salt in large bowl; make a well in center of mixture. Add egg mixture, stirring just until moistened. Fold in blueberries and walnuts. Pour batter into greased and floured 9" x 5" x 3" loaf pan; bake at 350° for 1 hour or until a wooden toothpick inserted in center comes out clean. Cool in pan 10 minutes, remove from pan and cool completely.

Submitted by:

Mary's Country Inn
Route 2, Box 4
Edinburg, Virginia 22824
(703) 984-8286
Mary & Jim Clark
$60.00 to $260.00 (entire inn)

Full breakfast
6 rooms, 3 private baths
Children allowed
No pets
Restricted smoking
Mastercard & Visa

A large country Victorian which has housed the milling families of this charming Shenandoah Valley town since 1850. Wraparound porch with its swing and rockers is a favorite spot for our guests. Rooms are bright and cheerful; antiques abound. Bountiful breakfast buffet.

CHOCOLATE APPLESAUCE BREAD

- **2 cups sugar**
- **3/4 cup butter**
- **3 unbeaten eggs**
- **25 oz. unsweetened applesauce**
- **4 cups unsifted flour**
- **2 1/2 teaspoons soda**
- **3/4 teaspoon salt**
- **1 teaspoon cinnamon**
- **4 tablespoons cocoa**
- **Chocolate chips for topping**

Cream sugar and butter, add eggs, then applesauce. Mix well. Measure next 5 ingredients and sift. Add to above mixture until mixed. Pour into 3 well-greased loaf pans 4" x 8", sprinkle with chocolate chips. Bake 1 hour at 350°.

A favorite breakfast bread.

Submitted by:

The Inn on South Street
South Street, Box 478A
Kennebunkport, Maine 04046
(207) 967-5151
Jacques & Eva Downs
$75.00 to $105.00

Full breakfast
3 rooms, 3 private baths
Children, over 10
No pets
Restricted smoking
Am Ex

Comfortable elegance in early 19th century home. Spacious guest rooms, one with fireplace, tastefully decorated with period antiques. Sumptuous breakfast, good conversation & views of the river & ocean. On a quiet side street, close to restaurants, shops & beach.

COCONUT INN BANANA BREAD

1/4 cup butter
1 cup sugar
1 egg
1/2 teaspoon baking soda
1/2 teaspoon salt
3 peeled, mashed bananas
2 cups flour
1/2 cup nuts

Combine all ingredients, mix, and bake at 300° for 40 minutes. Makes 1 loaf.

Origin: Simplicity at its very finest, an original recipe.

Submitted by:

Coconut Inn
181 Hui Road 'F'
Napili, Maui, Hawaii 96761
(808) 669-5712
$69.00 to $99.00

Continental breakfast
40 rooms, 40 private baths
Children allowed
No pets
Smoking allowed
Mastercard & Visa

A charming two-story, 40 unit retreat above Napili Bay. Each unit has a T.V., telephone, and a fully-equipped kitchen. Amenities include a free form pool, oversized spa, quiet garden areas, and daily maid service. Fine restaurants in neighborhood. Short stroll to beach.

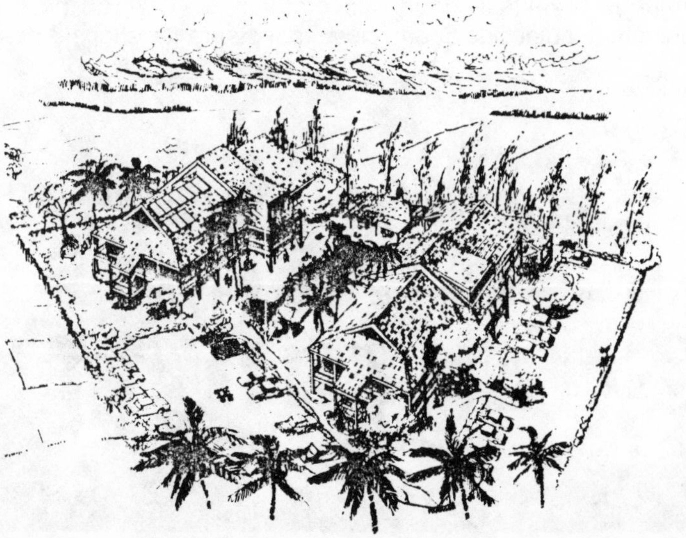

CRANBERRY BREAD

1 cup halved cranberries
1/4 cup sugar
1 cup chopped walnuts
2 eggs, beaten
1 cup firmly packed brown sugar
3 tablespoons salad oil
1 medium orange, ground
3/4 cup orange juice
3 cups sifted flour
1/2 teaspoon soda
3 teaspoons baking powder
1 teaspoon salt

Combine cranberries, sugar and walnuts. Cream eggs and brown sugar until fluffy. Add salad oil, ground orange and orange juice. Sift together flour, soda, baking powder, and salt. Stir into creamed mixture. Fold in sugared cranberries and nut mixture. Bake in greased loaf pan at 350° for 50 - 60 minutes.

Submitted by:

Halfway House
Bed & Breakfast
Route #2, Box 80
Oxford, Wisconsin 53952
(608) 586-5489
Dr. J. A. & Genevieve Hines
$28.00 to $42.00

Full breakfast
4 rooms
No children
No pets
No smoking

We were once a stop on the logging road that went north out of Portage in the 1800's. A comfortable, peaceful working farm with Herefords in the pastures; there are wild birds and animals. Your host is a veterinarian, working with all animals, but mostly dairy cattle.

DATE NUT BREAD

1 - 8 oz. pkg. dates
1 cup hot water
3 eggs
2 cups sugar
3/4 cup vegetable oil
2 cups plain flour
1/2 teaspoon salt
2 teaspoons baking powder
1 teaspoon ground cloves
1 teaspoon allspice
1 teaspoon cinnamon
1 cup chopped nuts

Soak dates in hot water. Meanwhile, beat eggs and add sugar and oil. Stir in dry ingredients and mix lightly. Add nuts, and dates in their soaking water, and mix just to combine. Pour batter into a greased and lined loaf pan. Bake at 325° for one hour, or until toothpick inserted in the center comes out clean.

Submitted by:

Cedar Grove Mansion
2300 Washington Street
Vicksburg, Mississippi 39180
(800) 862-1300 (outside MS.)
(800) 448-2820 (inside MS.)
Estelle Mackey
$75.00 to $130.00

Full breakfast
17 rooms, 17 private baths
Children, over 6
No pets
Restricted smoking
Mastercard, Visa, Am Ex

1840's mansion, with gaslit chandeliers, Italian marble mantels & gold leaf mirrors. Union cannonball is lodged in parlor wall. Mississippi's finest inn, 4 acres of formal gardens, fountains, gazebos, courtyards, pool and spa. Magnificent views, and AAA 4-Diamond rating.

EXQUISITE EASY STICKY BUNS

1 cup light sour cream
1 1/2 tablespoons dry yeast
1/4 cup warm water
2 tablespoons melted butter
1 teaspoon salt
3 tablespoons sugar
1/8 teaspoon soda
1 egg
3 cups flour

Filling:
3 tablespoons melted butter
3/4 cup brown sugar
1 teaspoon cinnamon
1 cup chopped pecans

Syrup:
1/2 cup sugar
3 tablespoons water
1 stick butter or margarine

Heat sour cream to lukewarm. Dissolve yeast in warm water, add to butter, salt, sugar, soda and egg. Stir in flour and blend well. Knead dough on floured board for 1 minute. Form into ball, let rest 5 minutes. Roll in 18" x 24" rectangle. Filling: Brush dough with melted butter, sprinkle with mixture of brown sugar and cinnamon. Sprinkle with nuts. Starting with long side, roll (as a jelly roll) and cut into 1 1/2" slices. Syrup: Simmer sugar in water until dissolved. Add butter, boil until thick and sticky. Drop 1 tablespoon of syrup into bottom of buttered muffin cups. Place dough slices in muffin cups. Let rise in warm place about 1 hour. Bake at 350° for 10 - 12 minutes. Invert on rack upon removing from oven. Makes 16 buns.

Submitted by:

The Heirloom
214 Shakeley Lane
Ione, California 95640
(209) 274-4468
Melisande Hubbs & Patricia Cross
$50.00 to $85.00

Full breakfast
6 rooms, 4 private baths
Children, over 10
No pets
Restricted smoking

1863 colonial antebellum brick in California gold country. Spacious English garden, century-old trees, magnolias, gardenias & wisteria, on 1 1/2 acres. Heirloom antiques, fireplaces, gracious hospitality.

GERMAN COFFEE BRAID

1 cup scalded milk, cool slightly
1 1/2 cups sugar
1 1/2 sticks melted butter
3 pkgs. yeast (dissolved in 1/2 cup - 115° water)
4 eggs & 1 yolk (reserve)
2 teaspoons anise seed, or fresh lemon rind zest from 2 large lemons
5 - 6 cups flour
1 cup raisins (regular or golden)

Combine milk, sugar, melted butter and dissolved yeast. Add 4 eggs, beat well. Add anise seed or lemon zest. Gradually add flour and raisins to make a moderately stiff dough. Knead 5 minutes. Let rise 1 - 1 1/2 hours. Punch down. Divide in half. Roll three 15" ropes from each half; braid and tuck ends. Let rise until double. Brush with beaten egg yolk, sprinkle sugar between cracks. Bake at 350° for 30 minutes on greased pan.

Origin: Traditional, authentic family recipe brought from Germany.

Submitted by:

Woodstock Inn
Bed & Breakfast
1212 W. Lexington
Independence, Missouri
64050
(816) 833-2233
Lane & Ruth Harold
$38.50 to $55.00

Full breakfast
11 rooms, 11 private baths
Children allowed
No pets
No smoking
Mastercard & Visa

Renovated 1900's home in the heart of historic city. Tasteful decor & air-conditioning. Near Truman Library & Home, theme parks, religious centers & sports stadiums. 2 handicapped-accessible rooms. Good food (special diets okay), hospitality & German language capability.

HOMESTEAD CINNAMON ROLLS

Dough:
1/2 cup lukewarm water
1 1/2 tablespoons yeast
1 cup mashed potatoes
2 teaspoons salt
2 eggs
1 cup sugar
1 tablespoon vanilla
1 1/2 cups milk
2/3 cup butter
7 - 8 cups bread flour
Cinnamon-sugar mixture for top of rolls

Filling:
1 cup brown sugar
1/2 tablespoon cinnamon
4 tablespoons butter
1 tablespoon milk

Caramel Icing:
1 cup butter
1 cup light brown sugar
2 teaspoons vanilla
2 tablespoons milk
4 cups sifted powdered sugar

Dough: Mix yeast in water, set aside. Cream together potatoes, salt, eggs, sugar and vanilla. Heat milk and butter together until butter melts. Add to mixture. Then add yeast. Pour over 1/2 of flour and mix. Add remaining flour a little at a time. Let rise until doubled. Punch down, roll out flat 1/4" thick. Mix filling ingredients and spread over entire dough. Roll up and cut and lay in about 6 pie pans, 3 - 4 per pan. Sprinkle with cinnamon-sugar. Let rise again 1/2 hour. Bake at 350° for 20 minutes. Icing: Melt butter in microwave until it bubbles. Add brown sugar and stir well. Add vanilla and milk, stirring until blended together. Add powdered sugar. Ice rolls while warm.

Submitted by:

Homestead Inn
7830 Pine Forest Road
Pensacola, Florida 32506
(904) 944-4816
Neil & Jeanne Liechty
$49.00 to $69.00

Full breakfast
5 rooms, 5 private baths
Children allowed
No pets
No smoking
Mastercard, Visa, Am Ex

Williamsburg atmosphere, with delicious Mennonite-prepared food, now famous in northwest Florida. Outside gazebo-courtyard area is perfect for reading, or quietly catching your breath. Near Pensacola Beach, Historic Downtown, Naval Air Museum & the USS Lexington.

HOT CROSS BUNS

1 cup sugar
1/2 cup melted butter, plus 2 tablespoons
4 eggs, separated, use yolks only
2 1/4 cups lukewarm milk
1 pkg. dry yeast sprinkled over milk
8 cups flour
1 1/2 teaspoons salt
1 teaspoon nutmeg
1/4 teaspoon powdered cloves
1 cup candied fruit
1 cup raisins

Mix sugar, 1/2 cup melted butter, egg yolks, milk and yeast, and 4 cups flour. Add salt, nutmeg, cloves and 4 more cups flour. Add fruit and raisins, and mix. Knead in bowl with hands 2 minutes. Punch down dough. Store in refrigerator overnight. Next day, remove from bowl, let stand 1 hour, and knead again. Divide dough into 32 pieces (balls), place on baking sheet 1" apart, and let rise until size of small oranges. Bake 25 minutes at 375°. Melt 2 tablespoons butter and 1 tablespoon water, brush on top of rolls.

Origin: Family recipe for 50 years or more. Made all year-round at the inn.

Submitted by:

Buckmaster Inn
R.R. #1, Lincoln Hill Road
Shrewsbury, Vermont 05738
(802) 492-3485
Sam & Grace Husselman
$45.00 to $60.00

Full & continental breakfast
4 rooms, 2 private baths
Children, over 8
No pets
Restricted smoking
Travelers checks

Built in 1801 as a stagecoach stop, we stand on a knoll in the heart of the Green Mts., overlooking a picturesque red barn & valley. Center hall, grand staircase and wide-pine floors show off family antiques. Country kitchen with fireplace, 4 other fireplaces, library, 2 porches.

IRISH SODA BREAD

3 1/2 cups all-purpose flour
1/2 cup sugar
1 teaspoon salt
1/2 teaspoon baking soda
2 teaspoons baking powder
2 large eggs
1 pint sour cream
1 cup dark raisins
2 teaspoons caraway seeds

Preheat oven to 350°. Grease and flour a round 8" cake pan. Mix together flour, sugar, salt, baking soda and baking powder. Fold in eggs and sour cream. Add the raisins and caraway seeds. Do not overbeat. Shape in cake pan, cut slit in top. Bake 1 hour.

Origin: Mrs. Fleming's Irish Soda Bread.

Submitted by:

Battle Island Inn
R.D. #1, Box 176
Fulton, New York 13069
(315) 593-3699
Richard & Joyce Rice
$50.00 to $75.00

Full breakfast
6 rooms, 6 private baths
Children allowed
No pets
No smoking
Mastercard & Visa

Battle Island Inn, circa 1840, is located across from the Oswego River just 7 miles from historic Oswego on Lake Ontario. The inn is furnished with period antiques throughout and a full breakfast is served in our elegant Empire dining room.

JAM BREAD

- 7/8 cup sugar (scant cup)
- 3 eggs
- 1/2 cup oil
- 2 1/2 cups self-rising flour
- 1 cup or 8 oz. jar jam (blackberry, strawberry, red raspberry, etc.)
- 1/4 cup sour cream
- 1/2 teaspoon cream of tartar
- 1/2 teaspoon vanilla
- 1 - 2 oz. pkg. pecans, chopped

Mix sugar, eggs and oil together in large bowl. Blend in flour, jam, sour cream and cream of tartar. Add vanilla and nuts. Mix well. Grease and flour one standard or two small loaf pans. Turn batter into pan, bake 45 - 60 minutes at 275°. Cool in pan 10 minutes.

Origin: Variation of a recipe from the Harley Hotel.

Submitted by:

P.T. Baker House
Bed & Breakfast
406 Highland Avenue
Carrollton, Kentucky 41008
(502) 732-4210
Bill & Judy Gants
$45.00 to $75.00

Full breakfast
3 rooms, 3 private baths
Children, over 10
No pets
Smoking allowed
Mastercard & Visa

1882 Eastlake Victorian home, overlooking the Carroll County Courthouse Square. Elaborate gingerbread exterior decoration, beautiful original interior features. Greeted with homemade cookies and fruit bowls in room. Walk to antique and gift shops, sports & restaurants.

KICKAPOO EGG BREAD

1 cup sifted cake flour
1 teaspoon baking powder
1/2 teaspoon salt
1/3 cup melted butter
1 cup whole milk
2 large eggs, beaten
4 large hard-boiled eggs

Sift together all dry ingredients; add melted butter and mix together thoroughly until mixture is crumbly. In separate bowl, beat milk and eggs together. Add to dry ingredients and stir thoroughly. Heat oiled casserole pan in oven. Slice over bottom of pan the hard-boiled eggs; pour batter over them. Bake at 450° until slightly puffed. Reduce heat to 350° and bake 25 minutes longer. Serves 4 - 6.

Origin: An original recipe, a favorite of our family. We use eggs and milk from the family farm and butter from the Amish cheese factory.

Submitted by:

Trillium
Route 2, Box 121
La Farge, Wisconsin 54639
(608) 625-4492
Rosanne Boyett
$45.00 to $65.00

Full breakfast
Private cottage, 1 bath
Children allowed
No pets
Smoking allowed

Completely furnished cottage, with woods & fields to explore. Wildlife & domestic livestock. Hammock under the apple tree. Large porch overlooking the garden & orchard. An original stone fireplace in the living room for chilly weather. In a thriving Amish community.

LETTUCE LOAF BREAD

1 1/2 cups flour
2 teaspoons baking powder
2 teaspoons baking soda
1/8 teaspoon mace
1/8 teaspoon ginger
1 cup sugar
1/2 cup oil
1 1/2 teaspoons grated lemon peel
1 cup chopped lettuce
2 eggs
1/2 cup walnuts (optional)

Sift dry ingredients. Combine sugar, oil and lemon peel. Add flour combination and lettuce. Add eggs one at a time, beating after each addition. Stir in nuts if desired. Turn into greased loaf pan and bake at 350° for 1 hour or until done. Cool in pan for 15 minutes and remove.

Origin: My grandmother used to make this bread. It's a puzzler, because no one knows what's in it!

Submitted by:

High Meadows
Bed & Breakfast
Route 101
Eliot, Maine 03903
(207) 439-0590
Elaine Raymond
$50.00 to $60.00

Full breakfast
5 rooms, 3 private baths
Children, over 12
No pets
Restricted smoking

Built in 1736 on the side of a hill in a country setting, by a merchant ship builder and captain. All the modern conveniences with the charm of the past. Minutes away from historic Portsmouth, New Hampshire and outlet shopping malls.

MAJOR'S ZUCCHINI BREAD

- 2 cups flour
- 2 cups sugar
- 2 teaspoons baking soda
- 2 teaspoons baking powder
- 1/8 teaspoon salt (opt.)
- 1/8 teaspoon nutmeg
- 3 teaspoons ground cinnamon
- 1/8 teaspoon allspice
- 8 eggs
- 1 1/2 cups vegetable oil
- 2 cups ground zucchini
- 1/4 cup chopped walnuts
- 1/4 cup raisins
- 1/4 cup blueberries

Preheat oven to 325°. Mix dry ingredients in large bowl. Add eggs, oil, zucchini, walnuts, raisins, blueberries. Pour into greased and floured pan. Bake for 60 - 70 minutes, until toothpick inserted comes out clean. Cool on wire rack for 10 minutes. Makes 2 loaves.

Submitted by:

Inn at Thatcher Brook Falls
R.D. #2, Box 62
Waterbury, Vermont 05676
(802) 244-5911
Kelly Fenton & Peter Varty
$75.00 to $125.00

Full breakfast
24 rooms, 24 private baths
Children, over 2
No pets
Restricted smoking
Mastercard & Visa

1899 Victorian mansion on Historic Register. Romantic get-away atmosphere with canopy beds, fireplaces, whirlpool tubs, antiques. Fine dining accented with candlelight & elegance. Central location.

MANSION HILL'S COUNTRY CINNAMON ROLLS

6 - 7 cups flour
1/2 cup sugar
2 teaspoons salt
3 tablespoons dry yeast
1/2 cup very warm water
1 1/2 cups warm milk
1/2 cup butter or margarine
2 eggs, beaten

Filling:
1/2 cup melted butter
1/2 cup milk
Cinnamon to taste
1 lb. brown sugar
1/2 cup chopped pecans

Icing:
1 lb. powdered sugar
1/4 teaspoon vanilla
1/2 cup heavy cream

Sift flour, sugar and salt into mixing bowl. Place yeast into small mixing bowl with warm water. Into large mixing bowl knead flour mixture, yeast mixture, warm milk, butter and beaten eggs. Knead on floured board for 1 minute; dough must rise for 20 minutes. After rising, roll out on a floured board and cut into portions. Sprinkle filling mixture onto dough. Place on greased baking sheet. Bake at 335° for 30 minutes. Top with icing.

Submitted by:

Mansion Hill Country Inn
Mansion Hill Drive
Bonne Terre, Missouri 63628
(314) 358-5311
Doug & Cathy Georgens
$60.00 to $80.00

Full breakfast
5 rooms, 2 private baths
Children, over 12
No pets
Restricted smoking
Mastercard, Visa,
Am Ex, Discover

1902 historical mansion, with 32 rooms, lovingly renovated. Huge fireplaces in the great rooms to warm on a frosty night. Also boasting a gourmet restaurant with unlimited menu.

MERRY MORNING RING

3/4 cup warm milk
1/4 cup sugar
1 teaspoon salt
1/4 cup shortening
2 beaten eggs

1 pkg. yeast mixed with
2 1/4 cups flour,
1/2 teaspoon mace, &
1/2 teaspoon nutmeg

For bottom crust:
Brown sugar

Maraschino cherries or pineapple chunks
Walnuts or pecans

Beat milk, sugar, salt, shortening, eggs, and yeast mixture 1 minute by hand. Cover with plastic wrap and let rise until light. Stir down. Grease angel food pan heavily with lots of butter and put a generous amount of brown sugar on the bottom. Arrange cherries or pineapple and walnuts or pecans all the way around the bottom. Pour batter into pan and let rise until light, about 45 minutes. Bake at 350° for 30 minutes. Turn out immediately on large plate. Let cool for 5 minutes, slice and serve. Can be made night before, and reheated in microwave before serving.

Submitted by:

Secluded Bed & Breakfast
19719 N. E. Williamson Road
Newberg, Oregon 97132
(503) 538-2635
Durell & Del Belanger
$35.00 to $50.00

Full breakfast
2 rooms, 1 private bath
Children, under 1 or over 6
No pets
Restricted smoking

Secluded country home on 10 acres, 25 miles west of Portland, Oregon. Restful retreat with hiking, and seasonal wildlife. Near fine eating establishments, air conditioned. Oregon coast 1 hour's drive.

MOM'S CARROT TEA BREAD

2 cups sugar
3/4 cup vegetable oil
4 eggs, unbeaten
2 cups flour
2 teaspoons baking powder
1 1/2 teaspoons baking soda
1 teaspoon salt
2 teaspoons cinnamon
3 cups raw grated carrot

Carrot Bread Icing:
1/2 cup soft butter
8 oz. soft cream cheese
1 lb. box confectioners sugar
1 teaspoon vanilla
1 cup chopped pecans

Cream sugar and oil until fluffy. Add eggs and beat well. Sift together flour, baking powder, baking soda, salt and cinnamon. Add dry ingredients to creamed mixture. Fold in grated carrots. Bake in large oiled and floured loaf pan at 300° for 50 - 55 minutes. Cool bread. Icing: Beat butter and cream cheese together until light (soft). Gradually add sugar, mix well. Add vanilla and nuts. Frost the cooled bread loaf.

Submitted by:

Century House
10 Cliff Road
Nantucket Island, Mass. 02554
(508) 228-0530
Gerry Connick & Jean E. Heron
$65.00 to $145.00

Continental plus breakfast
10 rooms, 8 private baths
Children allowed
No pets
Restricted smoking

Originally opened in 1833, we offer authentically restored, beautifully appointed rooms. In the residential Historic District, near beaches, restaurants, galleries, theatre, bicycle rentals and tennis facilities.

PERSIMMON OAT BREAD

2/3 cup raisins
1 cup hot water
1 cup packed brown sugar
4 teaspoons vegetable oil
2 eggs
2 cups persimmon pulp
2 cups whole wheat flour
2 cups all-purpose flour
2 cups rolled oats
8 teaspoons baking powder
1/2 teaspoon soda
1/2 teaspoon salt
1/2 teaspoon cinnamon or pumpkin pie spice

Mix together and cool first 4 ingredients. Add eggs and persimmon pulp. Add to this mixture all of the dry ingredients. Bake at 350° for 1 hour and 10 minutes. Test with pick for doneness. Makes 1 bundt pan or 2 loaf pans.

Origin: Our daughter Michel has persimmon trees on her farm. She created this bread; very, very popular with our guests.

Submitted by:

The Columbus Inn
445 Fifth Street
Columbus, Indiana
47201
(812) 378-4289
Paul A. Staublin
$79.00 to $225.00

Full breakfast
34 rooms, 35 private baths
Children allowed
No pets (special arrangement)
Restricted smoking
Mastercard, Visa,
Am Ex, Discover

History, hospitality & comfort in former 1895 city hall. Victorian elegance with ornate woodwork, elaborate tin ceilings & ornamental tile. Attention to detail expected in a premier hotel, with intimate atmosphere - feel like a V.I.P. Only AAA 4 Diamond B & B in the Midwest.

PINEAPPLE MACADAMIA NUT BREAD

2 cups all purpose flour
1 1/2 tablespoons baking powder
1/2 teaspoon salt
1/4 teaspoon nutmeg
1/4 cup unsalted butter
3/4 cup granulated sugar
2 eggs, room temperature
2/3 cup milk
1 teaspoon vanilla
1 cup crushed pineapple
1 cup macadamia nuts
1 tablespoon granulated sugar

In a bowl sift together flour, baking powder, salt and nutmeg. In another bowl cream butter and 3/4 cup sugar and beat in eggs, one at a time. Stir in flour mixture alternately with milk, and stir in vanilla. Fold in drained pineapple and nuts, and turn batter into a well-buttered and floured 7-cup loaf pan. (9 1/2" x 5" x 2 3/4") Sprinkle the remaining 1 tablespoon of sugar over batter and bake in a preheated 350° oven for 45 - 55 minutes, or until tester comes out clean. Let bread cool in pan on a rack for 10 minutes, turn it out onto rack, and cool completely. Makes 1 loaf.

Submitted by:

Pearl Street Inn
1820 Pearl Street
Boulder, Colorado 80302
(303) 444-5584
Yossi Shem-Avi &
Cathy Surratt
$68.00 to $98.00

Continental breakfast
7 rooms, 7 private baths
Children allowed
Pets allowed
Smoking allowed
Mastercard, Visa, Am Ex

A restored 1895 Victorian blends an inn ambiance with amenities of a luxury hotel. Guest rooms are laced with understated elegance, each with fireplace. 3 blocks from famous pedestrian mall with city's finest shops, galleries & restaurants. Nestled in the foothills of the Rockies.

PINEAPPLE NUT LOAF

1/2 cup butter
1 cup brown sugar
1 egg, beaten
1 cup crushed pineapple
3 tablespoons milk
2 cups sifted whole wheat flour
1 teaspoon baking powder
1/2 teaspoon baking soda
1/2 cup chopped walnuts

Grease a 9" x 5" x 3" loaf pan. Beat butter, brown sugar and egg in large bowl until fluffy. Combine pineapple and milk in a bowl. Sift flour, baking powder and baking soda onto waxed paper. Stir into sugar mixture alternately with pineapple-milk mixture. Stir in nuts. Place in pan. Bake in 350° oven 1 hour, or until center is springy to touch. Cool in pan on wire rack 5 minutes. Turn out of pan and cool completely.

Origin: Aunt Minnie.

Submitted by:

Casa de la Paz
22 Avenida Menendez
St. Augustine, Florida 32084
(904) 829-2915
Harry Stafford & Brenda Sugg
$65.00 to $135.00

Continental plus breakfast
5 rooms, 5 private baths
Children, over 8
No pets
No smoking
Mastercard, Visa, Am Ex

On the bayfront in the Historic District, we are a Mediterranean villa with Spanish walled courtyard. Central to all attractions. Completely renovated for an elegant stay in the oldest city.

PINEAPPLE TURNOVERS

6 cups sifted flour
2 cups lard, no substitute
1 tablespoon sugar
3 eggs, well-beaten
1 cake yeast (dissolved in 1/2 cup warm water)

Filling:
1 cup sugar
3 tablespoons cornstarch
1 can crushed pineapple

Mix first 4 ingredients as for piecrust. Add yeast mixture and chill overnight. Cook all filling ingredients until clear, then let chill. Roll chilled dough on sugared board. Cut into 3" squares and fill in center of squares. Lap over opposite ends in middle, over the filling. Bake on ungreased cookie sheet at 400° for 10 - 14 minutes, or until lightly browned. Yields 18 turnovers.

Submitted by:

Abendruh Bed & Breakfast
Swisstyle
7019 Gehin Road
Belleveille, Wisconsin 53508
(608) 424-3808
Mathilde Jaggi
$35.00 to $55.00

Full breakfast
3 rooms, 2 private baths
No children
No pets
No smoking
Mastercard & Visa

European hospitality by a Swiss hostess, in a peaceful get-away on a quiet country lane. Cool and relaxing in summer, cozy and warm in winter. Fireplaces, cable television, VCR, piano, large recreation area. Tourist attractions and year-round recreational activities nearby.

PUMPKIN BREAD WITH CREAM YOGURT SAUCE

3 cups sugar
1 cup vegetable oil
4 eggs, beaten
1 1/2 lb. canned pumpkin
3 1/2 cups flour
2 teaspoons soda
2 teaspoons salt
1/2 teaspoon ground cloves
1 teaspoon allspice
1 teaspoon nutmeg
2 1/2 teaspoons cinnamon
2/3 cup water

Sauce:
2 cartons peach yogurt
1 cup heavy whipping cream
3 tablespoons powdered sugar

Beat sugar, oil and eggs until creamy. Add pumpkin. Add dry ingredients. Add water and stir just till mixed. Pour into two very lightly greased and floured 9" x 5" loaf pans. Bake at 350° for 1 hour. Beat sauce ingredients until creamy, serve over bread or fruit.

Origin: The bread is my Amish grandmother's recipe, and the sauce is mine.

Submitted by:

Nicki's Country Place
31780 Edson Creek Road
Gold Beach, Oregon 97444
(503) 247-6037
Nicki & Carl Roten
$47.00 to $49.00

Full breakfast
2 rooms, 1 private bath
Children allowed
No pets
No smoking
Mastercard & Visa

Nestled among trees, we combine country French surroundings with the openness & warmth of a wilderness lodge. Cathedral ceilings & fireplace. Views of the surrounding mountains. Deer & squirrels play in yard. Whale watching, hiking, excellent dining & beach combing.

QUICK CROISSANTS

1 pkg. yeast, active dry or compressed
1 cup warm water
3/4 cup evaporated milk, undiluted
1 1/2 teaspoons salt
1/3 cup sugar
1 egg
5 cups unsifted all purpose flour
1/4 cup melted & cooled butter or margarine
1 cup (1/2 lb.) firm cold butter or margarine
1 egg beaten with 1 tablespoon water

Soften yeast in water. Add milk, salt, sugar, egg, 1 cup flour, and melted butter; set aside. In large bowl, cut 1 cup firm butter into remaining flour until particles are size of dried kidney beans. Pour yeast batter over top, blend carefully with a spatula, until all flour is moistened. Cover and refrigerate at least 4 hours to 4 days. On floured board, press into compact ball and knead about 6 turns just to release bubbles. Divide dough into 2, 3, or 4 parts, depending on size of rolls you want. Shape one lot at a time, refrigerating remainder. Shaping: On floured board roll dough into circle 17" - 22". Cut into 8 equal pie-shaped wedges. Roll toward point, shape into croissant, place on ungreased baking sheet with point down. Allow 1 1/2" between each roll. Let rise until almost doubled in bulk. Bake at 325° for 35 minutes or until lightly browned. Brush with egg mixture 5 minutes before they are finished baking. May also freeze baked rolls.

Submitted by:

Chaffin's Balmoral Farm
Bed & Breakfast
1245 W. Washington Road
Ithaca, Michigan 48847
(517) 875-3410
Sue Chaffin
$20.00 to $40.00

Full breakfast
2 rooms, 2 private baths
Children allowed
No pets
No smoking

Turn of the century farmhouse furnished with family quilts & antiques. Located on historic farm with stone fence and restored hip roof barn. Free tours of working farm operation available. Country breakfast.

RAISED COFFEE BREAD

2 cakes yeast or 2 pkgs. dry yeast
1/3 cup lukewarm water
1 cup milk
1/3 cup granulated sugar
2 teaspoons salt
1/3 cup shortening
2 eggs, beaten
4 cups sifted all-purpose flour
Melted shortening
3 tablespoons brown sugar
1 tablespoon cinnamon

Glaze:
3/4 cup confectioners sugar
1 teaspoon water
Topping: Chopped nuts

Crumble yeast into water. In large saucepan scald milk; add sugar, salt and shortening, cool to lukewarm. Stir in yeast and eggs. Add flour by cups, beating well after each addition until dough is stiff enough to handle. Brush with melted shortening, cover with towel, let rise in warm place (80 - 85°) until double in bulk. Knead on lightly floured board until smooth, with more flour if needed. Divide into six parts, roll out 3, each to 1/4" thick. Combine brown sugar & cinnamon, sprinkle 1/2 over 3 parts of dough. Roll each part up like jelly roll, starting at long side, and twist. Place in greased bread pan about 4" x 8". Braid twists loosely, pinching ends together. Brush with melted shortening. Repeat entire procedure with remaining 3 parts of dough, rolling each out, & sprinkling with cinnamon-sugar. Nuts, cherries, raisins or cooked drained prunes may be added before rolling. Cover, let rise until double in bulk. Bake at 375° for 30 minutes or until done. Mix glaze until smooth. Frost while warm, sprinkle with nuts. Makes 2 loaves.

Submitted by:

Henry Farm Inn
P.O. Box 646
Chester, Vermont 05143
(802) 875-2674
J. Bowman
$50.00 to $80.00

Full breakfast
7 rooms, 7 private baths
Children allowed
No pets
Restricted smoking
Mastercard & Visa

A 1780's stagecoach stop, nestled on 50 acres of rolling hills and woods. Spacious bedrooms, original widepine flooring and 8 fireplaces, a beehive oven, and early American ambiance.

THREE SEED BREAD

2 cups melted margarine
4 cups sugar
8 eggs, beaten
5 cups flour
4 teaspoons baking powder
2 teaspoons salt
2 cups milk
1 cup sunflower seeds
1/4 cup poppy seeds
1/4 cup caraway seeds

Mix margarine and sugar. Then add beaten eggs. Add alternately: flour (mixed with baking powder & salt) and milk. Then add the seeds. Bake at 325° in greased bread pans. Check doneness at 45 minutes. This recipe makes 6 loaves. They freeze well.

Origin: We invented this recipe a few years ago and have been using it happily ever since. Our guests love this bread.

Submitted by:

Lothrop Merry House
Owen Park, Box 1939
Vineyard Haven, Mass. 02568
(508) 693-1646
John & Mary Clarke
$65.00 to $145.00

Continental breakfast
7 rooms, 4 private baths
Children allowed
No pets
Smoking allowed
Mastercard & Visa

Charming 18th century B&B, on Martha's Vineyard, featured in The Best Places to Stay in New England. Overlooks Vineyard Haven Harbor, with private beach & sunny flower-bordered terrace. Harbor views and fireplaces. Close to the ferry, fine shops and restaurants.

VERMONT PEAR BREAD

9 tablespoons sweet butter, at room temp.
1 cup sugar
2 large eggs
2 cups flour
1/2 teaspoon salt
1/2 teaspoon baking soda
1 teaspoon baking powder
Pinch of nutmeg
1/4 cup buttermilk
1 cup coarsely-chopped cored pears
1 teaspoon vanilla
1/2 cup chopped walnuts

Cream butter, gradually beat in sugar. Add eggs one at a time, beating well after each additon. Combine dry ingredients and add to egg mixture alternately with buttermilk. Fold in pears and vanilla. Add nuts. Pour into prepared loaf pan. Bake at 350° for 1 hour. Cool and slice.

Origin: One fall, a friend delivered over a bushel of ripe Vermont pears to us. Once again, this recipe proves that "Necessity is the mother of - - -"

Submitted by:

The Governor's Inn
86 Main Street
Ludlow, Vermont 05149
(802) 228-8830
Charlie & Deedy Marble
$170.00 to $180.00

Full breakfast
8 rooms, 8 private baths
No pets
Restricted smoking
Mastercard & Visa

An elegant Victorian country inn. Potpourri-scented air, soft strains of classical music, & family heirlooms. National recognition & awards for excellence and superb cuisine only add to the warm hospitality.

VERY LEMONY LEMON BREAD

1/2 cup shortening
1 cup sugar
2 eggs, slightly beaten
1 1/4 cups flour (sifted before measuring)
1 teaspoon baking powder
1/2 teaspoon salt
1/2 cup milk
1/2 cup finely chopped nuts
Grated peel of 1 lemon

Topping:
1/8 cup sugar
Juice of 1 lemon

Cream shortening with sugar. Mix in eggs. Sift flour again with baking powder and salt. Alternately add flour mixture and milk to shortening mixture, stirring constantly. Mix in nuts and lemon peel. Bake in greased 5" x 9" loaf pan for about 50 minutes at 350°. As soon as the bread comes out of the oven, poke holes in the top with a fork and spoon the topping over it. NOTE: Mix the topping just prior to use or it will not be smooth.

Submitted by:

The Gingerbread Mansion
400 Berding Street
Ferndale, California 95536
(707) 786-4000
Wendy Hatfield & Ken Torbert
$85.00 to $165.00

Continental breakfast
9 rooms, 9 private baths
Children, over 10
No pets
Restricted smoking
Mastercard & Visa

Northern California's most-photographed inn, we boast twin, claw-footed tubs for "his & her" bubble baths, fireplaces, bicycles, 4 guest parlors, afternoon tea and colorful gardens. Attention to detail, elegance and warm hospitality make this the ultimate special experience.

WHEAT GERM ZUCCHINI BREAD

3 eggs
1 cup salad oil
1 cup sugar
1 cup brown sugar
3 teaspoons vanilla flavoring
2 cups shredded zucchini (packed)
1/2 cup wheat germ
2 teaspoons baking soda
1 teaspoon salt
1 cup chopped nuts

Combine eggs, oil, sugars and flavoring, beat well. Stir in zucchini. Combine remaining ingredients, mixing first; then add to other ingredients, mixing only until blended. Bake in two 5" x 9" loaf pans 50 - 60 minutes at 350°. Remove from pan after 5 minutes.

Origin: Of necessity, if you raise zucchini in your garden. Some guests take a giant zucchini with them, when they leave.

Submitted by:

The Old Reynolds Mansion
100 Reynolds Heights
Asheville, N.C. 28804
(704) 254-0496
Fred & Helen Faber
$40.00 to $75.00

Continental breakfast
10 rooms, 8 private baths
Children, over 12
No pets
Smoking allowed

1855 antebellum mansion surrounded by 4 acres of trees on a knoll of Reynolds Mountain. Beautiful view of mountains. Some rooms have working fireplaces. Swimming pool on grounds. Near Biltmore Estate, hiking, rafting, horseback riding, & Blue Ridge Parkway.

WILD PERSIMMON WALNUT BREAD

8 - 10 eggs
2 cups oil
1 1/2 cups orange juice (or apple juice)
1 1/2 cups sugar (more or less as desired)
2 cups whole oats
5 cups whole wheat flour
4 cups unbleached white flour
1 cup cornmeal
5 teaspoons baking soda
4 teaspoons baking powder
8 - 10 cups ripe, pitted & mashed persimmons
1 - 2 cups soaked raisins
1 tablespoon chopped lemon rind
2 cups chopped walnuts

Butter & flour loaf tins. In large bowl or wok, mix eggs, oil, orange juice and sugar. Gradually add oats, flours and cornmeal, while sifting in baking soda and powder. When thick batter is thoroughly mixed, pour in mashed persimmons, raisins, lemon rind, and walnuts. Bake 1 hour at 350° or until knife inserted comes out clean. Makes 5 medium-sized loaves. A bread ideal for freezing.

Origin: Created upon realizing we had a tree loaded with sweet wild persimmons. The extra toil of picking and mashing is well worth it!

Submitted by:

Acorn Inn, Inc.
P.O. Box 431
Nellysford, Virginia 22958
(804) 361-9357
Kathy Plunket Versluys & Martin Versluys
$35.00 to $85.00

Continental breakfast
10 rooms plus 1 cottage
Children allowed
No pets
Restricted smoking
Visa

We are remembered most for healthy breakfasts, the rejuvenating, rural mountain setting & friendly hospitality. Martin is from Holland; has bicycled through nearly 100 countries. Kathy is a photographer and printmaker. We love swapping stories with our traveling guests.

YEAST BISCUITS

1 pkg. dry yeast
2 tablespoons lukewarm water
2 cups self-rising flour
2 tablespoons sugar
1/4 teaspoon baking soda
1/2 cup shortening
3/4 cup buttermilk

Dissolve yeast in lukewarm water, let stand 5 minutes. Stir sifted flour, sugar and baking soda together. Add shortening and cut in with pastry blender or two knives. Add yeast to buttermilk, then add to flour mixture a little at a time, stirring with fork. Turn dough onto lightly floured cloth or board and knead several times. Roll out to 1/2" thick, cut, and place on ungreased baking sheet. Bake at 450° for 10 - 12 minutes. Note: If plain flour is used, add 2 1/2 teaspoons baking powder and 1 teaspoon salt.) Makes 12 - 16 biscuits 2" in diameter.

Submitted by:

Rosswood Plantation
Highway 552
Lorman, Mississippi 39096
(601) 437-4215
Jean & Walt Hylander
$75.00 to $90.00

Full breakfast
4 rooms, 4 private baths
Children allowed
No pets
Restricted smoking
Mastercard & Visa

An authentic columned antebellum mansion, built 1857, on a former cotton plantation (now Christmas trees), near Natchez and Vicksburg. Civil War history, antiques, slave quarters, charm & true hospitality. AAA 3-Diamond award, a Mississippi landmark, on National Register.

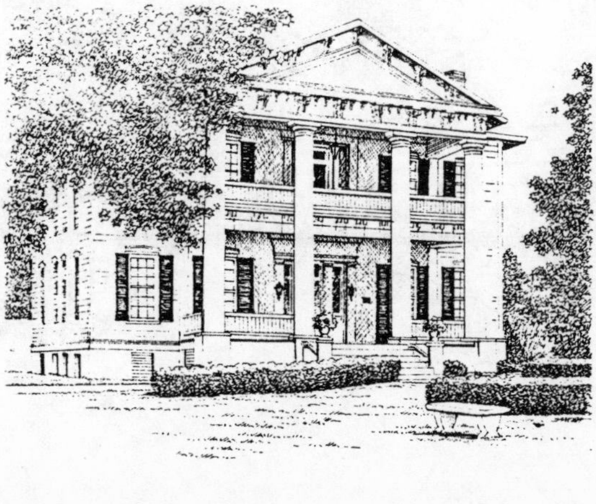

ZUCCHINI MORNING BREAD

- **1 cup sugar**
- **1/2 cup oil**
- **2 eggs**
- **1 teaspoon baking powder**
- **1 teaspoon salt**
- **2 teaspoons baking soda**
- **1 teaspoon vanilla**
- **1/4 teaspoon cinnamon**
- **1/4 teaspoon cloves**
- **1 cup shredded zucchini**
- **2 cups flour**

Mix all ingredients, adding flour last. Bake in loaf pan at 400° for 50 minutes or until knife inserted comes out clean.

Origin: Received raves when used in our restaurant.

Submitted by:

The Gables Inn
103 Walker Street
Lenox, Mass. 01240
(413) 637-3416
Frank Newton
$60.00 to $135.00

Continental breakfast
17 rooms, 17 private baths
Children, over 12
No pets
Smoking allowed
Mastercard, Visa, Am Ex

Home of authoress Edith Wharton, built in 1885, furnished in period style. Special theme rooms: Show Business, Presidents', & Mrs. Wharton's. Indoor swimming pool, private tennis court, quiet garden. Shopping, gracious dining and the discovery of living history in town.

ZUCCHINI PINEAPPLE BREAD

1 cup oil
3 eggs
2 cups sugar
1 1/4 teaspoons vanilla
2 cups grated zucchini
3 cups flour
1 teaspoon baking soda
1 teaspoon baking powder
1 cup crushed pineapple, drained
1/2 cup raisins, optional
1 cup nut meats

Beat together oil, eggs, sugar and vanilla. Add zucchini and dry ingredients. Stir in pineapple, raisins and nuts. Pour into 2 greased and floured loaf pans. Bake 1 hour at 350°.

Submitted by:

Kintner House Inn
101 South Capitol
Corydon, Indiana 47112
(812) 738-2020
Mary Jane Bridgwater
$55.00 to $85.00

Full breakfast
14 rooms, 14 private baths
Children allowed
No pets
No smoking
Mastercard, Visa , Am Ex

Completely restored inn, circa 1873, furnished in Victorian & country antiques, a National Historic Landmark. Breakfast buffet. Nearby are craft and specialty shops, antique malls, Indiana's first state capitol, Zimmerman Glass Factory, 3 major caves, and Wyandotte Woods.

OTHER BAKED GOODS

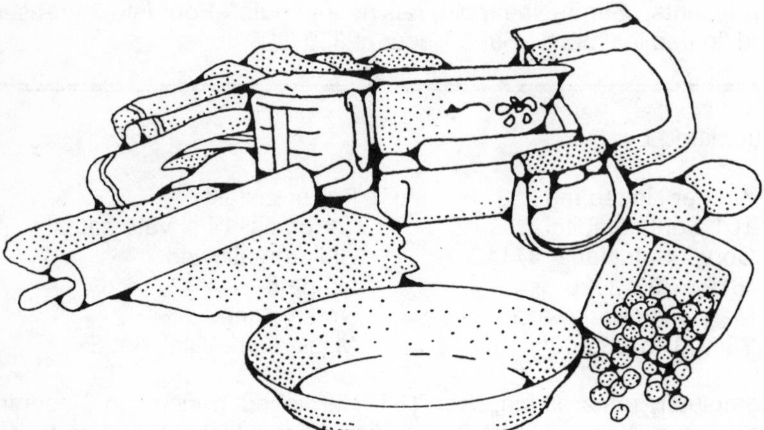

ALMOND BISCOTTI

3 cups flour
1 1/2 cups sugar
12 oz. whole blanched almonds
Grated peel of 2 lemons
6 oz. sweet melted butter
5 eggs, beaten

Hand mix flour, sugar and almonds in large bowl. Add lemon peel, melted butter and eggs and mix. Turn dough onto floured board, blend with fingers and add flour until dough doesn't stick. (About 2 cups more flour). Make 2 rolls of dough and flatten. Bake on floured cookie sheet at 350° until golden, approximately 1/2 hour. Remove from oven, slice at an angle. Separate on cookie sheet and return to oven until golden brown, 1/2 hour longer. Cookies are hard, crunchy, and good with coffee.

Origin: From one of our guests and her Italian grandmother. We often exchange recipes with our guests.

Submitted by:

Preston House
Bed & Breakfast
106 Faithway Street
Santa Fe, New Mexico 8750l
(505) 982-3465
Signe Bergman
$45.00 to $125.00

Continental plus breakfast
9 rooms, 9 private baths
No children
Pets allowed
Restricted smoking
Mastercard, Visa, Am Ex

Queen Anne style house, on the Historic Register and furnished with antiques, yet updated with all modern conveniences. 3 blocks from Santa Fe's Plaza on a quiet dead-end street. Enjoy breakfast on the garden patio in summer or near the dining room fireplace in winter.

APPLE-RASPBERRY CHEDDAR CRISP

2 cups (4 sticks) butter softened and unsalted
2 tablespoons cinnamon
1 1/2 cups brown sugar
4 cups all-purpose flour
1 1/2 cups grated Cheddar cheese
15 apples, peeled and sliced
3 cups raspberries (or other berries)
1 tablespoon cinnamon
2 tablespoons lemon juice

In large mixing bowl combine butter, cinnamon and sugar, until well-blended. Gradually add flour, starting with 2 cups and adding until mixture is crumbly and dry to the touch. Add Cheddar and mix well. Spread 1/2 mixture in large ungreased roasting pan. Combine apples and berries and spread evenly over crumb mix. Sprinkle with cinnamon and lemon juice. Top with rest of crumbs. Bake at 350° for 25 - 30 minutes. Serve with fresh whipped cream.

Origin: We grow our own berries; this is a perennial favorite of our guests.

Submitted by:

The Hilltop Inn
Main Street Route 117
Sugar Hill, N.H. 03585
(603) 823-5695
Mike & Meri Hern
$25.00 to $37.50

Full breakfast
6 rooms, 2 private baths
Children allowed
Pets allowed
Smoking allowed
Mastercard, Visa, Am Ex

Victorian inn filled with antiques. Peaceful & homey. Large country breakfasts, English flannel sheets, lovely views. Ten minutes to White Mountain National Forest. Skiing, hiking, swimming, golf and tennis nearby. 2 1/2 hours from Boston. Brochure & rates available.

APPLE TART

1 homemade or good-quality store pastry
1/2 cup powdered non-dairy coffee creamer
1/2 cup firmly packed brown sugar
1/2 cup sugar
1/3 cup all-purpose flour
1 teaspoon ground cinnamon
1/4 teaspoon salt
1/2 teaspoon ground nutmeg
1/4 cup butter or margarine
6 cups apple slices (1/2" thick)
2 tablespoons lemon juice

Make pastry very thin and put in 12" tart pan. Combine coffee creamer and next 6 ingredients. Sprinkle 1/2 of this mixture over crust. Cut butter into remaining mixture; set aside. Arrange apple slices in a circle in pastry shell, overlapping slices. Sprinkle with lemon juice and remaining sugar mixture. Bake at 450° for 30 minutes.

Origin: This is an adapted recipe for a guest who wanted good homemade pie; and it was such a success, I now use it regularly.

Submitted by:

Prospect Hill Farm
Bed & Breakfast
P.O. Box 135
Gerrardstown, W.V. 25420
(304) 229-3346
Charles & Hazel Hudock
$75.00 to $95.00

Full breakfast
2 rooms, plus cottage
Children allowed in cottage
No pets
Restricted smoking
Mastercard & Visa

1789 antebellum mansion on a working farm in the Shenandoah Valley. Hallway has an oil painting of colonial scenes stretching from the front door to the third floor. 20' x 24' rooms with air-conditioning & fireplaces. Near historic Harper's Ferry, Martinsburg & Winchester.

AUSTRALIAN TEA RING

2 cups sifted all-purpose flour
1 tablespoon baking powder
1/4 cup shortening
3/4 cup milk
1/4 cup melted butter
1/2 cup sugar
1 tablespoon cinnamon
1/4 cup coconut
1/2 cup chocolate chips

Mix flour and baking powder together. Cut in shortening and add milk, mix well. Roll out on a floured surface into large rectangle 1/4" thick. Brush top side with butter and sprinkle with sugar-cinnamon mixture. Sprinkle rectangle with coconut and chips. Roll up jelly-roll fashion and curl into circle. Place in greased pie tin. Slit top at 1" intervals. Bake at 350° for 30 minutes. Makes 1 ring.

Origin: Richard's mother has made this recipe for years in Australia, varying the filling with the seasons. Now a favorite at the inn.

Submitted by:

The Walkabout Inn
837 Village Road
Lampeter, Penn. 17537
(717) 464-0707
Richard & Margaret Mason
$45.00 to $85.00

Full breakfast
4+ rooms, 3 private baths
Children allowed
No pets
Restricted smoking
Mastercard, Visa, Am Ex

Owned & operated by an Australian & his family, an authentic British-style B&B inn, in the heart of Amish country. Antique furnishings, quilts & hand-painted stencilings. Pastries, muffins & jellies. Enjoy restaurants, golf, farm markets or shopping on your own "walkabout".

BLUEBERRY BOY BAIT

2 cups flour
1 1/2 cups sugar
3/4 cup shortening
2 egg yolks (reserve whites)
1 cup milk
1 teaspoon salt
2 teaspoons baking powder
1 teaspoon vanilla
1 pint fresh or frozen blueberries

Preheat oven to 325°. Mix flour, sugar & shortening to resemble coarse cornmeal. Set aside 1 cup for topping. Mix egg yolks, milk, salt, baking powder and vanilla well, and add to dry mixture. In separate bowl beat egg whites, then fold into mixture. Pour into greased and floured 9" x 13" baking dish. Spread blueberries evenly over top. Sprinkle with crumb topping. Bake for 40 minutes or until done.

Submitted by:

Marina Guest House
230 Arbutus
Manistique, Michigan 49854
(906) 341-5147
Margaret A. Beach
$35.00 to $50.00

Full breakfast
5 rooms, 3 private baths
Children allowed
No pets
No smoking

Marina Guest House is a revived bed & breakfast which was active for 14 years during the Depression. The original 1905 home is being redecorated and furnished with a sprinkling of antiques. We are finishing our sixth season of bed & breakfast.

CRANBERRY CRISP

1 cup sugar
3/4 cup flour
1/3 cup softened butter
1 - 16 oz. can whole cranberry sauce

Blend sugar, flour, and butter in food processor. Pour cranberry sauce into well-buttered 8" square pan. Cover with pastry mix. Bake at 350° for 30 - 40 minutes.

Origin: Nantucket has huge cranberry bogs with brilliant color at harvest time.

Submitted by:

The Four Chimneys
38 Orange Street
Nantucket Island, Mass.
02554
(508) 228-1912
Betty York
$98.00 to $155.00

Continental breakfast
10 rooms, 10 private baths
No children
No pets
Smoking allowed
Mastercard, Visa, Am Ex

Very large 1835 Merchant mansion, from days of the whalers and China Clippers. Double drawing room, spiral staircase, harbor views and porches. Continental breakfast served in room. Period antiques, canopy beds and oriental rugs.

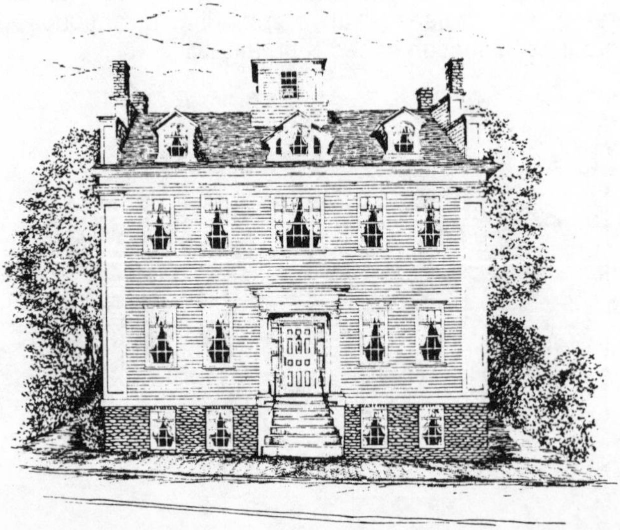

EAGLES' NESTS

1 can (21 oz.) Comstock apple pie filling
1 cup apple juice (plain or spiced)
1 teaspoon cinnamon
1 tablespoon red hots (candy)
1 small box raisins
1 tablespoon granola
1 cup vanilla yogurt

Combine first five ingredients and divide into four ramekins. We use miniature enamel pie pans. Sprinkle granola in center of apples. Bake 30 minutes at 350°. Serve warm with flavored yogurt on the side. We found small round baskets to put the pie pans in - hence the name, as they look like nests. Serves 4.

Origin: Because of our high altitude at 1 mile, we had a problem baking apples; so we invented this easy, popular dish.

Submitted by:

Eagles Landing
Bed & Breakfast
27406 Cedarwood
Lake Arrowhead, California
Mail to: Box 1510,
Blue Jay, California 92317
(714) 336-2642
Dorothy & Jack Stone
$75.00 to $125.00

Full breakfast
4 rooms, 4 private baths
No children
No pets
No smoking

European-style hospitality at its best, by the shores of beautiful Lake Arrowhead in the San Bernadino Mountains. Common room & decks overlook sparkling blue waters. Enjoy boating, fishing & swimming, toasty fires, skiing & skating, in season. Have a mountain adventure!

GIFFORD FAMILY TART

Base:
1 1/2 cups flour
1/4 cup sugar
1 egg yolk
1 stick butter
1/2 teaspoon vanilla

Fruits in season:
cherries,cranberries, raisins, apples, plums, grapes, peaches, blueberries or combinations
Toppings:
Apricot or orange glaze
Powdered sugar

Prepare base in food processor. Put into porcelain quiche pan. Then place fresh fruit in an attractive arrangement. Bake at 350° for 30 minutes. Top with apricot or orange glaze or powdered sugar. Note: Egg yolk can be substituted with Scramblers; butter can be substituted with corn oil margarine.

Origin: We have enjoyed this tart for over 150 years in America. We use only turn-of-the century & earlier "receipts", with modifications.

Submitted by:

The Edge of Thyme
6 Main Street, P.O. Box 48
Candor, New York 13743
(607) 659-5155
Frank & Eva Mae Musgrave
$45.00 to $65.00

Full breakfast
7 rooms, 2 private baths
Children allowed
No pets
No smoking

A Georgian home, in Victorian style, with leaded glass windowed porch, marble fireplaces, parquet floors, beautiful stairway, gardens, arbor, and gracious atmosphere. In the Finger Lakes area, near Watkins Glen, colleges, state parks and Elmira's Mark Twain country.

GLORIA'S FRUIT KUCHEN

1/2 cup softened butter or margarine
1 pkg. yellow cake mix
1/2 cup flaked coconut
2 1/2 cups sliced, pared fruit (apples, peaches, pears, papaya, mango, etc.), fresh or canned
1/2 cup sugar
1 teaspoon cinnamon
1 cup sour cream
2 egg yolks or 1 egg

Cut butter into dry cake mix until crumbly. Mix in coconut. Pat mixture lightly into ungreased 9" x 13" Pyrex baking dish, building up slight edges. Bake 10 minutes. Arrange fruit slices on warm crust. Mix sugar and cinnamon, sprinkle on fruit. Blend sour cream and egg; drizzle over fruit. (Topping will not completely cover fruit.) Bake at 350° for 25 minutes or until crust is light brown. Serve either warm or chilled. Makes 12 - 15 servings.

Origin: Gloria & her husband received this old rural Ohio recipe while serving Sycamore United Church of Christ, and hosting parishioners.

Submitted by:

Gloria's Spouting Horn
Bed & Breakfast
4464 Lawai Beach Road
Poipu, Kauai, Hawaii 96756
(808) 742-6995
Gloria & Bob Merkle
$55.00 to $95.00

Continental breakfast
5 rooms, 3 private baths
Children, over 14
No pets
Restricted smoking
Mastercard & Visa

Intimate oceanfront retreat on the sunny south shore of Kauai; relax in a hammock under coconut palms, or whale watch from your bed with the surf 40 feet from your deck! The Tea House has romantic Japanese-style soaking tub and koi (exotic Japanese carp) pond.

GOLDEN CORNBREAD

- 1 lb. - 10 oz. yellow cornmeal
- 1 lb. corn flour
- 2 lbs. - 12 oz. bread flour
- 4 1/2 oz. baking powder
- 2 lbs. - 8 1/2 oz. granulated sugar
- 1 1/4 oz. salt
- 1/4 oz. nutmeg
- 4 lbs. liquid milk
- 1 lb. - 9 oz. melted shortening
- 1 lb. whole eggs, plus 1 yolk

Preheat oven to 375°. Blend dry ingredients together, add milk slowly till slightly smooth. Add melted shortening, mix on slow speed. Add eggs and mix on slow speed until smooth. Remove from mixer. Place approximately 24 oz. of batter into 9" x 9" x 1 1/3" greased pan. Bake until golden brown.

Origin: Found in an old book in the Jefferson Inn.

Submitted by:

Jefferson Inn
R.D. 2, Box 36, Route 171
Main Street
Thompson, Penn. 18465
(717) 727-2625
Doug & Mary Stark
$25.00 to $50.00

Full breakfast
6 rooms, 3 private baths
Children allowed
Pets allowed, with restrictions
Restricted smoking
Mastercard & Visa

Situated in the rolling hills of Northeast Pennsylvania, our 1871 inn offers uniquely decorated rooms and a warm atmosphere. Near fishing, boating, deer & turkey-hunting. Also skiing, snowmobiling, horseback riding, golfing.

ORANGE SCONES

2 cups flour
1/4 cup sugar
1 tablespoon baking powder
1/2 teaspoon salt
1/4 cup chilled butter, cut into pieces
1/2 cup currants (dried currants if possible)
1 teaspoon grated orange peel
1 egg
1 egg, separated
2/3 cup whipping cream

Preheat oven to 400°. Combine first 4 ingredients in food processor. Add butter pieces and cut in using on/off turns until mixture resembles coarse meal. Transfer to large bowl. Mix in currants and orange peel. Beat whole egg with egg yolk (of separated egg) in small bowl. Whisk in cream. Add to flour mixture and stir until dough pulls away from sides of bowl. Turn dough out on lightly floured surface and knead gently until smooth. Roll or pat out to 1" thickness, cut into 3" rounds. Transfer rounds to baking sheet, spacing 1" apart. Brush tops with egg white. Bake until puffy and golden brown, about 18 minutes. Cool on rack. Serve warm or at room temperature. These scones freeze well. Makes 8 - 15 scones.

Submitted by:

Ye Olde Nantucket House
2647 Main Street
South Chatham, Mass. 02659
(508) 432-5641
Norm Anderton
$60.00 to $72.00

Continental breakfast
5 rooms, 5 private baths
Children, over 8
No pets
Smoking allowed
Mastercard & Visa

A classic Greek Revival style home, brought to its present location in 1867. A short walk to a Nantucket Sound beach and only three miles from the charming seaside village of Chatham, with its fine shops, dining, summer band concerts and picturesque lighthouse.

PALMER INN'S APPLE PIE

Pie Crust:
2 cups all purpose flour
1 teaspoon salt
3/4 cup shortening
1 tablespoon cider vinegar
4 - 5 tablespoons ice cold water

Apple Pie Filling:
1/2 cup white sugar
1/2 cup light brown sugar
1/4 cup orange juice
3 tablespoons flour
1 tablespoon dark corn syrup
1/8 teaspoon allspice
1/4 teaspoon ground nutmeg
1/2 teaspoon ground cinnamon
1/8 teaspoon ginger
6 - 7 cups peeled, cored, thinly sliced Macoun or Cortland apples

Pie Crust: Mix flour and salt. Cut in shortening. Add vinegar and sprinkle with water until flour is moistened and cleans side of bowl. Divide in half and roll to circle 1/8" thick, on floured board. Fold in quarters and place in 9" glass pie plate. Pie Filling: Mix all ingredients except apples, until smooth. Stir in apples. Spoon into shell. Roll other half of crust to 1/8" thick, slit, and place on top of apple mixture. Bake at 450° for 15 minutes; reduce to 350° and bake another 35 minutes.

Submitted by:

The Palmer Inn
25 Church Street
Noank, Connecticut 06340
(203) 572-9000
Patricia W. Cornish
$95.00 to $175.00

Continental breakfast
6 rooms, 6 private baths
Children, over 16
No pets
Restricted smoking
Mastercard & Visa

Elegant seaside 1907 Victorian mansion, 1 block to the water and 2 miles to Mystic. Walking distance to tennis, sailing, art galleries, and a fine Lobster House. Gracious lodging, and personalized service.

PEACH PRALINE PIE

3/4 cup sugar
3 tablespoons all-purpose flour
4 cups peeled & sliced fresh peaches
1 1/2 teaspoons lemon juice
1/3 cup brown sugar, firmly packed
1/4 cup all purpose flour
1/2 cup chopped pecans
3 tablespoons butter
1 unbaked pie shell

In large mixing bowl, combine sugar and 3 tablespoons flour, mix together. Add peaches and lemon juice. In small bowl, combine brown sugar, 1/4 cup flour and pecans, cut the butter in until the mixture becomes crumbly. Sprinkle 1/3 of the nut mixture in an unbaked pie shell until it becomes a layer on the bottom. Cover with peach mixture and sprinkle the remaining nut mixture over the peaches. Bake at 400° until the peaches are tender. If pie browns too quickly, lower oven temperature. Serves 6.

Submitted by:

Bradford Inn
RFD 1, Box 40 - Main Street
Bradford, New Hampshire 03221
(603) 938-5309
Connie & Tom Mazol
$59.00 to $99.00

Full breakfast
12 rooms, 12 private baths
Children allowed
Pets allowed, with limitations
Smoking allowed
Mastercard, Visa, Am Ex, Discover

The Bradford Inn is an historic country hotel which opened in 1898 in a scenic rural village. Savory breakfasts and sumptuous suppers, skiing, hiking, auctions, antiques, state parks, lake cruises, summer playhouse, and foliage, all in Lake Sunapee area of state.

PINEAPPLE SPOONBREAD

3/4 cup sugar
1 stick butter
4 eggs, beaten

5 slices white bread, decrusted & cubed
1 - 20 oz. can crushed pineapple, drained

Cream together sugar and butter thoroughly. Stir in eggs, bread and pineapple. Pour into a 10" quiche dish or large pie plate, greased with Crisco. Bake át 350° for 40 - 45 minutes. Serves 12.

Submitted by:

The Aerie
509 Pollock Street
New Bern, N.C. 28560
(919) 636-5553
Rick & Lois Cleveland
$55.00 to $80.00

Full breakfast
7 rooms, 7 private baths
Children allowed
No pets
Restricted smoking
Mastercard, Visa, Am Ex

A Victorian style home built in 1882, located on a quiet street one block from Tryon Palace. Elegant accommodations include antique furnishings, sitting room with player piano, complimentary beverages and light refreshments, and our generous country breakfast.

PRUNE TEA RING

1/2 cup scalded milk
3 tablespoons shortening
2 tablespoons sugar
1/2 teaspoon salt
1/2 cup water
1 egg
3 cups flour
1 cup prunes, chopped
1 tablespoon lemon juice
1/4 cup sugar
1/8 teaspoon salt
Glaze:
4 teaspoons milk
1 cup powdered sugar
1/4 teaspoon vanilla

Combine first 7 ingredients, let stand 15 minutes. Simmer next 4 ingredients until thickened. Roll dough 14" x 12". Spread with prune mixture. Roll as jelly roll, joining ends in ring on greased baking sheet. Cut deep slits 1" apart and turn ends up. Bake at 350° for 30 minutes. Glaze while warm.

Submitted by:

Adams Inn Bed & Breakfast
1744 Lanier Place, N.W.
Washington, D. C. 20009
(202) 745-3600
Gene & Nancy Thompson
$45.00 to $95.00

Continental plus breakfast
25 rooms, 12 private baths
Children allowed
No pets
No smoking
Mastercard, Visa, Am Ex

We are located near a multi-cultural restaurant area, bus lines, subway, all tourist sites and convention sites. A sitting parlor is available for our guests' relaxation; all rooms are furnished homestyle. Comfortable surroundings and hospitality in a personal atmosphere.

PUMPKIN ROLL

Batter:
3 eggs
1 cup sugar
2/3 cup pumpkin
1 teaspoon baking soda
1 teaspoon cinnamon
3/4 cup flour

Filling:
8 oz. cream cheese
4 tablespoons butter
1 cup powdered sugar
1 teaspoon vanilla

Mix eggs and sugar together. Add remaining ingredients. Bake on a greased cookie sheet (grease pan and put waxed paper on top, then grease and flour waxed paper). Bake at 350° for 15 minutes. (This bakes very quickly, so keep an eye on it.). Remove warm cake from pan onto a dishtowel covered with powdered sugar. Wrap up and let cool. Mix filling ingredients. Unwrap and spread with filling. Roll up like jelly roll and wrap in aluminum foil and keep refrigerated. Slice and serve.

Submitted by:

Kaltenbach's Bed & Breakfast
R.D. #6, Box 106A,
Stony Fork Road
Wellsboro, Penn. 16901
(717) 724-4954
Lee & Tim Kaltenbach
$50.00 to $89.50

Full breakfast
11 rooms, 8 private baths
Children allowed
No pets
No smoking
Mastercard & Visa

A 72 acre, Tioga County farm with a sprawling ranch house offering comfortable lodging, home-style breakfasts & warm hospitality. Forests, meadows, picnic tables, outdoor grills, playground, domestic animals & wildlife. Near skiing, snowmobiling trails, hunting & fishing.

RAISIN AND COTTAGE CHEESE BUNS

1 cup cottage cheese
3 tablespoons milk
1 egg, separated
1/3 cup oil
1/3 cup sugar
1 cup whole wheat flour
1/2 cup white flour
2 teaspoons baking powder
1/2 cup raisins
1/2 cup chopped nuts
5 tablespoons sugar
1 teaspoon cinnamon

Mix together cottage cheese, milk, egg yolk, oil and sugar. Mix flours and baking powder together and add to cottage cheese mixture. Mixture will be sticky. Knead on lightly floured board for short time and roll into a 17" x 8" rectangle. Baste with egg white. Sprinkle with raisins, nuts, sugar, and cinnamon. Roll up tightly to make a long cylinder and cut into 12 pieces. Place in greased pan and bake at 350° for about 25 minutes. These nutritious buns can be served warm with a white icing.

Submitted by:

Deerfield Inn
The Street
Deerfield, Mass. 01342
(413) 774-5587
Karl & Jane Sabo
$115.00

Full breakfast
23 rooms, 23 private baths
Children allowed
Pets allowed
Restricted smoking
Mastercard, Visa, Am Ex

Our inn, built in 1884, is a National Historic Landmark, one of many historic houses lining the mile-long Street. A gracious and elegant home with an award-winning restaurant. Nearby are antique shops, state parks, golfing, boating, fishing, swimming and buggy rides.

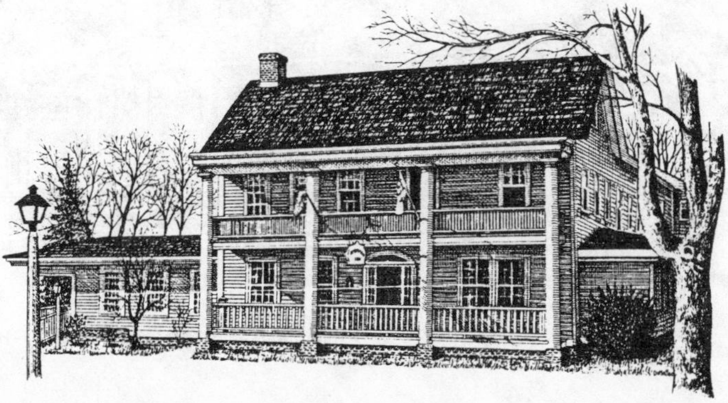

RHUBARB CRISP

4 cups rhubarb
1/2 teaspoon salt
1 1/2 cups sugar
1/4 cup flour
1 tablespoon cinnamon
1/3 cup butter

Cut rhubarb into small pieces and place in a buttered 10" x 6" pan. Mix salt, sugar, flour, cinnamon and butter until crumbly, then sprinkle over fruit. Bake at 350° for 20 - 25 minutes.

Submitted by:

Sutter Creek Inn
75 Main Street, Box 385
Sutter Creek, Calif. 95685
(209) 267-5606
Jane Way
$45.00 to $92.00

Full breakfast
19 rooms, 20 private baths
Children, over 15
No pets
Restricted smoking

Located on Highway #49 in California's gold country. 10 of the inn's rooms have fireplaces, 4 have swinging beds that can be stabilized. A hot breakfast is served family style in front of the fireplace each morning. Small, lovely dinner houses within walking distance.

RHUBARB CUSTARD KUCHEN

Crust:
1/2 cup butter
1 egg yolk
1 1/4 cups flour
1 teaspoon salt
1 tablespoon sugar
1 tablespoon flour

Filling:
2 cups rhubarb (cut into 1/2" pieces)
2 eggs & 1 egg white
1 1/2 cups sugar
1/2 cup cream
Dash of salt

Crust: Cream butter and egg yolk with a spoon. Add flour and salt, using a fork to blend. Put into greased 7" x 11" pan, working dough flat and up the sides. Combine sugar & flour, and sprinkle on crust. Filling: Fill crust-lined pan with rhubarb. In small bowl, blend and beat eggs. Add remaining ingredients and mix well. Pour on top of rhubarb in crust. Bake at 350° for 45 minutes. Add whipped cream and serve.

Submitted by:

The Renaissance Inn
414 Maple Drive
Sister Bay, Wisconsin 54234
(414) 854-5107
John & Jo Dee Faller
$55.00 to $70.00

Full breakfast
5 rooms, 5 private baths
Children, over 14
No pets
Restricted smoking
Mastercard, Visa, Am Ex

Our lobby and reception area, graced with antiques, welcome guests with the warmth of stepping back in time. The inn has five small rooms and a parlor on the second floor, decorated with European furniture and Renaissance art. We feature a five-course breakfast.

RUSSELL-COOPER RUGULA

1 large loaf Pepperidge Farm Bread
2 - 8 oz. pkgs. softened cream cheese
1 cup melted butter
White sugar & cinnamon mix (4 cups sugar to 2 tablespoons cinnamon)

Trim crusts from bread. With a rolling pin, flatten each piece. Spread with softened cream cheese and roll into logs. Dip logs into melted butter and sugar-cinnamon mix. Place close together on large cookie sheet and freeze. To bake, remove as many logs as needed directly from freezer and bake at 350° for 15 minutes, cutting the logs into thirds after first 5 minutes. Serve hot.

Submitted by:

The Russell-Cooper House
115 East Gambier Street
Mount Vernon, Ohio 43050
(614) 397-8638
Tim & Maureen Tyler
$45.00 to $60.00

Full breakfast
6 rooms, 6 private baths
Children, over 13
No pets
Restricted smoking
Mastercard & Visa

National award-winning Victorian B&B, is nestled in the heart of America's hometown. Candlelit breakfasts, inn and historic walking tours, antique & gift shops, museums, canal boat rides, Indian mounds, tennis, golfing, hunting, fishing, hiking & cultural events.

SANDY'S ENGLISH SCONES

- 4 cups flour
- 3 tablespoons baking powder
- 1 teaspoon salt
- 1 teaspoon cream of tartar
- 3 tablespoons sugar
- 1 cup butter or margarine
- 1 cup currants (or firm fresh strawberries or raisins or pecans)
- 1 1/3 cups milk
- Egg wash

Mix first 6 ingredients well in food processor. Put in large bowl and mix in currants. Add milk and mix very gently. On floured board knead 10 - 15 times. Roll to 1 1/4". Cut with 3" cutter. Brush with egg wash. Bake on ungreased cookie sheet in preheated 425° oven 12 minutes. Makes 15 scones. Or divide dough in half and put into 2 ungreased 9" cake pans, and cut each into 8 wedges. Serve warm with butter and your very best homemade jam.

Origin: First prize, New York State Fair, 1984. Many guests say they return year after year just for these wonderful scones.

Submitted by:

The Red House Country Inn
Finger Lakes National Forest
Picnic Area Road
Burdett, New York 14818
(607) 546-8566
Joan Martin & Sandy Schmanke
$47.00 to $75.00

Full breakfast
6 rooms
Children, over 12
No pets
Restricted smoking
Mastercard, Visa, Am Ex

1844 inn in the Finger Lakes National Forest, containing 28 miles of hiking & cross-country ski trails. Beautifully appointed rooms, public room & veranda, acres of lawns and gardens, and an inground pool.

SCOTTISH OATMEAL SCONES

6 oz. plain flour (1 1/2 cups)
2 oz. medium oatmeal (1/3 cup)
1/4 teaspoon salt
1 level teaspoon bicarbonate of soda
2 level teaspoons cream of tartar
2 oz. margarine (1/4 cup)
About 1/4 pint milk (2/3 cup)

Mix all dry ingredients together. Add margarine cut into small pieces. Rub into flour, stir in sufficient milk to make a soft but not sticky dough. Knead lightly until smooth. Roll out and cut using 2 1/2" fluted cutter or shape into 8" circle and cut into eight wedges. Bake on lightly greased cookie sheet at 425° for about 10 minutes. Serve with butter and strawberry jam. Makes 7 - 8.

Origin: A Scottish recipe hundreds of years old.

Submitted by:

Brae Loch Inn
5 Albany Street (U.S. Route 20)
Cazenovia, New York 13035
(315) 655-3431
H. Grey & Doris Barr
$59.00 to $125.00

Continental breakfast
12 rooms, 12 private baths
Children allowed
No pets
Smoking allowed
Mastercard, Visa, Am Ex, Diner's Club

Family-owned and operated since 1946. Originally built in 1805, as close to a Scottish inn as you will find this far west of Edinburgh. Victorian antiques, mellow tartan plaids, original stained glass, all delight the eye and relax the mind. Near shopping, golf and beach.

SIMON'S SCONES

3 cups flour (unbleached white, whole wheat pastry or a mixture)
1/3 cup sugar
1/2 teaspoon soda
2 1/2 teaspoons baking powder
3/4 cup cold butter
1 cup buttermilk
Small amount of milk or cream for tops
Cinnamon-sugar (1 cup sugar to 4 tablespoons cinnamon)

In mixing bowl stir together flour, sugar, soda and baking powder. Drop pieces of cold butter into bowl and "cut in" either with 2 forks or with fingers until mixture is the texture of cornmeal. Make a well in the center, and add buttermilk. Stir with a fork until mixture leaves the sides of the bowl. Add more buttermilk (about 1 spoon) if necessary, to bind the mixture. Divide into 2 equal portions. Shape each into a 3/4" high round on greased cookie sheet. Both will fit on 1 sheet. Score each round with knife, cutting almost to the bottom of dough, making 6 or 8 equal sections. Brush tops of bread with a little milk or cream, then sprinkle with cinnamon-sugar until lightly covered. Bake at 350° - 400° until golden brown, about 30 minutes. Serve warm with butter, jam or lemon curd.

Submitted by:

Old Thyme Inn
779 Main Street
Half Moon Bay, Calif. 94019
(415) 726-1616
Anne & Simon Lowings
$60.00 to $150.00

Full breakfast
7 rooms, 5 private baths
Children, over 8
Pets allowed at inn's discretion
No smoking
Mastercard, Visa, Am Ex

We are a family run B&B located on the Pacific Ocean, just 45 minutes from San Francisco. The inn has an herbal theme and guests are invited to walk in Anne's herb garden. Some rooms have whirlpool tubs for two and fireplaces. We serve a full breakfast.

SUPER SIMPLE CINNAMON ROLLS

1 tablespoon butter or margarine
1 cup cinnamon-sugar mixture (1 cup sugar to 4 teaspoons cinnamon)
1/2 cup nuts (broken or chopped)
2 packages flaky biscuits (10 each)
1 - 8 oz. package cream cheese cut into 20 cubes
More melted butter to sprinkle on biscuit tops

Preheat oven to 325°. In an oven safe dish, melt 1 tablespoon butter or margarine. Sprinkle bottom of dish with 1 tablespoon cinnamon-sugar and 1 tablespoon nuts. Open biscuits. Take one biscuit, indent with thumb. Place in indentation 1/2 teaspoon cinnamon-sugar and 1 cube cream cheese. Draw ends of biscuit together and pinch closed. Place in center of dish. Repeat with remaining biscuits, arranging in a spiral around center. Sprinkle 1 tablespoon (or more) melted butter or margarine over biscuits. Follow with 2 - 3 tablespoons cinnamon-sugar, and remaining nuts. Bake until browned and tops are crunchy, about 15 - 20 minutes. Allow to cool about 10 minutes, as cream cheese center becomes very hot.

Submitted by:

Gibson's Lodgings
110 - 114 Prince George St.
Annapolis, Maryland 21401
(301) 268-5555
Holly Perdue
$55.00 to $120.00

Continental breakfast
20 rooms, 8 private baths
Children allowed
No pets
Smoking allowed
Mastercard, Visa, Am Ex

Located in Historic District of Annapolis on the Chesapeake Bay, circa 1750's, next to the U. S. Naval Academy. Popular with corporate and government groups holding conferences and meetings as well as individuals touring the area by land or sea.

SWEDISH TEA ROLLS

2 teaspoons baking powder
1/2 teaspoon salt
2 cups sifted flour
1/2 cup butter
2/3 cup milk
1/3 cup sugar
1 teaspoon cinnamon

Add baking powder and salt to flour, cut in shortening. Add milk all at once, stir until all flour is dampened. Stir again, turn out, knead 30 seconds. Roll 1/4" thick and cut into 2 1/2 " squares. Fold squares in half. Press edges into sugar & cinnamon. Place on ungreased baking sheet. Bake at 450° for 15 minutes. Yields 15 - 18 rolls.

Submitted by:

Captain Hawkins Inn
321 Terryville Road
Terryville, New York 11776
(516) 473-8211
Ralph & Anne Cornelius
$62.00 to $105.00

Full & continental breakfast
9 rooms, 7 private baths
Children, over 12
No pets
Restricted smoking
Mastercard & Visa

An 1867 Victorian mansion, which features reproductions and period furniture, spacious guest rooms, 5 with fireplaces, and a pool. Near Bridgeport, Connecticut, & the Port Jefferson Ferry to New England.

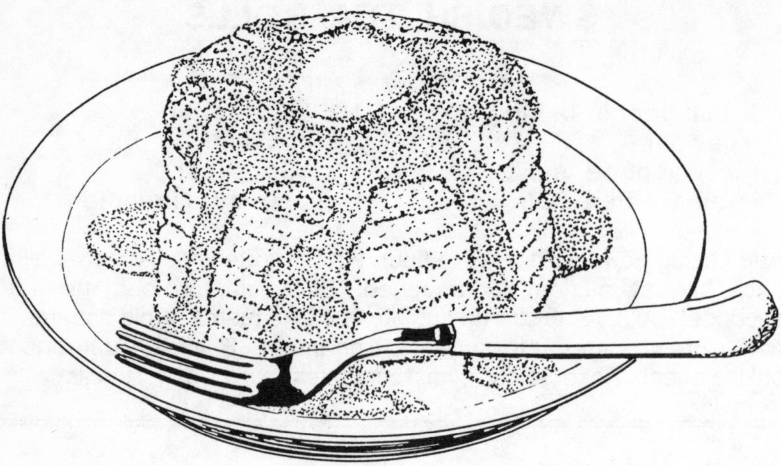

PANCAKES, WAFFLES & PASTRIES

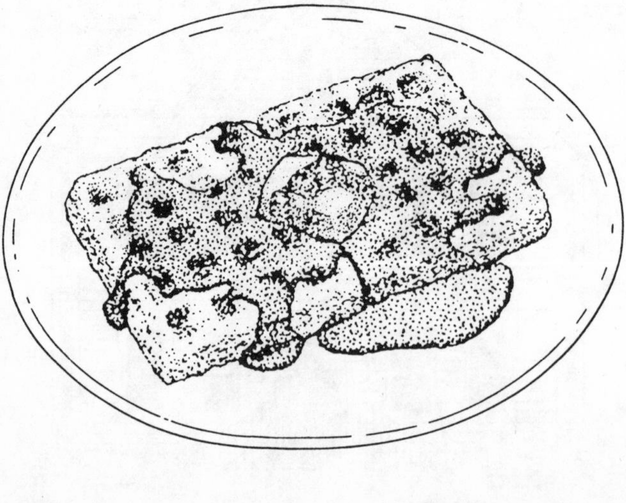

APPEL INN'S PHYLLO PASTRIES

1 box frozen phyllo leaves
15 oz. ricotta cheese
2 eggs
1/4 cup sugar
Melted butter
Strawberry or apricot jam

Thaw phyllo according to directions. Mix ricotta, eggs, sugar and 1 tablespoon melted butter. With pastry brush, brush butter on sheet of phyllo. Top with another sheet and brush with butter again. Cut phyllo into 3 strips lengthwise. Put teaspoon of cheese at top of each. Fold over like a triangle, and keep folding to bottom of the strip. Repeat until all phyllo or cheese is finished; it should be pretty close. You may freeze at this point. To bake, preheat oven to 350°. Put pastries on greased cookie sheet, brush with a little butter. Bake 20 - 25 minutes until golden brown. Brush with melted jelly or jam just before serving. Makes about 36 pastries.

Submitted by:

Appel Inn
Box 18, R.D. #3, Route 146
Altamont, New York 12009
(518) 861-6557
Laurie & Gerd Beckmann
$40.00 to $60.00

Full breakfast
4 rooms
Children allowed
No pets
Restricted smoking
Mastercard & Visa

1765 home on State & National Registers. Wide plank floors, antique beds, down comforters, fireplaces, solarium & private porches. Near antiquing, sightseeing, skiing, ice skating, hiking, golf & swimming pools. Perfect for honeymoons, anniversaries or "just because".

APPLEBUTTER PANCAKES

2 cups all-purpose flour
1 tablespoon baking powder
3 tablespoons sugar
1 teaspoon salt
2 eggs
1 cup milk
3 tablespoons oil
1/2 cup applebutter
1 teaspoon ground cinnamon
3 tablespoons butter
2 cans apple pie filling (1 lb. - 4 oz.)

Mix dry ingredients and eggs, milk, oil and applebutter for pancake batter. In saucepan, heat cinnamon, butter and apple pie filling. Treat griddle with shortening or non-stick spray. Heat to 350°. Pour pancake batter to form 3" - 4" cakes. Turn when edges brown. Serve with pie filling mixture, to be spooned over cakes. Yields 12 - 16 pancakes.

Origin: Recipe created by Marcia Norton.

Submitted by:

The Rock House
380 W. Washington Street
Morgantown, Indiana 46160
(812) 597-5100
Doug & Marcia Norton
$45.00 to $85.00

Full breakfast
5 rooms (1 suite), 3 private baths
Children, by prior arrangement
No pets
Restricted smoking

Enjoy a unique home, good food and the companionship of other guests, in a traditional B&B 'homestay'. The home's exterior has dice, geodes, doorknobs, dishes, etc., which were set into the molds for the concrete blocks from which the house was built.

APPLE CHEESE PANCAKES

6 large eggs, separated
1/2 teaspoon salt
16 oz. cottage cheese
3 tablespoons sugar
1 teaspoon allspice
1 teaspoon cinnamon
3 medium Red Delicious apples, peeled & sliced
Butter for frying

In food processor beat egg whites with salt until stiff. Transfer to large bowl. In processor, add egg yolks, cottage cheese, sugar, allspice, cinnamon and apples. Process until smooth. Fold into egg whites. Melt butter in skillet, brown both sides of pancake. Yields 24 - 3" pancakes.

Submitted by:

Tulip Tree Inn
Chittenden Dam Road
Chittenden, Vermont 05737
(802) 483-6213
Ed & Rosemary McDowell
$60.00 to $95.00

Full breakfast
8 rooms, 8 private baths
No children
No pets
Restricted smoking
Mastercard & Visa

This is the way you have always pictured a country inn. Warm and charming guest rooms, many with their own jacuzzi. Secluded in the Green Mountain National Forest, we offer a bit of backwoods luxury. Fine candlelight dining.

APPLE-FILLED GERMAN PANCAKE FOR 4

Filling:
2 - 3 cups peeled & sliced apples
2 tablespoons butter or margarine
2 1/2 tablespoons brown sugar
1/4 teaspoon cinnamon
1/4 teaspoon nutmeg

Pancake:
3 tablespoons melted butter
2 eggs
1/2 cup milk
1/2 teaspoon vanilla
1/2 cup flour
1/4 teaspoon salt

Filling: Combine apples and butter in saucepan. Cook 5 - 10 minutes over medium heat. Stir in sugar and spices. Cover and simmer until tender. Pancake: Put 1 tablespoon butter in 10" skillet. Place in preheated 450° oven to heat. Beat eggs. Add milk and vanilla. Gradually mix in flour and salt until blended. Pour batter in heated skillet. Bake 10 - 15 minutes until puffed and golden brown. Brush with 1 tablespoon butter. Place filling over half of pancake, fold in half. Brush with last 1 tablespoon butter. Cut into 4 wedges. Dust with powdered sugar and serve with warm maple syrup.

Submitted by:

Village Green Inn
40 West Main Street
Falmouth, Mass. 02540
(508) 548-5621
Linda & Don Long
$65.00 to $95.00

Full breakfast
5 rooms, 5 private baths
Children, over 15
No pets
Restricted smoking

Gracious Victorian near fine shops and restaurants, in historic Village Green. Picturesque bike path to beaches, tennis and Woods Hole. 19th century charm and warm hospitality. Breakfast features house specialities. Explore Cape Cod and the Islands. Open year-round.

BAKED SWEDISH PANCAKE

1/2 stick margarine
6 eggs
1 cup milk
1 cup flour
Dash of salt

Toppings: Maple syrup, butter, fresh-sliced strawberries, jam, powdered sugar, or cranberry-orange relish

Heat oven to 400° and place margarine in 9" x 13" casserole to melt. Mix other ingredients into a batter and pour into hot pan. Bake 20 minutes. It will puff up and edges will curl in and brown when done. Cut in squares and serve with a variety of toppings. Makes 10 slices per pan, serves 6 - 8.

Origin: A combination of several family recipes. A tradition here on Sunday.

Submitted by:

Sjöholm Bed & Breakfast Inn
17 Chase Road, Box 430
West Falmouth (Cape Cod),
Massachusetts 02574
(508) 540-5706
Barbara Eck Menning
$50.00 to $75.00

Full breakfast
15 rooms, 5 private baths
Children, over 5
No pets
Restricted smoking

An 1850's farmhouse in quiet Cape Cod, open year-round. Decorated in a country motif. Reasonable rates include country breakfast. Near excellent ocean beaches, shopping, golf, cycling & ferries to Martha's Vineyard.

BARNEY'S BAKED APPLE PANCAKE

2 tablespoons melted butter
3 eggs, lightly beaten
3/4 cup milk
1 tablespoon sugar
1/2 teaspoon vanilla
1/4 teaspoon cinnamon
1/4 teaspoon salt
1/2 cup flour
2 medium apples, peeled
3 tablespoons butter
1 tablespoon flour
3 tablespoons brown sugar
Powdered sugar

Combine first 8 ingredients, mix. Set aside. Sauté or microwave apples, 3 tablespoons butter and 1 tablespoon flour. Spread over 10" pie plate. Pour in batter. Sprinkle with brown sugar. Bake 25 minutes at 450°. Dust with powdered sugar before serving.

Submitted by:

Mountain Meadows Inn
28912 State Road 706E
Ashford, Washington 98304
(206) 569-2788
Tanna Barney
$50.00 to $70.00

Full breakfast
3 rooms, 1 private bath
Children, over 10
No pets
Restricted smoking
Mastercard & Visa

1910 Craftman-style home nestled among towering cedar trees, furnished with antiques. Full veranda porch overlooking pond. Friendly farm animals and "Oscar" the llama. Near Mt. Rainier National Park & Scenic Railroad. Gracious hospitality - create your own adventure!

BLACKBERRY INN BLINTZES

Crepes:
1 1/2 cups flour
1 1/2 cups milk
2 eggs
2 tablespoons vegetable oil
1 teaspoon margarine for frying crepes

Filling:
1 cup cottage cheese
1/2 cup sour cream
1/3 cup sugar
1 teaspoon vanilla
3 tablespoons butter for frying filled blintzes

Sauce:
4 teaspoons cornstarch
2 tablespoons water
1/2 cup sugar
2 cups fresh or frozen blackberries

Combine all crepe ingredients except margarine in blender until smooth. In 6" - 7" crepe pan, melt butter over medium heat. Make thin pancakes, cooking only on 1 side. Cool on wire rack before stacking. Filling: In medium bowl, beat cottage cheese until very smooth. Beat in sour cream, sugar and vanilla. Place 2 tablespoons in center of cooked side of crepe. Fold in opposite edges about 1", then fold in remaining edges to enclose, making a rectangular envelope. Heat butter in large frying pan. Place blintzes in pan, seam side down. Fry carefully, turning once, until golden brown. Top with sauce and garnish with orange medallions. Sauce: Mix cornstarch and water until smooth, add sugar and blackberries in medium saucepan, lightly crushing half or so of the berries with spoon; cook over medium heat. Watch carefully as sauce thickens rapidly. Thin with more water if necessary. Makes 6 - 8 blintzes.

Submitted by:

Blackberry Inn
82 Elm Street
Camden, Maine 04843
(207) 236-6060
Vicki & Ed Doudera
$50.00 to $100.00

Full breakfast
8 rooms, 8 private baths
Children, in Carriage House
No pets
No smoking
Mastercard & Visa

Stately Italianate Victorian in a lovely coastal village. Relax in our sunny parlors, before heading out to sail, swim or stroll.

BLUEBERRY BLINTZES

Crepes:
4 eggs
1 cup milk
1 1/4 cups flour
1 tablespoon brown sugar
1/4 teaspoon almond extract
1/2 - 2 teaspoons butter

Filling:
16 oz. cottage cheese
1 egg
3 tablespoons honey
1 tablespoon orange peel, finely grated
1/2 cup chopped almonds
2 teaspoons butter

Blueberry Sauce:
1/4 cup sugar
1 tablespoon cornstarch
1/3 cup orange juice
2 cups blueberries, fresh or frozen
Sour cream or yogurt
1/2 cup sliced almonds

Combine all crepe ingredients except butter in blender. Whirl until smooth. Heat 8" fry pan, coated with 1/2 teaspoon butter, over medium heat. Add 3 - 4 tablespoons batter, tilt pan to cover bottom, cook until light brown. Cook other side, stack on plate with waxed paper between crepes. Fry remaining batter, adding butter as needed. Mix filling ingredients, except almonds & butter in blender. Whirl until smooth. Add almonds & process fine. Fill each crepe with heaping tablespoon of filling. Roll, & place in lightly buttered shallow baking pan. Cover with foil, bake 15 minutes at 350°. Mix sugar & cornstarch in small saucepan. Stir in juice. Add blueberries and cook over medium heat until sauce boils and thickens. Pour sauce over blintzes, serve with sour cream and almonds. Makes 12 - 16.

Submitted by:

Goose Chase
200 Blueberry Road
Gardners, Penn. 17324
(717) 528-8877
Marsha & Rich Lucidi
$55.00 to $70.00

Full breakfast
3 rooms, 1 private bath
Children, over 12
No pets
No smoking
Mastercard & Visa

Restored 1762 home on 25 acres, furnished in the Williamsburg tradition. Gourmet breakfast, breathtaking views, pool, woodland trails. Near Gettysburg Battlefield, skiing, antiquing, and golf.

BLUE CORN PANCAKES WITH BLUEBERRY SYRUP

1 cup blue cornmeal
2 teaspoons baking powder
1/2 teaspoon salt
1/2 cup chopped nuts
1 cup flour
1/4 cup sugar
1/2 teaspoon baking soda
2 eggs
1/4 cup oil
2 cups sour milk or buttermilk

Blueberry Syrup:
2 cups blueberries, fresh or frozen
1 1/2 cups sugar
1/4 cup fresh lemon juice

Pancakes: Mix dry ingredients together. Beat eggs with oil and milk and combine all ingredients. Cook on a hot griddle 2 tablespoons at a time to make small pancakes. Syrup: Combine all ingredients in saucepan and heat gently until all sugar is dissolved, or cook for a few minutes in a bowl in microwave. Serve with bacon or sausage. Makes 12 - 18 4" pancakes.

Submitted by:

Peppertrees Bed & Breakfast
724 E University Boulevard
Tucson, Arizona 85719
(602) 622-7167
Marjorie Martin
$60.00 to $120.00

Full breakfast
4 rooms
Children, over 12
No pets
Restricted smoking

Unique 1905 Territorial home with a warm Western welcome. Gourmet breakfast and afternoon tea with homemade shortbread. Two blocks from University of Arizona Campus, walk to restaurants, theatres, museums, and shops. Main house and guest house.

BUTTERMILK PANCAKES

- 2 cups flour
- 1 teaspoon salt
- 1 teaspoon soda
- 1 teaspoon baking powder
- 1 1/4+ cups buttermilk
- 1 - 8 oz. carton sour cream
- 2 eggs
- 6 tablespoons butter

Mix flour, salt, soda and baking powder. In separate bowl mix 1 1/4 cups buttermilk and sour cream. Fold two mixtures together, add eggs and additional buttermilk to get a proper pancake consistency. Stir melted butter in well. Fry in a Teflon-coated pan. Serves 6 hungry adults!

Submitted by:

Blue Shadows Bed &
Breakfast Guest House
R.R. #2, Box 432
Greensboro, Alabama 36744
(205) 624-3637
Thad. & Janet May
$50.00

Full breakfast
3 rooms
Children allowed
No pets
No smoking
Personal checks

70 acres of gardens, fields, wildlife, & a nature trail with fishing pond. Main house surrounded by 100 year old trees, with circular driveway. Contemporary furnishings & antiques, with an unusual key collection. Near antebellum homes, historical sites, antique shops & churches.

CHEESE BLINTZES

Crepe Batter:
2 eggs
2 tablespoons salad oil
1 cup milk
3/4 cup sifted flour
1/2 teaspoon salt

Cheese Filling:
1/4 lb. cream cheese
2 egg yolks
1/4 lb. cottage or pot cheese
2 tablespoons sugar
1 teaspoon vanilla

Beat eggs, oil & milk. Add flour and salt, beating until very smooth. Chill 30 minutes; it should be like heavy cream. If too thick, add a little milk. Grease 8" hot skillet with light coating of butter. Pour 3 - 4 tablespoons batter into skillet, turning pan to coat it. Fry lightly on one side. Repeat with remaining batter. Stack crepes on waxed paper, brown side up. Beat filling ingredients together until smooth. Fill each crepe with 2 heaping tablespoons of filling and roll up egg roll style by folding in sides of crepe over filling. May be frozen at this point, then fried without defrosting. Melt 2 tablespoons butter over medium heat in larger skillet. Fry crepes until golden brown on all sides. Serve with sour cream and/or fruit preserves. Makes 10 - 12 crepes.

Submitted by:

Village Victorian Inn
31 Center Street
Rhinebeck, New York 12572
(914) 876-8345
Judy Kohler
$95.00 to $130.00

Full breakfast
5 rooms, 5 private baths
Children, over 16
No pets
Restricted smoking
Mastercard, Visa, Am Ex

Beautiful little private inn where the ambiance is gentle and romantic. Recapture a Victorian fantasy: antiques, laces, and canopy beds. The most spectacular place to stay in the Hudson Valley.

COTTAGE CHEESE HOTCAKES

3 eggs, separated
3/4 cup cottage cheese
1/4 cup flour
1/4 teaspoon salt
Sour cream
Jam

Beat egg yolks until thick. Add cottage cheese and beat well. Stir in flour and salt. Fold in stiffly beaten egg whites. Fry on 380° griddle. Make each hotcake about 3" in diameter. Serve immediately with 1 teaspoon sour cream and jam on each hotcake. Do not prepare this batter ahead. Serves 3.

Submitted by:

Log Castle Bed & Breakfast
3273 E. Saratoga Road
Langley, Washington 98260
(206) 321-5483
Senator Jack & Norma Metcalf
$60.00 to $80.00

Full breakfast
4 rooms, 4 private baths
Children, over 10
No pets
No smoking
Mastercard & Visa

Log lodge on a private secluded beach on Whidbey Island. Turret bedrooms, wood stoves, magnificent view. Peaceful and serene with sounds of gulls and the sea.

DUTCH BABIES

3 eggs
1/2 cup flour
1/2 cup milk
2 tablespoons melted butter
1/2 teaspoon salt
Lemon juice
Powdered sugar
Dab of strawberry jam

Beat eggs with French whip. Add flour in 4 additions, beating smooth each time. Add milk in 2 additions. Lightly beat in melted butter and salt. Thickly butter 2 - 9" glass pie pans and put 1/2 batter in each. Bake at 400° for 10 minutes, at 350° for 5 minutes longer. Combine lemon juice, powdered sugar and jam to a paste and drizzle over pan after it's removed from oven. A baked version of a cross between a crepe and a pancake. It should puff up and out on the sides so that it resembles a hat.

Submitted by:

Country Gardens
Bed & Breakfast
Lakeshore Drive
Branson, Missouri 65616
(417) 334-8564
Bob & Pat Cameron
$50.00 to $85.00

Full breakfast
3 rooms, 3 private baths
Children, over 12
No pets
Smoking allowed
Mastercard & Visa

Parklike gardens and a waterfall surround this wood frame & rock home on Lake Taneycomo. In fast-growing tourist area with beautiful sights & country music shows. Rose Suite has private spa, Dogwood is furnished in rustic cedar, and Bittersweet is comfortably Victorian.

FINNISH OVEN PANCAKE

1 stick oleo or butter
5 large or extra-large eggs
1 tablespoon sugar
1/2 teaspoon salt
2 cups milk
1 cup small curd cottage cheese
1 cup all-purpose flour
1 teaspoon baking powder
Garnishes of choice

Preheat oven to 425°. Melt butter in #10 size black iron skillet or 9" x 13" Pyrex baking dish. Use blender on medium - high to beat eggs, sugar, & salt for 1 minute. Slowly add milk, cottage cheese, flour and baking powder. Pour into pan and bake 35 minutes or until well-browned. Will be puffy and "jiggly", not set. Let cool 5 - 10 minutes. It will sink, leaving high sides. Cut into wedges and serve on silver tray or glass plate. Garnish with fresh fruit of choice and syrup, honey or powdered sugar.

Submitted by:

Frampton House
Bed & Breakfast
489 Powell Avenue
Healdsburg, California 95448
(707) 433-5084
Paula Bogle
$70.00 to $85.00

Full breakfast
3 rooms, 3 private baths
Children, over 12
No pets
Restricted smoking
Mastercard & Visa

Stately 1908 Victorian in heart of California wine country. Queen size beds, tubs-for-two, and views. Romantic "hideaway" has private deck with panoramic view of mountains. Fireplace, games, pool, spa, sauna, bikes, and ping-pong.

FLUFFY BLUEBERRY PANCAKES

1 1/2 cups flour
2 teaspoons sugar
2 teaspoons baking powder
1 teaspoon salt
2 eggs
1 cup milk
3/4 cup plain yogurt
3 tablespoons oil
1 cup fresh blueberries

Sift together flour, sugar, baking powder and salt. In another bowl lightly mix eggs, and add milk, yogurt and oil. Add wet ingredients to dry and mix until smooth. Add blueberries. Use 1/3 cup batter for each pancake. Cook until bubbles form and edges are dry; then turn and cook until golden brown on underside. Serve topped with fresh blueberries, a scoop of French vanilla ice cream and warmed Vermont maple syrup. Serves 4.

Submitted by:

Inn at Blush Hill
Blush Hill Road, Box 1266
Waterbury, Vermont 05676
(802) 244-7529
Pamela & Gary Gosselin
$60.00 to $100.00

Full breakfast
6 rooms, 2 private baths
Children allowed
No pets
Restricted smoking
Mastercard & Visa

1790 Cape Cod on 5 acres of Vermont countryside with beautiful mountain views. 4 fireplaces, large sitting room, library and lots of antiques. Each room is individually decorated. Skiing at Stowe, Sugarbush or Bolton Valley minutes away. Summer sports nearby.

FRENCH PANCAKES

1 1/2 cups flour
3/4 teaspoon salt
2 teaspoons baking powder
4 tablespoons powdered sugar
4 eggs
1 1/3 cups milk
2/3 cup water
1 teaspoon vanilla
Fillings: Sour cream, jam, butter, fresh fruit & brown sugar
Garnish: Powdered sugar

Sift together first 4 ingredients into large bowl. Beat eggs. Add milk, water and vanilla to eggs and beat together. Make a well in dry ingredients and pour in liquids. Mix lightly, ignoring the lumps. Pour mixture onto hot griddle for large, thin pancakes. Serve with bowls of sour cream, butter, jam, brown sugar and fresh fruit. Roll the pancakes up around these items and sprinkle powdered sugar over them. Serves 6.

Submitted by:

Highland House Inn
3 Highland Place
Lake Placid, New York 12946
(518) 523-2377
Teddy & Cathy Blazer
$45.00 to $85.00

Full breakfast
8 rooms, 5 private baths
Children allowed
No pets
Restricted smoking
Mastercard & Visa

Centrally located in lovely residential setting just above Main Street. Tastefully decorated rooms. Breakfast includes blueberry pancakes, a renowned specialty. Fully-equipped country cottage next door has fireplace.

FRESH CORN WAFFLES WITH CILANTRO BUTTER

1 cup all-purpose flour
1/2 cup yellow cornmeal
2 tablespoons sugar
2 teaspoons double-acting baking powder
1/4 teaspoon salt
1 large egg
2 tablespoons melted unsalted butter
1/2 cup water
1 cup fresh corn (remove from cob)
1 teaspoon vanilla

Cilantro butter:
1/4 lb. softened sweet butter
1/4 cup fresh-cut cilantro

In large bowl, mix flour, cornmeal, sugar, baking powder and salt. In separate bowl whip together egg, melted butter, water, corn, and vanilla. Add egg mixture to flour mixture, and mix until just combined. Heat waffle iron, oil and cook waffle. Whip cilantro and butter together until smooth and creamy. Serve waffle with cilantro butter and real maple syrup. Yield: 4 - 6 waffles.

Submitted by:

The Hotel Carter
301 L Street
Eureka, California 95501
(707) 444-8062
Mark & Christi Carter
$69.00 to $250.00

Continental breakfast
20 rooms, 20 private baths
Children allowed
No pets
No smoking
Mastercard, Visa, Am Ex

Oriented toward the business or vacation traveler, with fine views of Humboldt Bay. A Victorian charmer, our cheerfully decorated rooms offer antique pine, jacuzzis, television, telephones and fireplaces.

FRUITED GRIDDLECAKES WITH HONEY-RUM SYRUP

1 3/4 cups flour
1/4 cup sugar
2 teaspoons baking powder
4 tablespoons melted butter
1 egg
1 1/2 cups milk
1/2 cup blueberries
1/2 cup peaches
1/2 cup chopped apples
1/2 cup chopped bananas
(Or 2 cups other fruit)

Honey-Rum Syrup:
1 cup honey
1 cup maple syrup
1 tablespoon butter
1 tablespoon rum flavoring (extract)

Combine flour, sugar and baking powder. Stir in butter, egg, milk, beat until smooth. Fold in fruit. Ladle 1/4 cup batter onto greased hot grill. Cook until small bubbles appear, then flip. Makes 12 - 4" griddlecakes. Honey-Rum Syrup: Mix all ingredients in saucepan. Stir over low heat for 3 - 5 minutes. Serve hot. Can be stored in covered container for several weeks.

Submitted by:

Henry Ludlam Inn
Cape May County
R.D. #3, Box 298
Woodbine, New Jersey 08270
(609) 861-5847
Ann & Marty Thurlow
$65.00 to $90.00

Full breakfast
5 rooms, 3 private baths
Children, over 12
No pets
Restricted smoking
Mastercard & Visa

1800 historic home on 55 acre lake. Furnished with fireplaces & antiques. Creative breakfast served fireside, enjoyable conversation, relaxed atmosphere, candlelight and music. Antiquing, biking, boating, zoo, beaches, ice skating and cross-country skiing.

GINGER PANCAKES WITH FRESH PEACHES

3 cups water
3 fresh peaches
1 tablespoon butter
2 tablespoons maple syrup
1 1/2 cups flour
1 teaspoon baking soda
1 tablespoon ground ginger
3 tablespoons melted butter or oleo
1 1/4 cups buttermilk
1 egg, slightly beaten

Boil 3 cups water in medium saucepan. Add peaches, boil 1 minute, and place in cold water. When cool, peel and slice. Heat 1 tablespoon butter in medium frying pan, add peach slices and maple syrup. Keep on low temperature, stir occasionally. Combine flour, baking soda, and ginger in large mixing bowl. Mix well. Add melted butter, buttermilk and egg all at once, and stir until batter is moist but still lumpy. Heat griddle, and pour approximately 1/4 cup batter for each pancake on griddle. Turn when small bubbles appear on edges. Place 3 - 4 pancakes on plate, put hot peaches on top. Serves 4.

Submitted by:

Silas Griffith Inn
R.R. #1, Box 66F
Danby, Vermont 05739
(802) 293-5567
Paul & Lois Dansereau
$65.00 to $78.00

Full breakfast
17 rooms, 11 private baths
Children allowed
No pets
Restricted smoking
Mastercard, Visa, Am Ex

Gracious 1891 mansion & carriage house on Historic Register. Unique 8' round cherry wood pocket door, cherry and oak woodwork, stained glass windows, furnished with Victorian antiques. In Green Mtn. National Forest, spectacular views, hiking, biking, skiing nearby.

GRAMMA'S CREAM PUFFS

Pastry:
1 cup water
1/2 cup margarine
1 cup flour
4 eggs

Filling:
1 - 3 1/2 oz. pkg. instant banana pudding mix
1 3/4 cups milk
1 envelope Dream Whip
1/3 cup milk

Glaze:
1/4 cup margarine
1 1/2 tablespoons cocoa
3 tablespoons milk
2 cups powdered sugar

Pastry: Combine water and margarine, bring to boil. Add flour, stir quickly until mixture forms ball. Cool, add eggs one at a time, stir with fork until mixture is smooth. Divide dough into 12 amounts. Drop onto cookie sheet. Bake at 400° for 15 minutes, reduce heat to 325° and bake 40 minutes longer. Filling: Beat pudding mix and 1 3/4 cups milk, until smooth. Then, beat Dream Whip and 1/3 cup milk until stiff. Fold pudding and Dream Whip together. Cut off tops from cooled pastries. Fill with pudding mixture. Glaze: Heat margarine, cocoa and milk. Do not boil. Beat in powdered sugar until smooth. Drizzle over pastries, and refrigerate.

Origin: Created when I was a young mother; my family still loves them!

Submitted by:

Gramma's House
Route 3, Box 410
Marthasville, Missouri 63357
(314) 433-2675
Judy & Jim Jones
$45.00 to $60.00

Full breakfast
3 rooms, 1 private bath
Children allowed
Pets allowed
Restricted smoking
Mastercard & Visa

Charming 150 year old farm house will bring back memories of the good times spent at your Gramma's house. Near antique shops, restaurants, and historical Daniel Boone home and monument.

GRAMMA'S PANCAKES

1/4 cup wheat germ
3/4 cup graham flour
1 teaspoon baking soda
1/4 teaspoon salt
1 tablespoon molasses
2 eggs, separated
1 cup cultured sour cream
Water

Mix dry ingredients. Add molasses, egg yolks, and sour cream. Beat, and add water to batter consistency (medium - not thin). Beat whites not too stiff and fold into batter. Cook on medium hot griddle. Yield: 10 - 3" pancakes.

Origin: Recipe from Great-grandmother Smith.

Submitted by:

The Maine Stay Inn
22 High Street
Camden, Maine 04843
(207) 236-9636
Peter & Donny Smith & Diana Robson
$45.00 to $86.00

Full breakfast
8 rooms, 2 private baths
Children, over 10
No pets
No smoking
Mastercard & Visa

Built in 1802, this colonial is one of the oldest of the 66 houses in the High Street Historic District. Nestled between the mountains and the sea, a 5 minute walk to the harbor and the center of the village. The innkeepers are happy to share any recipe with house guests.

MAINE SOUR CREAM BLUEBERRY PANCAKES

1 cup milk
1 egg
1/4 cup sour cream
1 cup flour
1 tablespoon baking powder
1 tablespoon sugar
1/4 teaspoon salt
2 tablespoons melted butter
1/2 - 1 cup fresh Maine blueberries

Combine milk, egg and sour cream in medium bowl. In separate bowl stir together flour, baking powder, sugar and salt. Add all but 2 tablespoons of this mixture to milk, and beat until large lumps disappear. Add butter; toss blueberries in remaining flour mixture, then fold into batter. Cook on hot griddle 2 - 3 minutes per side. Yield: 12 - 4" pancakes.

Origin: Wild blueberries are plentiful when hiking; now our guests enjoy picking the fruit and eating the pancakes as well!

Submitted by:

Admiral Peary House
9 Elm Street
Fryeburg, Maine 04037
(207) 935-3365
Nancy & Ed Greenberg
$87.00 to $96.00

Full breakfast
4 rooms, 4 private baths
No children
No pets
No smoking
Mastercard & Visa

Former residence of Arctic explorer, Robert E. Peary. Clay tennis court, spa, bicycles, library, billiards, with spacious grounds and perennial gardens. Near the White Mountains, hiking, canoeing, skiing, antiquing, theater, and golf.

MT. ADAMS HUCKLEBERRY HOTCAKES

3 cups all-purpose flour
3/4 cup uncooked oatmeal (old fashioned)
1/4 cup All-Bran cereal
4 teaspoons baking powder
2 teaspoons baking soda
1 teaspoon salt
4 eggs, beaten
4 cups buttermilk
4 tablespoons oil
1 cup huckleberries, fresh or frozen

In large bowl, mix dry ingredients. Beat eggs, then add buttermilk and oil, mixing well. Stir egg mixture into dry ingredients until just moistened. Add more liquid if too thick. Gently fold in berries. Pour 1/4 cup portions onto moderately greased hot griddle. Flip cakes when bubbles appear. Serves 8.

Origin: From Ilse Lloyd, who has made these at the ranch for 45 years.

Submitted by:

Flying L Ranch
25 Flying L Lane
Glenwood, Wash. 98619
(509) 364-3488
Darvel Lloyd
$49.00 to $64.00

Full breakfast
12 rooms, 8 private baths
Children allowed
Pets allowed
Restricted smoking
Mastercard, Visa
Diner's Club, Carte Blanche

This 160 acre retreat is nestled in the Ponderosa pines & meadowlands at the base of majestic 12,276 foot Mt. Adams. Built by the Lloyd family in 1945, and operated as a bed and breakfast since 1960. Wide variety of outdoor activities year-round, on & near ranch.

ORANGE WAFFLES

2 cups sifted all-purpose flour
3 teaspoons baking powder
2 tablespoons granulated sugar
1/2 teaspoon salt
4 eggs, lightly beaten
1 cup milk
4 tablespoons melted butter
3 tablespoons grated orange rind

Sift together dry ingredients. Combine eggs, milk and butter; add orange rind. Add to the dry ingredients, 1/2 of total amount at a time. Beat well after each addition until the batter is smooth. Pour about 3/4 to 1 cup of batter at a time onto preheated waffle iron, following manufacturer's directions. Bake until waffles are golden brown. Serves 8.

Submitted by:

Manor House
P.O. Box 447, Maple Avenue
Norfolk, Connecticut 06058
(203) 542-5690
Hank & Diane Tremblay
$70.00 to $150.00

Full breakfast
9 rooms, 7 private baths
Children, over 12
No pets
Restricted smoking
Mastercard, Visa, Am Ex

Included in Fodor's 100 Best in the U.S.A., an 1898 Tudor Victorian set on 5 park-like acres. Tiffany windows, antique-decorated guest rooms, and fireplaces, with horse-drawn sleigh and carriage rides, winter and summer activities; music festivals and antiquing nearby.

PATTI'S PUFFCAKES AND FRUIT

3 eggs
1/2 teaspoon salt
1/2 cup flour
1/2 cup milk
2 tablespoons butter
1/2 cup shredded Cheddar or Swiss cheese
1 cup fresh berries, sliced
1 tablespoon powdered sugar

Heat oven to 450°. Place 2 - 8" layer cake pans in oven. Beat eggs and salt for 1 minute at high speed. Add flour and milk in 3 separate additions, mixing at low speed for 1 minute. Remove pans from oven and brush with butter. Pour batter into pans equally. Bake 15 minutes, reduce heat to 350°, and bake 5 more minutes. Sprinkle each cake with cheese, top with berries and dust with powdered sugar. Serves 2.

Submitted by:

The Tar Heel Inn
205 Church Street
P.O. Box 176
Oriental, N.C. 28571
(919) 249-1078
Patti & Dave Nelson
$65.00 to $75.00

Full breakfast
7 rooms, 7 private baths
Children allowed
No pets
No smoking

Built in 1899, restored as an English style country inn, with heavy beams, comfortable gathering rooms, country fabrics and wallpaper. Poster, cannonball and pencil post beds & antiques. 2 patios, lawns, lawn games, bicycles, and breakfast "from scratch" each morning.

PUFF PANCAKE WITH HOT FRUIT SAUCE

- 1/4 cup butter
- 1 cup unbleached white flour
- 1 tablespoon bran
- 1 tablespoon cornmeal
- 1 cup cream
- 4 whole eggs
- 1/4 teaspoon salt
- 1 tablespoon baking powder
- 1 quart fresh or frozen blueberries, or other fruits, sweetened to taste

With oven at 400°, melt butter in 10" heavy cast iron skillet about 3 - 5 minutes. Meanwhile mix remaining ingredients, except blueberries, in blender or mixer until smooth, and pour into hot sizzling butter in skillet. Bake 20 - 25 minutes until puffed, golden brown with crispy edges pulled away from skillet. While baking, heat blueberries until juice runs, but don't cook long. Serve pancake hot, in skillet, and serve berries in a bowl. Cut into wedges, split horizontally, open up, and pour on berry sauce. Serves 4.

Submitted by:

West Shore Farm
Bed & Breakfast
2781 West Shore Drive
Lummi Island, Wash. 98262
(206) 758-2600
Polly & Carl Hanson
$50.00 to $60.00

Full breakfast
2 rooms, 2 private baths
Children allowed
No pets
No smoking
Mastercard & Visa

Visitors will enjoy and remember: quiet beach with island and sunset views, passing boats, seabirds, eagles, seals, the Canadian mountains, octagonal owner-built home of native woods, healthy meals served family-style.

PUMPKIN PUFF PANCAKES

2 eggs, separated
1 cup milk
1/2 cup cooked or canned pumpkin
2 1/3 cups buttermilk biscuit mix
2 tablespoons sugar
1/4 teaspoon cinnamon
1/4 teaspoon nutmeg
1/4 teaspoon ginger
1/4 cup vegetable oil
Toppings: Butter, warmed maple syrup & pecans (optional)

Beat egg whites until soft peaks form, then beat in egg yolks. In separate bowl, blend milk and pumpkin, and all remaining ingredients. Beat with mixer until blended. Batter will be stiff. Thoroughly fold in beaten eggs. Drop batter by tablespoons onto hot, greased griddle. When puffed and browned, turn and cook on other side. Serve with butter and warm syrup. May sprinkle with pecans if desired. Makes about 12 pancakes.

Submitted by:

Walden Acres Bed & Breakfast
R.R. #1, Box 30
Adel, Iowa 50003
(515) 987-1338 or 987-1567
Phyllis Briley
$50.00 to $55.00

Full breakfast
2 rooms
Children allowed
Restricted smoking

English style brick home with handsome walnut woodwork, built in 1940 by Cleveland Indians' pitcher, Bob Feller. On 40 acres of beautiful woods with a lake. Convenient location, 15 minutes west of Des Moines. Open all year.

RENATE'S HOMEMADE APPLE PANCAKES

4 eggs, separated
1 cup flour (Arrow Head Mills unbleached organic flour)
3/4 cup half & half
1 tablespoon sugar
Dash of salt
2 medium apples, peeled and sliced thin
Butter
Sugar for apples

Beat 4 egg whites until stiff. In separate bowl combine flour, egg yolks, half & half, sugar and salt. Fold stiff egg whites with second mixture. Heat well-buttered frying pan (low heat), spoon in batter and add apple slices lengthwise onto batter. Add a little butter to top of apples. Turn pancakes, fry till golden brown and apples are cooked. Sprinkle sugar on top of apples and keep warm in oven on serving platter. Makes 16 oval pancakes (3" x 5") for 4 servings. Serve with additional sour cream and syrup.

Submitted by:

Leduc's Bed & Breakfast
41 Arrow Drive
Sedona, Arizona 86336
(602) 282-6241
Klaus & Renate Leduck
$55.00 to $75.00

Full breakfast
3 rooms, 3 private baths
No children
No pets
Restricted smoking

Relax with us in peace and quiet. Our guest rooms are individually decorated. Honeymoon Suite has king size bed with fireplace and jacuzzi tub. Full breakfast & afternoon refreshments. Pool in season.

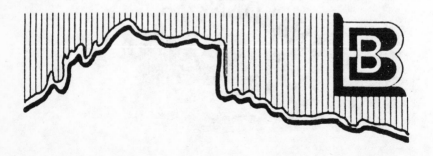

ROBERT'S CINNAMON-APPLE WHOLE-WHEAT PANCAKES

2 cups whole wheat flour
1 teaspoon salt
2 tablespoons sugar (preferably Turbinado sugar)
4 teaspoons baking powder
2 eggs
2 1/4 cups lowfat milk
2 oz. melted unsalted butter
2 peeled, cored apples, thinly sliced in rings & coated in cinnamon

Combine all dry ingredients except apples and cinnamon. Add eggs and milk, whisk until smooth. Stir in melted butter. Place approximately 1/4 cup batter on preheated, buttered griddle; place apple ring in center and cook until bubbles appear. Turn and cook other side. Serve apple-side-up with warm Vermont maple syrup. Yield: 12 - 14 pancakes 3" in diameter.

Submitted by:

Manchester Highlands Inn
P.O. Box 1754, Highland Ave.
Manchester, Vermont 05255
(802) 362-4565
Robert & Patricia Eichorn
$80.00 to $98.00

Full breakfast
15 rooms, 12 private baths
Children allowed
No pets
Restricted smoking
Mastercard, Visa, Am Ex

An 1898 Queen Anne Victorian home perched on a hill overlooking Manchester and Mt. Equinox, offering a warm, relaxed atmosphere. Large outdoor pool and rocking chairs on front porch, game room for guests' enjoyment.

SOURDOUGH PANCAKES

Sourdough starter minus 5 tablespoons
2 eggs
1 teaspoon salt
1 tablespoon oil
2 teaspoons baking soda

Use existing or make starter: Dissolve 1 pkg. dry yeast in 1/2 cup warm water. Stir in 2 cups lukewarm water, 2 cups flour, 1 teaspoon salt, 1 tablespoon sugar. Beat until smooth. Let stand at room temperature 4 - 5 days. Stir twice a day, cover at night. Store in jar and refrigerate. For pancakes: Night before, to 5 tablespoons of starter add 2 cups flour, 1 1/2 cups milk, 1 tablespoon sugar. Stir and cover with plate overnight. In morning, return 5 tablespoons to refrigerator in separate container. Add to mixture eggs, salt, oil, and soda listed above. Blend and cook on griddle at 350°. 4" pancakes serve 6 - 8.

Submitted by:

Limestone Inn
Bed & Breakfast
33 E. Main Street
Strasburg, Penn. 17579
(717) 687-8392
Jan & Dick Kennell
$59.00 to $69.00

Full breakfast
6 rooms, 2 private baths
Children, over 12
No pets
Restricted smoking
Am Ex

An 18th century home with 20th century touches, in the heart of Amish country. Built for a merchant, it served as an orphanage following the Civil War. Share memories of the colonial past.

SPICED APPLE PANCAKES

- 2 cups all-purpose flour
- 1/2 cup sugar
- 1 tablespoon baking powder
- 1 teaspoon baking soda
- 1/2 teaspoon nutmeg
- 1/4 teaspoon ground cloves
- 1/2 teaspoon cinnamon
- 1/4 teaspoon allspice
- 3 eggs, separated
- 1 cup buttermilk
- 1/2 teaspoon vanilla
- 2 medium Granny Smith apples, peeled & diced
- 1/2 cup raisins (optional)

Mix dry ingredients (first 8 ingredients). Make a well in the center. Whisk together yolks, buttermilk and vanilla. Put egg yolk mixture into well, and slowly incorporate into flour mixture. Whip egg whites to stiff peaks. Fold into other ingredients. Fold in diced apples and raisins (if desired). Ladle onto griddle in 3" rounds. Serves 4 - 5.

Origin: Chef Tim Blackwell.

Submitted by:

Barrows House
Dorset, Vermont 05251
(802) 867-4455
Sally & Tim Brown
$155.00 to $200.00

Full breakfast
30 rooms, 29 private baths
Children allowed
Pets allowed in 2 cottages
Restricted smoking
Personal checks

Early 19th century inn and eight buildings, set on 11 acres. Tennis courts, a heated swimming pool, bicycles, cross-country ski shop, and a gourmet restaurant are all available on the property.

SPICED PANCAKES

- 1 1/4 cups flour
- 1/8 cup sugar
- 1 teaspoon baking powder
- 1/2 teaspoon baking soda
- 1/2 teaspoon cinnamon
- 1/4 teaspoon nutmeg
- 1/4 teaspoon salt
- 1 egg
- 1 1/4 cups buttermilk
- 2 tablespoons oil

Toppings:

- Whipped butter
- Warm maple syrup
- Sliced bananas (opt.)

Sift together dry ingredients in large mixing bowl. In separate bowl, mix egg, buttermilk and oil. Make a well in dry ingredients and add liquid, stir until blended. Spoon 1/4 cup batter onto hot griddle or skillet for each pancake, turning once when edges become dry. Serve with sliced bananas if desired, whipped butter and warm maple syrup. Especially good on cold northern New England mornings. Makes 8 - 10 pancakes.

Origin: Concocted in our kitchen one very cold night!

Submitted by:

Sunny Side Inn
Seavey Street
North Conway, N.H. 03860
(603) 356-6239
Chris & Marylee Uggerholt
$40.00 to $65.00

Full breakfast
10 rooms, 3 private baths
Children allowed
No pets
Restricted smoking
Mastercard & Visa

An 1850's restored farmhouse with views of the White Mtns. from flower-trimmed porches in summer. Relax by fireplace or wood stove in winter, minutes from restaurants & outlet shopping. Hiking, rock climbing, swimming, fishing, golf, and skiing at four nearby ski areas.

THE TASTIEST-HEALTHIEST WAFFLE IN THE WORLD

1/2 cup whole wheat pancake mix
1/2 cup oat bran
1 1/2 teaspoons "Egg Replacer" (available at health food stores)
1/2 - 2/3 cup pecan pieces
1 cup apple juice
Optional:
Garnish with fresh berries in season

Mix ingredients together. Spray waffle iron lightly with Pam. For a tastier, crispier waffle, allow it to cook for 30 seconds longer than suggested time of waffle iron manufacturer. Top sparingly with maple syrup. Contains no cholesterol, no fat, no animal products. High in fiber, complex carbohydrates, protein and vitamins. The oat bran helps to reduce cholesterol. Yield: 2 waffles.

Origin: Developed by Dr. & Mrs. Mel Rosenthal, our owners.

Submitted by:

Jefferson House Bed & Breakfast
The Strand at the Wharf
Historic New Castle, Delaware 19720
(302) 323-0999 / Cellar Gourmet Restaurant
Chris at the Cellar Gourmet Restaurant
$55.00 to $75.00

Full breakfast
3 rooms, 3 private baths
Children allowed
No pets
Smoking allowed
Mastercard & Visa

200 year old river front hotel-residence in Historic District, near museums, antique markets, craft fairs and outlet shopping.

WHOLE WHEAT BANANA PANCAKES

- **2 cups buttermilk or 1 cup lowfat milk**
- **1 cup plain yogurt**
- **3 large eggs**
- **2 tablespoons honey**
- **2 cups whole wheat flour**
- **2 tablespoons wheat germ**
- **2 tablespoons baking soda**
- **1 teaspoon salt**
- **2 tablespoons oil**
- **3 mashed bananas**

Beat together milk, yogurt, eggs and honey until smooth. Blend in flour, wheat germ, soda, salt and oil. Add mashed bananas. Pour batter by large spoonfuls onto hot, lightly greased griddle. Bake until bubbles form on top. Turn and brown other side. Serve with real maple syrup. Serves 6 - 8.

Origin: Mailed to us by an "anonymous" guest, and we love it. So, thank-you, whoever you are!

Submitted by:

Snowvillage Inn
Snowville, New Hampshire
03849
(603) 447-2818
Frank, Trudy & Peter Cutrone
$40.00 to $80.00

Full breakfast
19 rooms, 19 private baths
Children, over 7
No pets
Restricted smoking
Mastercard, Visa, Am Ex

Romantic getaway, set on a mountainside with an exhilarating view of the Presidential Range. We are known for our fine food. Tennis, sauna, and cross-country skiing on the grounds. Swimming nearby.

WHOLE WHEAT BANANA WALNUT PANCAKES

3/4 cup all-purpose flour
3 1/2 teaspoons baking powder
3/4 teaspoon salt
1/4 teaspoon baking soda
3 tablespoons sugar
3/4 cup whole wheat flour
1 egg, well-beaten
1 cup buttermilk
3 tablespoons peanut or vegetable oil
1 banana, mashed
1/2 cup chopped walnuts

Sift flour; measure; add baking powder, salt, soda and sugar, sift again. Add whole wheat flour. Combine egg, milk and oil. Mix in mashed banana. Pour into flour mixture and stir just enough to moisten dry ingredients. Add chopped walnuts. Do not beat. Bake on hot griddle. Serve hot with syrup. Makes 1 - 1 1/2 dozen.

Origin: Combination of an old 1940 recipe and my mother's fritter recipe.

Submitted by:

The Corners
601 Klein Street
Vicksburg, Mississippi 39180
(800) 444-7421
Cliff & Bettye Whitney
$65.00 to $130.00

Full breakfast
9 rooms, 9 private baths
Children allowed
Pets allowed
Restricted smoking
Mastercard, Visa, Am Ex

Greek Revival & Victorian mansion with original parterre gardens & a 68' long gallery across the front with river & valley views. Plantation breakfast in formal dining room & tours of mansion garden. Host weddings, receptions and luncheons. AAA Four Diamond Award.

WILD RICE & RICOTTA GRIDDLE CAKES

- 1/2 cup wild rice
- 1 cup ricotta cheese (8 oz.)
- 3 eggs, separated
- 1 tablespoon sugar
- 1/8 teaspoon salt
- 1/4 cup margarine, melted
- 1 tablespoon lemon zest
- 1/4 cup flour

Cook rice until tender, cool. Beat cheese, egg yolks, sugar, and salt until smooth, add to rice. Stir in 1/4 cup melted butter. Add lemon zest, then flour. Beat egg whites to soft peaks, fold into batter. Heat griddle or skillet, coated with 1 teaspoon of oil. Scoop 1/3 cup of batter and spread to 3" - 4" circle. Serve with syrup, yogurt, or sour cream. Makes 12 - 3" pancakes.

Submitted by:

Villa Cardinale
P.O. Box 649
Oracle, Arizona 85623
(602) 896-2516
Judy & Ron Schritt
$35.00 to $45.00

Full breakfast
4 rooms, 4 private baths
Children, over 10
Pets allowed
Restricted smoking

A Spanish hideaway with red tile roofs & courtyard with fountain; a world away from the city's fast pace. Spacious rooms, private entrance and fireplace. In Catalina Mtns.,with clear, cool starry nights. Minutes from Biosphere II, Aravaipa Canyon, and The Arizona Trail.

Villa Cardinale

WILD RICE WAFFLES

- 3 eggs, beaten
- 1 1/2 cups buttermilk
- 1 teaspoon soda
- 2 teaspoons baking powder
- 1 teaspoon salt
- 1 3/4 cups all-purpose flour
- 1 stick melted oleo
- 1 - 2 cups cooked wild rice

Beat first two ingredients well. Add next four ingredients and mix. Add melted oleo. Stir in 1 - 2 cups cooked wild rice. Cook in waffle iron. Makes 6 - 8 small waffles.

Origin: Created by Mary Martin, co-owner.

Submitted by:

Canterbury Inn
Bed & Breakfast
723 Second St. S.W.
Rochester, Minnesota 55902
(507) 289-5553
Mary Martin & Jeffrey VanSant
$60.00 to $75.00

Full breakfast
4 rooms, 4 private baths
Children, over 8
No pets
Restricted smoking
Mastercard & Visa

Victorian charm with all modern comforts, walking distance to Mayo Clinic. Gracious 1890 home, central air-conditioning, off-street parking, telephones, and gourmet breakfast. Good local antiquing, many beautiful day trips.

YUMMY WAFFLES

- 2 cups Bisquick
- 2 teaspoons baking powder
- 2 teaspoons baking soda
- 1/2 cup wheat germ
- 1 tablespoon sugar
- 4 eggs, separated
- 1 cup milk
- 2 cups buttermilk
- 1/2 cup Crisco oil
- 4 tablespoons vanilla

Mix dry ingredients. Add egg yolks and liquid ingredients, and mix well. Beat egg whites until they peak (add dash of cream of tartar if necessary), then fold into mixture. Cook in waffle iron. Top with fruit or flavored yogurt. Serves about 8.

Submitted by:

Singleton House
Bed & Breakfast
11 Singleton Street
Eureka Springs, Ark. 72632
(501) 253-9111
Barbara Gavron
$55.00 to $65.00

Full breakfast
5 rooms, 5 private baths
Children allowed
No pets
Restricted smoking
Mastercard, Visa,
Am Ex, Discover

An old-fashioned Victorian with a touch of magic. Whimsically decorated with an eclectic collection of unexpected treasures & antiques. Breakfast on the balcony overlooking the fantasy garden & fishpond below. In the Historic District, 1 1/2 blocks to shops & cafes.

FRENCH TOAST

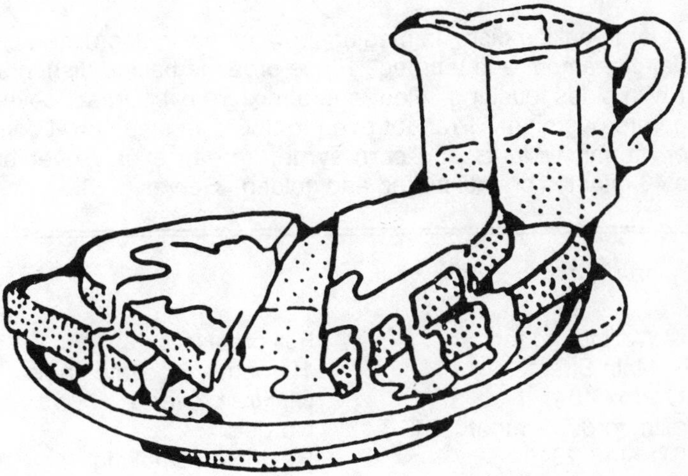

BAKED FRENCH BREAD SUZANNE

- 6 large eggs
- 1 1/2 cups milk
- 1 cup light cream or half & half
- 1 1/4 teaspoons vanilla
- 1/4 teaspoon cinnamon
- 1/4 teaspoon nutmeg
- 1 loaf French bread (cut 1" thick diagonally)
- 1/4 cup softened butter
- 1/2 cup firmly packed light brown sugar
- 1/2 cup chopped walnuts (optional)
- 1 tablespoon light corn syrup

Butter large baking dish. In medium bowl combine eggs, milk, cream, vanilla, cinnamon, and nutmeg. Place bread in baking dish in single layer with sides touching. Pour entire mixture over bread, cover and refrigerate overnight. Preheat oven to 350°. In small bowl combine butter, sugar, walnuts and corn syrup, spread evenly over bread. Bake 40 minutes or until puffed and golden. Serves 6 - 8.

Submitted by:

The Wallingford Inn
9 N. Main Street
P.O. Box 404
Wallingford, Vermont 05773
(802) 446-2849
Kathy & Joe Lombardo
$50.00 to $70.00

Full breakfast
10 rooms, 8 private baths
Children, over 3
No pets
Restricted smoking
Mastercard & Visa

1876 Victorian with arched marble fireplaces, oak woodwork, elegant chandeliers and polished wood floors. Guest rooms furnished in period decor. Candlelit dining rooms, where the fare is hearty, the conversation entertaining, and the mood informally relaxed.

BAKED FRENCH TOAST

1 loaf French bread
4 eggs
1 cup milk
1 teaspoon vanilla
1/2 teaspoon nutmeg
1/2 cup butter (1 stick)

Slice French bread into 1" slices. Arrange 8 slices on an edged baking sheet. Beat eggs in large bowl. Add milk, vanilla, and nutmeg. Pour mixture over bread, covering both sides and soaking well. Freeze on pan, then store in plastic zip-lock bags. In the morning, preheat oven to 475°. Spread both sides of bread with butter and bake for 8 minutes on one side, and 7 on the other. Serve with maple syrup and walnuts.

Origin: Passed along by Bill & Mary O'Conner who started the Dutch Treat House. It gets great reviews!

Submitted by:

Dutch Treat House
1220 31st Street
Anacortes, Wash. 98221
(206) 293-8154
Mike & Melanie Coyne
$35.00 to $55.00

Full breakfast
4 rooms
Children, over 8
No pets
No smoking
Mastercard & Visa

Comfortable lodging in a beautifully restored Dutch Colonial home built in 1930. Breakfasts made with all natural ingredients will start you out with plenty of energy for a day enjoying the beauty of nearby natural attractions.

DULWICH MANOR STUFFED FRENCH TOAST

8 eggs
1 1/2 cups milk
1 teaspoon vanilla
1/2 teaspoon orange extract
1 loaf French bread
Thin-sliced ham
Thin-sliced Swiss cheese
Butter or margarine
Crushed Corn Flakes
Confectioners sugar

In bowl mix first four ingredients, whipping slightly. Add more milk if too thick. Slice French bread diagonally 1/2" thick, then slice through middle of each slice lengthwise to form pocket. Place slice of ham & cheese into pocket. Arrange bread in shallow pan and pour egg mixture over top. Let set 10 minutes, then turn over and refrigerate overnight. Next day, preheat oven to 325°. Melt butter in fry pan. Dip bread into crushed Corn Flakes, coating well. Brown lightly on both sides, then place in hot oven to finish baking for 15 - 20 minutes. Remove to hot serving dish, dust with sifted confectioners sugar. Serve with hot maple syrup. Serves 8.

Submitted by:

Dulwich Manor Bed & Breakfast Inn
Route 5, Box 173A
Amherst, Virginia 24521
(804) 946-7207
Bob & Judy Reilly
$55.00 to $75.00

Full breakfast
5 rooms, 3 private baths
Children allowed
Pets allowed
Restricted smoking

Elegant English-style manor house in the foothills of the Blue Ridge Mountains, at the end of a lovely country lane. Fireplaces, window seats or bay window, with private whirlpool in master suite. Country breakfast.

ELEGANT FRENCH TOAST

- 2 tablespoons sliced almonds
- 2 - 3 oz. pkgs. softened cream cheese
- 1/4 cup and 2 tablespoons milk
- 12 slices cinnamon-raisin bread
- 3 tablespoons apricot preserves
- 3 eggs
- 1 tablespoon sugar
- 1 teaspoon vanilla
- 4 tablespoons butter
- Confectioners sugar

Toast almonds until golden in small skillet. Set aside. In small bowl, mix cream cheese with 2 tablespoons milk until well blended. Spread cream cheese on 6 slices bread. Spread apricot preserves on top of cream cheese. Top with remaining 6 slices bread. In a pie plate, mix eggs, sugar, vanilla and 1/4 cup milk. In skillet over medium-high heat, melt 2 tablespoons butter. Dip 3 sandwiches in egg mixture, brown on both sides. Repeat with remaining butter and sandwiches. Cut in half diagonally and sprinkle with confectioners sugar and almonds. Serves 6.

Submitted by:

Bedford Inn
805 Stockton Avenue
Cape May, New Jersey 08204
(609) 884-4158
Cindy & Alan Schmucker
$60.00 to $125.00

Full breakfast
11 rooms, 11 private baths
Children, over 7
No pets
Restricted smoking
Mastercard & Visa

Restored 1881 Italianate cottage sits a short block from the Atlantic Ocean. Victorian antiques, hearty sit-down breakfast in dining room or parlor with fireplace. Near restaurants, carriage rides, swimming, fishing, and tennis.

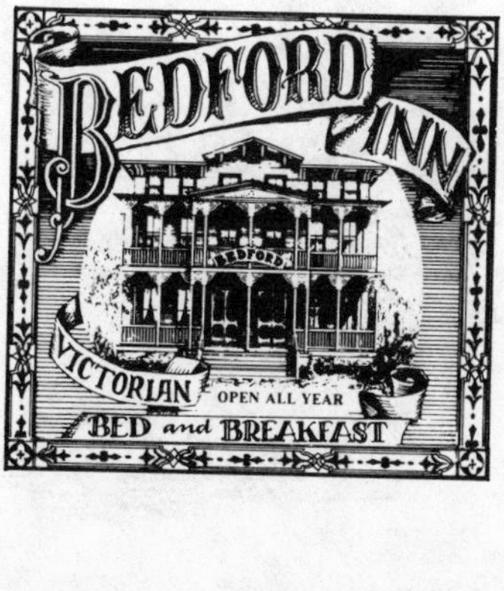

FERRY POINT HOUSE STUFFED FRENCH TOAST

8 oz. cream cheese
1/2 cup walnuts
2 teaspoons vanilla
4 large eggs, beaten
3/4 cup heavy cream
Dash of nutmeg
Butter for frying

Bread: sourdough bread, egg bread, walnut bread, Vienna bread or homemade white bread, sliced 1/2" - 1" thick

Spread mixture of cream cheese, walnuts and 1 teaspoon vanilla on six slices of bread, then close each "sandwich" with another slice of bread. Dip each "sandwich" into a mixture of eggs, cream, 1 teaspoon vanilla and nutmeg. Grill in butter in fry pan or on non-stick grill until golden brown on both sides. Cut into points and serve with sliced bananas and blueberries or raspberries. Serve with warmed maple syrup or apricot-orange sauce. Mix 12 oz. jar apricot preserves with 1/2 cup orange juice for sauce. Heat in microwave.

Submitted by:

Ferry Point House
Route #1, Box 335
Laconia, N.H. 03246
(603) 524-0087
Joe & Diane Damato
$55.00 to $65.00

Full breakfast
5 rooms, 3 private baths
Children allowed
No pets
Restricted smoking

150 year old Victorian furnished with antiques, reflecting the charm of the past. 60 foot veranda with panoramic views of Lake Winnisquam and the White Mountains. Relax, or enjoy the many activities of the region.

FRENCH TOAST FONDUE

- 1 1/2 cups powdered sugar
- 1/2 cup butter
- 1/2 cup maple syrup
- 1 egg yolk
- 1 egg white, stiffly beaten
- 2 cups milk
- 6 eggs
- 1 cup flour
- 1 1/2 tablespoons sugar
- 1/4 teaspoon salt
- Pinch of nutmeg
- 1/2 teaspoon vanilla
- French bread slices
- Hot oil for frying

Cream powdered sugar and butter. Add maple syrup, then egg yolk. Fold in beaten egg white. Set aside. In a blender, combine milk, eggs, flour, sugar, salt, nutmeg and vanilla, and mix. Dip chunks of French bread into batter, then into hot oil in fondue pot until golden. Serve with maple syrup mixture.

Origin: A favorite of our guests. Each likes to dip his/her own, while chatting with others at the table.

Submitted by:

Roundtop Bed & Breakfast
Box 258, R.D. #2
Wrightsville, Penn. 17368
(717) 252-3169
Judith Blakey, owner
Joni Eberly, manager
$35.00 to $75.00

Full breakfast
6 rooms, 1 private bath
Children allowed
No pets
Smoking allowed

Romantic 1880 stone home, 800 feet above the Susquehanna River. Spectacular views, a true "getaway", but only 5 minutes from a renowned French restaurant. Unique setting on over 100 acres of woodland.

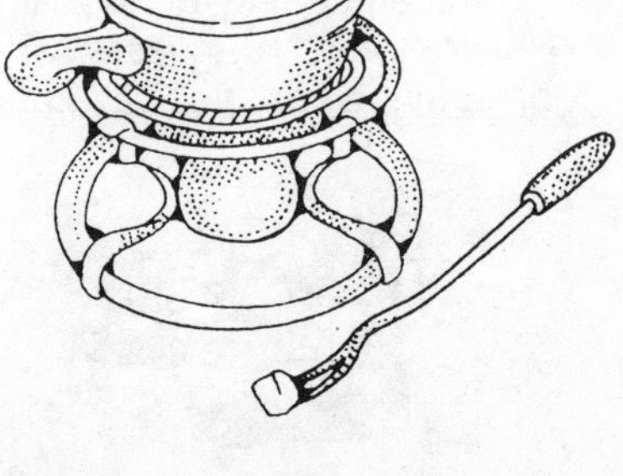

FRENCH TOAST STUFFED WITH APRICOTS AND PECANS

1/2 cup finely chopped dried apricots
1/4 cup orange juice
8 oz. cream cheese
1/4 cup coarsely chopped pecans
16 - 3/4" thick slices sourdough bread or challah (egg bread)
2 cups milk
1 cup half & half
6 eggs
5 tablespoons sugar
4 teaspoons grated orange rind
1 teaspoon vanilla
1 teaspoon salt
1/2 cup butter

Apricot-Orange Syrup:
18 oz. apricot preserves
3/4 cup orange juice

In saucepan combine apricots and orange juice, and bring to boil. Simmer for 10 minutes or until apricots are tender, then chill to room temperature. Mix cream cheese, pecans and apricot mixture in a small bowl. Spread over 8 slices of bread, forming 8 sandwiches. Mix milk, half & half, eggs, sugar, orange rind, vanilla and salt. Dip sandwiches in egg mixture to completely coat. Melt 2 tablespoons butter in skillet over medium heat. Cook sandwiches until golden brown, adding more butter as necessary. Transfer to plates. Apricot-Orange Syrup: Bring preserves & 3/4 cup juice to boil in heavy saucepan, stirring occasionally. Serve hot syrup over toast.

Submitted by:

Golden Plough Inn
Route 202
Lahaska, Pennsylvania 18931
(215) 794-4004
Earl Jamison
$85.00 to $200.00
Special rates available

Continental breakfast
45 rooms, 45 private baths
Children allowed
No pets
Restricted smoking
Mastercard, Visa, Am Ex

A newly renovated 18th century inn located along the old stage route between N.Y. & Philadelphia. Jacuzzis, air-conditioning, canopy beds, fireplace, & balcony. Near specialty shops, superb dining, and antiques.

GERMAN FRENCH TOAST (WITH SAUSAGE)

2 cups milk
3 eggs, separated
1 tablespoon lemon rind
1 tablespoon sugar (optional)
6 - 8 slices day-old French bread
1 cup bread crumbs
2 tart apples, peeled, cored & sliced
1 tablespoon lemon juice
Water
2 - 3 links smoked, sliced bratwurst
1/4 onion, sliced
Cinnamon-sugar mixture

Combine milk, egg yolks, lemon rind and sugar, if desired. Soak bread in this until saturated, then dip in egg whites, then in bread crumbs and place bread on greased cookie sheet. Place in preheated oven for 15 minutes at 425°, turn bread and bake for additional 10 - 12 minutes. Meanwhile, place apple slices and lemon juice in saucepan with water to cover, and bring to boil; then remove from heat. Also lightly sauté sliced bratwurst and onions until lightly browned. Place 2 slices of toast on each plate, sprinkle with cinnamon-sugar, cover with apples and serve with bratwurst.

Origin: Recipe from my grandmother who came from Alsace-Lorraine. She called it Arme Ritter, meaning "Poor Knights".

Submitted by:

Strawberry Creek Inn
P.O. Box 1818
Idyllwild, California 92349
(714) 659-3202
Diana Dugan & Jim Goff
$65.00 to $90.00

Full breakfast
9 rooms, 9 private baths
No pets
No smoking
Mastercard & Visa

Mountain home, elevation 5500', nestled amid the pine & cedar trees of the San Jacinto Mtns. Country antiques, hand-crafted items, queen-sized beds, fireplaces, and a glassed-in wraparound porch.

GOURMET FRENCH TOAST

For Toast:
2 large eggs
1 cup 1% milk
Dash of nutmeg
8 slices French baguette bread
Butter for frying

Syrup:
2 oz. butter
2 tablespoons sugar
1 cup fresh fruit (blackberries, nectarines, apples, blueberries)
1 cup boiling water
Arrowroot or cornstarch

For Syrup: In sauté pan or saucepan, melt butter. Add sugar and simmer 2 minutes on low heat. Add fresh fruit and 1 cup boiling water. Simmer for 10 minutes or until fruit is soft. If sauce is not thick, add a little prepared thickening mixture (arrowroot or cornstarch). For Toast: Blend eggs, milk and nutmeg together. In another pan melt 1 pat butter, dip bread slices in egg mixture and cook quickly on medium-high heat. Pour sauce over browned toast and serve. Garnish with nuts or powdered sugar.

Submitted by:

The Lincoln Inn
538 Lincoln
Port Townsend, Wash. 98368
(206) 385-6677
Joan & Robert Allen
$60.00 to $75.00

Full breakfast
3 rooms, 3 private baths
No children
No pets
Restricted smoking
Mastercard & Visa

Unique Victorian with original woodwork, brass chandeliers, Persian rugs and antique furniture. Each room has it's own color scheme. We cater to honeymooners, anniversaries or just plain "get away from it all". Near golf, tennis, boating, hiking, windsurfing, and antiques.

LOW CHOLESTEROL FRUITY FRENCH TOAST

6 slices French or Italian bread, cut diagonally
1 cup skim milk
1/2 teaspoon nutmeg
3/4 cup Egg Beaters
2 tablespoons strawberry, blueberry or peach preserves
Melted margarine
Topping: Fruit & confectioners sugar

Arrange bread in pan in single layer. Combine milk, nutmeg, Egg Beaters and preserves. Beat together and pour over bread. Turn bread once. Refrigerate overnight. Melt margarine, fry to light brown on each side. Top with fruit and confectioners sugar.

Submitted by:

Hopp-Inn Guest House
5 Man-O-War Drive
Marathon, Florida 33050
(305) 743-4118
Joan Hopp
$45.00 to $125.00

Full breakfast
5 rooms, 5 private baths
Children, over 12
No pets
Smoking allowed
Mastercard & Visa

Located on the ocean in the heart of the Florida Keys. All rooms have televisions and private entrances. Also have housekeeping villas which accommodate families. Scuba, snorkeling, swimming, tennis & biking nearby.

PEACHES AND CREAM FRENCH TOAST

12 eggs
3/4 cup peach preserves
3 cups half & half
24 slices French bread, cut 1/2" - 3/4" thick
1/3 cup peach preserves
1/2 cup softened butter
8 fresh peaches, peeled and sliced
Powdered sugar
1/2 cup toasted almonds
Butter for frying

In large bowl beat eggs and 3/4 cup preserves with whisk to blend. Beat in half & half (can use electric mixer). Place bread slices in single layer in 11" x 15" baking dish. Pour egg mixture over bread, cover and refrigerate overnight, until all liquid is absorbed. In small bowl beat 1/3 cup preserves and 1/2 cup butter on high with mixer until fluffy to make Peach Butter, set aside. Melt butter on large electric sandwich grill. Add bread slices and cook over medium heat until lightly browned, turning once. Remove and keep warm. Serve French Toast topped with 1 tablespoon Peach Butter & fresh peach slices. Sprinkle with toasted almonds and powdered sugar. Serves 2 slices each to 10-12 people. Serve with bacon or sausages.

Submitted by:

Windward House
Bed & Breakfast
6 High Street
Camden, Maine 04843
(207) 236-9656
Jon & Mary Davis
$70.00 to $95.00

Full breakfast
5 rooms, 5 private baths
Children, over 12
No pets
Restricted smoking
Mastercard & Visa

1854 Greek Revival home furnished with period antiques, above picturesque Camden Harbor. Enjoy the warm ambiance of the common rooms, our private gardens, and convenient location.

RENEE'S FRENCH DELIGHT

8 oz. cream cheese
12 slices thinly-sliced whole wheat bread or cinnamon bread or combination
1/2 cup chopped walnuts or pecans
1 teaspoon vanilla extract
4 eggs, beaten
3/4 cup half & half
Dash of nutmeg
Butter for frying

Apricot Sauce:
12 oz. apricot jam
1/2 cup orange juice
Garnish: Sliced bananas

Spread cream cheese on bread (works best on frozen bread). Sprinkle nuts on top. Top with slice of bread to form sandwich. Mix vanilla, eggs, half & half, and nutmeg for batter. Dip each sandwich. Fry in butter. Combine jam and orange juice and bring to boil. Cut toast diagonally. Garnish with bananas, serve apricot sauce on top.

Submitted by:

Partridge Brook Inn
P.O. Box 151, Hatt Road
Westmoreland, N.H. 03467
(603) 399-4994
Renee & Don Strong
$65.00 to $75.00

Full breakfast
5 rooms, 5 private baths
Children, over 6
No pets
No smoking

Historic 1790 home in serene setting, bears many reminders of a rich past. Authentic decor, mortise-and-tenon doors, original fireplaces, intricate woodwork and stenciling. Fishing, nature walks, horseback riding, skiing, swimming, boating, golf, and antiquing nearby.

STUFFED FRENCH TOAST

8 oz. cream cheese
1 cup grated mozzarella cheese
1/2 cup ricotta or cottage cheese
1/2 cup apricot preserves
8 slices 1 1/2" thick bread
6 eggs
1/2 cup heavy cream
1/2 teaspoon salt
Butter for frying

Apricot Sauce:
1 cup dried apricots
2 cups warm water
1/3 cup sugar
Pinch of salt
1/8 teaspoon almond extract

Cut and mix together the three cheeses and apricot preserves. Cut a pocket almost to the bottom crust in each slice of bread and stuff with the cheese mixture. Beat eggs, cream and salt together. Dip each piece of bread into egg mixture, soaking each side thoroughly. Melt butter on medium hot griddle, and cook toast approximately 8 - 10 minutes each side, or until golden brown and cheeses begin to melt. Sauce: Soak apricots in warm water for 1 hour. Cover and cook over low heat 15 - 20 minutes or until tender. Remove from heat. Pour apricots and liquid into blender. Blend until smooth and stir in remaining ingredients. Mix and serve warm over toast.

Submitted by:

Meadeau View Lodge
P.O. Box 356
Cedar City, Utah 84720
(801) 682-2495
Val & Harris Torbenson
$33.00 to $60.00

Full breakfast
9 rooms, 9 private baths
Children allowed
Small pets allowed
Restricted smoking
Mastercard & Visa

We blend harmoniously into the seemingly unending wilderness surrounding our lodge. 8,400' above sea level among aspens, pines, & wildflowers. Geode-faced circular fireplace in lobby, French doors, dormer windows. Near parks, lakes, skiing, and snowmobiling.

CASSEROLES

AUNT DIANA'S SAUSAGE STRATA

10 slices sourdough bread
3/4 lb. cooked, crumbled mild Italian sausage
1/2 lb. grated sharp Cheddar cheese
8 eggs
3 cups milk
1/4 teaspoon salt

Trim crusts from bread. Cube bread and put into ungreased 9" x 13" baking dish. Pile with cooked, drained sausage, and cheese. Beat eggs, add milk and salt. Pour mixture over bread. Cover with plastic wrap, and refrigerate overnight. Uncover, and bake at 350° for 45 minutes.

Stratas are wonderful, as they must be done the night before, leaving the cook with a little less to do in the morning!

Submitted by:

Calistoga Wayside Inn
1523 Foothill Boulevard
Calistoga, California 94515
(707) 942-0645
Deborah & Leonard Flaherty
$85.00 to $109.00

Full breakfast
3 rooms, 1 private bath
Children, over 8
No pets
Restricted smoking
Mastercard, Visa, Am Ex

Graceful 1920's Spanish-style hacienda in a park-like setting, in the Napa Valley. Short walk to town and famous hot spring resorts. Bicycles, picnic baskets, a hammock, hot tub, cozy fireplace - a relaxing vacation.

BEEF BRUNCH BAKE

- 2 large onions
- 1 lb. chopped beef
- 4 tablespoons butter
- 4 eggs
- 2 cups sour cream
- 1 teaspoon salt
- 1/4 teaspoon pepper
- 1/2 teaspoon caraway seeds
- 6 - 8 slices of bread

Sauté onions with chopped beef in butter. Beat eggs with sour cream, salt, pepper, and caraway seeds. Place bread in bottom of greased shallow casserole. Cover with meat and onions and pour on sauce. Bake at 375° for 20 - 30 minutes. Serves 6 - 8.

Submitted by:

Windward House
24 Jackson Street
Cape May, New Jersey 08204
(609) 884-3368
Owen & Sandy Miller
$80.00 to $115.00

Full breakfast
8 rooms, 8 private baths
Children, over 12
No pets
Smoking allowed
Mastercard & Visa

Edwardian seaside inn, in Historic District, with "an entry room & staircase that are perhaps the prettiest in town," says New Jersey Monthly, 1986. Antiques, queen beds, air-conditioned. 3 sun & shade porches, cozy parlor fireplace, 1/2 block to beach & shopping.

COLVMNS IRISH FRITTATA

1 lb. potatoes, cooked & diced
1 diced green bell pepper
1 diced red bell pepper
1 medium onion, diced
Butter
1 dozen eggs
1 cup heavy cream
1/2 cup milk
3 tablespoons flour
Salt & pepper to taste

Sauté vegetables together in butter. Mix other ingredients well. Place vegetable mixture in buttered glass 9" x 13" baking dish. Pour egg mixture over vegetables and bake at 425° for 30 - 35 minutes. Good with ham or sausage. Serves 8 - 10.

Origin: Trial & error with Potatoes O'Brien, with lots of input from our guests.

Submitted by:

COLVMNS By the SEA
1513 Beach Drive
Cape May, New Jersey 08204
(609) 884-2259
Barry & Cathy Rein
$95.00 to $135.00

Full breakfast
11 rooms, 11 private baths
Children, over 12
No pets
Restricted smoking
Mastercard & Visa

Elegant oceanfront mansion in historic Victorian seaside resort. Antiques of an era when a "cottage" had 20 rooms, coffered ceilings and hand-carved woodwork. Gourmet breakfast, high tea and bikes. Great for birders, history buffs, or just to relax.

DAIRYLAND MEXICALI

2 - 3 oz. cans chopped green chilies
1 lb. grated Monterey Jack cheese
5 eggs
1 1/4 cups milk
1/4 cup flour
1/2 teaspoon salt
Dash of black pepper
4 drops Tabasco sauce
4 cups (1 lb.) grated mild Cheddar cheese

Place chilies in an ungreased 9" x 13" glass baking dish. Cover with grated Monterey Jack cheese. Mix eggs, milk, flour, salt, pepper and Tabasco in blender, and pour over chilies and cheese. Sprinkle top with grated Cheddar cheese. Bake uncovered at 350° for 45 minutes. For a sharper taste, use sharp Cheddar cheese.

Submitted by:

Just-N-Trails Bed & Breakfast/
Farm Vacation
Route #1, Box 263
Sparta, Wisconsin 54656
(608) 269-4522
Don & Donna Justin
$50.00 to $85.00

Full breakfast
6 rooms, 5 private baths
Children allowed
No pets
No smoking
Mastercard & Visa

4 Laura Ashley-decorated guest rooms in 1920 farmhouse on dairy farm. 1988 "Little House on the Prairie" log cabin sleeps 4, with bath and air-conditioning. Near safe, scenic Elroy-Sparta Bike Trails or canoe La Crosse River. Cross-country skiing for classic or freestyle.

EGG & SAUSAGE BREAKFAST CASSEROLE

6 hard-boiled eggs, sliced
Salt & pepper to taste
1 lb. hot bulk sausage
1 1/2 cups sour cream
1/2 cup dry bread crumbs
1 1/2 cups grated Cheddar cheese

Place sliced eggs in buttered 9" x 13" glass casserole dish and season to taste with salt & pepper. Cook bulk sausage, drain well and sprinkle over eggs. Pour sour cream over the sausage. Combine dry bread crumbs and grated cheese. Sprinkle over casserole. Heat thoroughly in 325° oven for about 30 minutes and then brown top under the broiler. Serves 6.

Submitted by:

The Okemo Inn
Jct. Route 103 & 100 North
Ludlow, Vermont 05149
(802) 228-8834
Ron & Toni Parry
$40.00 to $65.00

Full breakfast
11 rooms, 11 private baths
Children, over 6
No pets
Smoking allowed
Mastercard, Visa, Am Ex

Classic, cozy inn with the charm and history of a more relaxed era. King-size sauna, summer swimming pool, color cable television, quiet times in our reading parlor, candlelight dinners and hearty country-style breakfasts. Bike rentals and gift shop.

EGGS À LA WEDGEWOOD

16 eggs
1 teaspoon nutmeg
Salt & pepper to taste
1 teaspoon fresh parsley
1/4 cup sour cream
1/4 cup finely chopped green onions
1/2 - 1 cup crisply fried bacon
16 button mushrooms
2 cups grated Cheddar cheese

Night before: In skillet scramble eggs and nutmeg. Add salt, pepper, and parsley. Place cooked eggs in greased baking or quiche dish as first layer. Now layer sour cream, green onions, bacon, mushrooms, and cheese. Refrigerate overnight. Next morning: Bake at 300° for 20 - 30 minutes until warm through, and cheese is melted. Serves 8. May be adapted to serve any number. Use 2 eggs per person and layer other ingredients generously.

Submitted by:

The Wedgewood Inn
11941 Narcissus Road
Jackson, California 95642
(209) 296-4300
Vic & Jeannine Beltz
$75.00 to $105.00

Full breakfast
6 rooms, 6 private baths
Children, over 12
No pets
Restricted smoking
Mastercard, Visa, Discover

Elegant 1987 Victorian replica with wraparound porch and swing, nestled on wooded acreage. Lavishly furnished with antiques and family heirlooms. Some balconies & wood burning stoves in rooms. Afternoon refreshments and gourmet breakfast. Romantic getaway!

EGGS MONTEREY

- **1 1/2 lbs. shredded Monterey Jack cheese**
- **1 lb. fresh mushrooms, sliced**
- **1 medium onion, chopped**
- **1/4 cup melted butter**
- **1 cup cubed ham**
- **7 eggs, beaten**
- **1 3/4 cups milk**
- **1/2 cup flour**
- **1 tablespoon chopped parsley**
- **1 tablespoon seasoned salt**

Place half the cheese in bottom of greased 9" x 13" baking dish. Sauté mushrooms and onion in butter until tender, spread over cheese. Sprinkle ham cubes over mushrooms and top with remaining cheese. May be covered and refrigerated overnight. When ready to bake, beat eggs, milk, flour, parsley and seasoned salt. Pour evenly over casserole. Bake at 350° for 45 minutes. Suitable for baking in individual ramekins. Garnish with a split cherry tomato and sprig of parsley. Serves 8 - 10.

Submitted by:

Benner House
Bed & Breakfast
645 Main Street
Historic Weston, Missouri
64098
(816) 386-2616
Ken & Karen West
$58.00 to $65.00

Full breakfast
4 rooms
Children, over 12
No pets
No smoking
Cash or check only

Gracious 1890's restored Victorian home within walking distance to downtown. Relax on charming wraparound porch, tour in a 1929 vintage auto or stroll along picturesque streets. Specialty & antique shops, fine art, museums, wineries, state park and winter skiing.

EGGS OLÉ

1 dozen eggs
1 1/2 cups cottage cheese
1/2 lb. grated Monterey Jack cheese
1/2 lb. grated Cheddar cheese
1 can chopped (diced) green chilies
1/2 cup flour
1 teaspoon baking powder
1 teaspoon salt (optional)

Mix all ingredients together. Bake in greased 9" x 13" dish at 350° for about 1 hour. Serve with salsa, chopped green onions and sour cream. Serves 12.

Submitted by:

Anaheim Country Inn
856 South Walnut
Anaheim, California
92802
(714) 778-0150
Lois Ramont & Marilyn Watson
$50.00 to $75.00

Full breakfast
8 rooms, 6 private baths
Children, over 12
No pets
No smoking
Mastercard, Visa,
Am Ex, Discover

1910 Princess Anne home with beveled, leaded glass windows and turn-of-the-century country furnishings. Relax on airy porches, wander through the garden and under the avocado trees. Near Disneyland, Knott's Berry Farm, Convention Center "Fun Bus" stop.

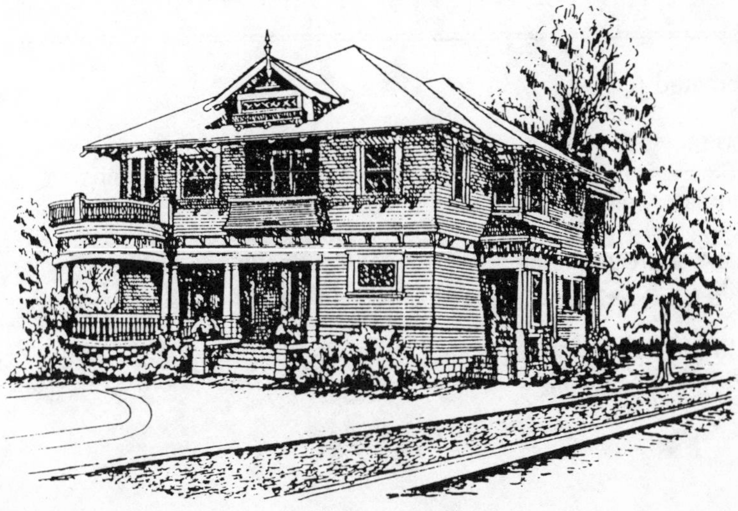

FRITTATA WITH DIJON-HOLLANDAISE SAUCE

- 8 oz. cream cheese
- 1/2 cup flour
- 1 dozen eggs
- 1 red onion
- 5 cloves garlic
- 3 zucchinis
- 4 chantrell mushrooms
- 1 yellow sweet pepper
- 1/4 cup fresh basil leaves (chopped & loosely packed)
- 1/4 lb. grated Swiss cheese
- 3/4 teaspoon salt
- 1/4 teaspoon white pepper

Dijon-Hollandaise Sauce:

- 3 egg yolks
- Juice of 1/2 lemon
- 1/4 teaspoon salt
- 2 dashes white pepper
- 1 dash cayenne pepper
- 1/2 cube unsalted butter
- 2 tablespoons coarse-grain dijon mustard

Frittata: Whip together cream cheese, flour and 4 eggs. Set aside. Chop, finely process, or grate red onion, garlic, zucchinis, mushrooms, sweet pepper and basil. Place mixture into a cloth napkin and squeeze out all excess moisture; put into large mixing bowl. Add to cream cheese mixture 8 more eggs, grated Swiss cheese, salt, & white pepper, and whip together well. Add cheese/egg mixture to chopped vegetables. Blend well. Pour batter into greased 12" tart pan with removable bottom. Bake at 300° for 1 hour. Sauce: In double boiler, whip egg yolks and lemon juice until mixture has custard-like consistency. Add salt, white pepper & cayenne pepper. In separate pan, melt butter and add it very slowly (a few drops at a time) to the egg yolk mixture, whipping constantly. Add dijon mustard and blend well. Top frittata with sauce.

Submitted by:

Carter House
1033 Third Street
Eureka, California 95501
(707) 445-1390
Mark & Christi Carter
$65.00 to $299.00

Full breakfast
7 rooms, 4 private baths
Children, over 8
No pets
No smoking
Mastercard, Visa, Am Ex

Victorian faithfully replicated, with marble fireplaces and bays. Oriental rugs, contemporary paintings and flowers, hors d'oeuvres.

GOURMET SAUSAGE FONDUE

1 1/2 lbs. bulk pork sausage
2 tablespoons minced green onion
1/4 cup chopped pimiento
Salt & pepper to taste
1 teaspoon dry mustard
12 slices wheat or white bread, crusts removed
6 eggs, beaten
3 cups milk
1/2 teaspoon salt
2 teaspoons Worcestershire sauce
Pimiento strips for garnish
6 stuffed green olives, sliced, for garnish

In frying pan, break apart and lightly brown sausage, draining off fat. Add onion, chopped pimiento, salt & pepper, and dry mustard, set aside. Line bottom of greased 8" x 12" pan with 6 bread slices. Fill in space with more bread if needed, to cover. Spoon sausage mixture over bread. Cover top with remaining 6 slices of bread. Combine eggs, milk, salt and Worcestershire sauce. Pour over bread, chill overnight. Set in pan of hot water and bake at 325° for 1 hour & 15 minutes. Garnish with pimiento strips and olives to form a poinsettia for Christmas, or with pimiento in heart shape for Valentine's Day.

Submitted by:

Coleen's California Casa
11715 S. Circle Drive
Whittier, California 90601
(213) 699-8427
Coleen Davis
$55.00 to $75.00

Full breakfast
3+ rooms, 3 private baths
Children, over 10
No pets
Restricted smoking

High above the city, but just 5 minutes from freeways. Quiet, residential area with deer and other wildlife nearby. Delightful conversation and privacy, near Disneyland, Knott's Berry Farm & most tourist attractions. Sincere hospitality.

HAM AND EGGS "TO DIE FOR"

24 hard-cooked eggs
2 cups ham cubes, the size of tiny dice
1/2 cup sliced black olives
4 tablespoons margarine
3 - 10 oz. cans white sauce
4 dashes Tabasco sauce
2 tablespoons Worcestershire sauce
2 tablespoons curry powder
2 cups grated Cheddar cheese

Slice hard-cooked eggs with a wire egg slicer. Put into casserole dish with tiny ham cubes and sliced olives. Melt margarine in large saucepan and add white sauce. Heat over low flame, stir out the lumps, and when sauce is smooth and bubbly, add Tabasco, Worcestershire and curry. Mix in all but 1/2 cup of Cheddar cheese and stir until cheese melts. Pour the sauce over the baking dish, and blend ingredients together. Sprinkle remaining grated cheese on top. Bake at 375° for 1/2 hour. Your guests are sure to exclaim with all the "Y" words: "Yippie!" "Yummy!" "Yowie!" Serves 8.

Submitted by:

The Mansion Hotel
2220 Sacramento Street
San Francisco, California 94115
(415) 929-9444
Robert C. Pritikin
$89.00 to $225.00

Full breakfast
20 rooms, 20 private baths
Children allowed
Pets allowed
Smoking allowed
Mastercard, Visa, Am Ex, Discover

Historic landmark: flowers in room, nightly concerts, billiard-game room, sculpture gardens, and the magic parlour. "Lovely, marvelous hospitality," said Barbra Streisand. ". . . Breathe an atmosphere of forgotten elegance," according to the Christian Science Monitor.

HAM/POTATOES O'BRIEN CASSEROLE

4 baking potatoes, baked
1 cup mayonnaise
1/2 cup grated Cheddar cheese
1/4 cup chopped green pepper
1/4 cup chopped scallions
1/4 cup chopped pimiento
14 oz. sliced ham, diced

Scoop baked potatoes from shell. Lightly toss with other ingredients. Bake in 9" x 13" casserole at 350° for 45 minutes or until potatoes are crispy brown. Optional: Top casserole with 1/4 cup grated Cheddar cheese. You can also substitute 14 oz. drained tuna for the ham.

Submitted by:

Valley Forge Mountain Home Bed & Breakfast
P.O. Box 562
Valley Forge, Pennsylvania 19481-0562
(215) 783-7838 or 783-7783
Carolyn & Dick Williams
$45.00 to $70.00

Full or continental breakfast
3 rooms, 2 private baths
Children allowed
Some pets allowed
Smoking allowed
Mastercard, Visa, Am Ex

French Colonial on 2 1/2 wooded acres, adjacent to Valley Forge Nat'l. Historical Park. Air-conditioning, cable television, telephone in guest rooms. Florida room & parlor with fireplace. Near Philadelphia, Longwood Gardens, Hopewell Village, and Brandywine Valley.

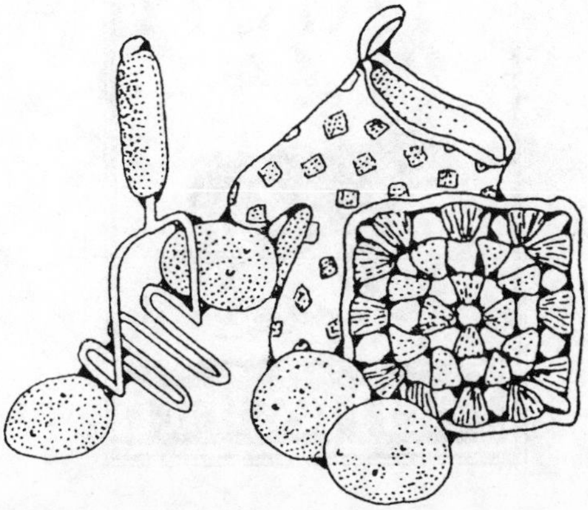

HASHBROWN CASSEROLE

2 lbs. shredded hashbrown potatoes
1 can cream of chicken soup
1 cup sour cream
1 cup chopped onions
1 cup shredded Cheddar cheese
1 stick melted margarine

Mix all ingredients together and spoon into buttered 2 1/2 quart casserole, or two or three smaller ones. Bake at 350° until done, 30 - 35 minutes.

Submitted by:

Parish Patch Farm & Inn
625 Cortner Road
Normandy, Tenn. 37360
(615) 857-3441
Richard Thomsen
$60.00 to $120.00

Full breakfast
14 rooms, 12 private baths
Children allowed
Pets allowed/Kennel available
Smoking allowed
Mastercard, Visa, Am Ex

150 acre farm on the Duck River, surrounded by cornfields and smokey blue hills, near Opryland USA, and the Tennessee Walking Horse Farm. Fireplaces, swimming pool, warm woods, bright prints, & air-conditioning. Public dining room. Hiking, fishing and canoeing.

PARISH
PATCH
farm&inn

JUDY'S BREAKFAST CASSEROLE

2 lb. bag Ore-Ida hash brown potatoes, thawed
1/2 teaspoon salt
1/2 lb. mild sausage
Chopped onions to taste
1/2 lb. shredded Swiss cheese
5 eggs
1 - 13 oz. can evaporated milk
1/4 teaspoon pepper
1/2 teaspoon nutmeg

Grease 9" x 13" baking dish. Press potatoes in bottom and on sides. Sprinkle with 1/2 teaspoon salt and brown lightly in oven. Brown sausage and onion and drain. Spread over potato crust. Sprinkle with cheese. Beat together remaining ingredients and pour into the crust. Bake at 425° (400° if using glass dish) for 20 - 25 minutes. Makes 10 servings.

Submitted by:

Teetor House
300 Main Street
Hagerstown, Indiana 47346
(317) 489-4422
Jack & JoAnne Warmoth
$50.00 to $85.00

Full breakfast
4 rooms, 4 private baths
Children allowed
No pets
Restricted smoking
Mastercard & Visa

Elegant historical mansion on 10 acres in charming small town. Walk to restaurants and shops, air-conditioned, with many unique amenities. Near golf, swimming, and fitness center. 1 hour from Indianapolis and Dayton, Ohio.

MARILYN'S SMASH

1 - 2 tablespoons margarine
1 cold baked potato, peeled & diced
2 tablespoons chopped green onion
4 - 6 sliced mushrooms
1 - 2 oz. sausage patty, fried & crumbled
2 oz. grated Cheddar cheese
1/2 teaspoon crushed fresh garlic or garlic salt, to taste
1/2 cup heavy cream
2 eggs, poached
Garnish: Sour cream & crumbled cooked bacon

Heat 1 - 2 tablespoons margarine in heavy skillet. Add diced potato, green onions and mushrooms, and brown lightly. Add cooked sausage, cheese, garlic and cream, and turn up heat so cream thickens and cheese melts. Pour into individually-sized baking dishes or casserole and place in oven to hold, while poaching eggs. Top casserole with eggs, sprinkle with bacon bits and serve with sour cream on the side.

Origin: Based on corned beef hash, this looks & tastes great, and it's easy!

Submitted by:

The Mansion of Golconda
515 Columbus
P.O. Box 339
Golconda, Illinois 62938
(618) 683-4400
Don & Marilyn Kunz
$45.00 to $75.00

Full breakfast
4 rooms
Children, over 12
No pets
Restricted smoking
Mastercard, Visa,
Am Ex, Discover

An 1894 gabled "mansion" in historic river town, minutes from Shawnee National Forest. Known state-wide for fine dining, this gracious building is on National Register of Historic Places, and is beautifully decorated throughout.

MARY ELIZABETH'S BRUNCH EGGS

12 slices Canadian bacon or ham
12 slices Swiss cheese
1 dozen eggs
Half & half to cover
Parmesan cheese
Hungarian paprika

Grease long glass baking dish. Cover bottom of pan with bacon or ham. Cover meat with Swiss cheese. Break open an egg on each layered slice of ham and cheese. Then cover entire pan contents with half & half, exposing only the yellow. Bake for 30 minutes at 375°. Take out of oven and sprinkle with Parmesan cheese and paprika. Bake for 5 more minutes.

Origin: A quick & favorite recipe of Sally's, that she's been using for years. The delicious trademark of our B&B!

Submitted by:

The Historical Hudspeth House
1905 Fourth Avenue
Canyon, Texas 79015
(806) 655-9800
Dave & Sally Haynie
$40.00 to $90.00

Full breakfast
8 rooms, 6 private baths
Children allowed
No pets
Restricted smoking
Mastercard & Visa

Historical landmark dedicated to the late Mary Elizabeth Hudspeth. Tremendous hospitality and beautiful atmosphere; guests feel extra-special. Near antique shops, art galleries, museum, parks, golf, Palo Duro Canyon and the magnificent Texas Drama in summer.

MEETING HOUSE SUNRISE

2 cups medium diced pan-fried potatoes
1 cup ricotta cheese
1/2 cup whipped cream cheese
1/2 cup grated Gruyère cheese
1 cup frozen chopped spinach, patted dry
1 cup cubed baked ham
8 eggs
1/4 cup heavy cream
Topping:
1/4 cup bread crumbs
Minced fresh basil
1/4 cup fresh grated Parmesan cheese
1 tablespoon melted butter
Fresh pepper

Fry potatoes. Can be prepared ahead. Use 4 ovenproof dishes. Place 1/2 cup potatoes in center of each dish. Combine ricotta cheese, cream cheese, Gruyère cheese, spinach and ham. Divide into fourths & place on top center of potatoes. (Do not flatten cheese). Place in oven to heat. Beat eggs and cream, divide into fourths. In small 7" omelet pan, cook portion gently. Do not turn or brown. When eggs are still moist on top, remove & slide on top of the heated cheese mixture. Combine topping ingredients. Top each dish with 1/4 crumbs, and bake at 350° for 10 minutes. Serves 4.

Submitted by:

Meeting House Inn and Restaurant
35 Flanders Road
Henniker, N.H. 03242
(603) 428-3228
June & Bill Davis and Cheryl & Peter Bakke, "a family affair"
$63.00 to $88.00

Full breakfast
6 rooms, 6 private baths
Children by permission
No pets
No smoking
Mastercard, Visa, Am Ex

A quiet, relaxed, and cozy atmosphere where special attention is paid to the comfort of guests. We have a personal commitment as innkeepers. Restaurant is noted for its gourmet food. Wide range of activities available, or "nothing" at all.

MEXICAN FRITTATA

4 tablespoons butter
1/2 cup onion, chopped
1 can (17 oz.) corn, drained
2 cans (8 oz.) chopped green chilies
18 large eggs
1 cup sour cream
1 1/4 teaspoons chili powder
1/2 teaspoon salt
Dash red pepper
1/3 cup all-purpose flour
3 cups shredded sharp Cheddar
2 1/2 cups shredded Monterey Jack cheese
Garnish: Bottle of medium salsa, drained, and sour cream

Sauté first 4 ingredients. Whisk eggs and 1 cup sour cream. Combine these 2 mixtures with next 6 ingredients and pour into 2 greased pie dishes. Cook at 350° for 1 hour. Cut into wedges and garnish with salsa and dab of sour cream. Serves 16.

Submitted by:

1837 Bed & Breakfast/
Tea Room
126 Wentworth Street
Charleston, S.C. 29401
(803) 723-7166
Sherri Weaver & Richard Dunn
$45.00 to $85.00

Full breakfast
8 rooms, 8 private baths
Children allowed
No pets
Restricted smoking
Mastercard, Visa, Am Ex

Cotton planter's home, with brick carriage house in Historic District. Antiques & period pieces, with owners' artistic backgrounds evident. Formal parlor with cornice moulding & wide heart pine floors. Walk to boat tours, old market, antique shops, restaurants and attractions.

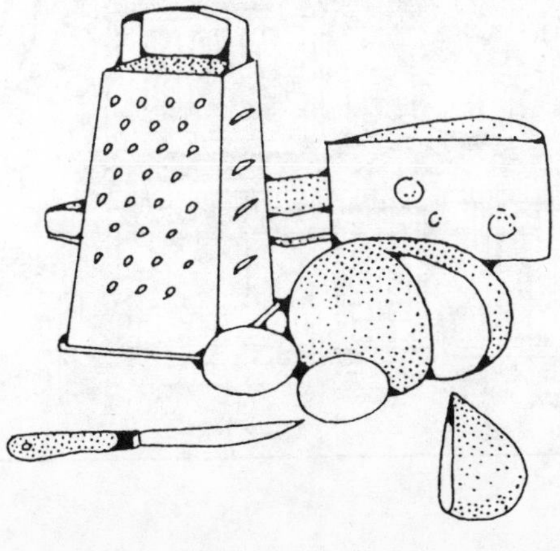

POTATO DELIGHT

8 cups cooked diced potatoes
6 slices diced bacon, uncooked
1 large onion, diced
1/4 lb. Velveeta cheese
1/4 cup chopped green olives
1 cup mayonnaise

Mix all ingredients and chill overnight. Bake in ungreased 9" x 13" casserole at 350° for 1 hour. Serves 10.

Origin: This recipe was given to us for use at our inn by a pair of delightful 70 year old twins.

Submitted by:

The Chicago Street Inn
219 Chicago Street
Brooklyn, Michigan 49230
(517) 592-3888
Karen & Bill Kerr
$50.00 to $69.00

Continental plus breakfast
4 rooms, 4 private baths
Children, over 13
No pets
Restricted smoking
Mastercard & Visa

Return to yesteryear. 1880's Victorian decorated with family and area antiques, located in the Irish Hills area. Close to antiquing, shopping, hiking, biking, county and state parks, swimming and golfing.

RANCHER'S EGG CASSEROLE

8 - 10 eggs
1/2 cup milk
4 - 5 slices white bread
1/2 - 1 lb. sausage or ham
1/4 lb. cheese

Spray 9" x 13" baking dish with Pam. Remove crusts from bread, lay in pan to cover bottom. Beat eggs and milk together until foamy. Pour over bread. Brown and crumble sausage or dice ham. Sprinkle on top of eggs. Cut cheese into 1/2" cubes. Distribute on top of casserole. Refrigerate overnight. Bake at 375° for 30 minutes or until set.

Submitted by:

Bessemer Bend
Bed & Breakfast
5120 Alcova, Rt., Box 40
Casper, Wyoming 82604
(307) 265-6819
Opal McInroy
$35.00 to $45.00

Full breakfast
2 rooms, 2 private baths
Children allowed
No pets
No smoking

On the Goose Egg Ranch, 1/2 mile from the site of an Oregon Trail crossing, the Red Butte Pony Express Station, & the first white man's cabin in Wyoming. Scenic area on North Platte River, with deer, bald eagles, pelicans, ducks and geese. Near Casper, a city of 50,000.

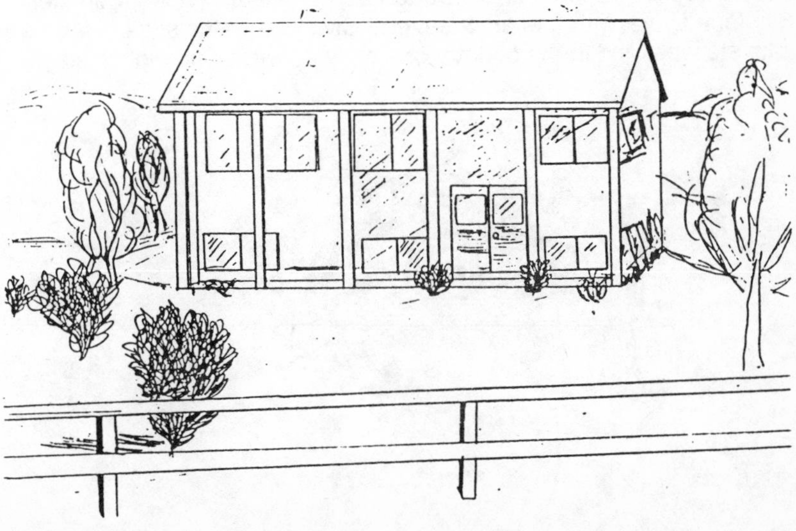

SMOKED SAUSAGE FRITTATA

1/4 cup vegetable oil
2 cloves garlic, finely chopped
1 green pepper, diced
1 red pepper, diced
2 stalks celery, diced
1 medium onion, diced
1 lb. smoked sausage
1 baked potato, peeled and diced
8 eggs, beaten
1/2 cup Parmesan cheese
2 tablespoons dried basil
Salt & pepper to taste

Sauté garlic, peppers, celery and onions in oil for 5 minutes. Cut sausage into bite-sized pieces, add to vegetables and cook 5 more minutes. Pour vegetables and sausage into lightly greased 9"x12" pan. Add diced potatoes. Beat eggs with cheese and spices, pour over vegetables. Bake at 375° for 45 minutes - 1 hour, until eggs are set. Serve warm. Reheats well in microwave. Makes 5 - 6 servings.

Submitted by:

The Hidden Inn
249 Caroline Street
Orange, Virginia 22960
(703) 672-3625
Ray & Barbara Lonick
$79.00 to $139.00

Full breakfast
9 rooms, 9 private baths
Children allowed
No pets
No smoking
Mastercard & Visa

1880's inn surrounded by 6 wooded acres. Near historic Monticello, Sky Line Drive, Montpelier, & several Civil War battle sites. Have an intimate weekend in the country or simply a refreshing night's stay.

SNAPPY CASSEROLE

7 - 8 slices old bread, cubed
2 - 3 oz. crumbled bacon, cubed ham or chopped beef
1 chopped onion
2 cups milk
3 eggs
Salt to taste
Pepper to taste
1 cup grated Cheddar (sharp or medium)
1/2 cup melted butter or margarine

Layer bread in buttered 9" x 13" pan. Cover bread with meat and onion. Beat milk, eggs, salt and pepper, and pour over bread. Sprinkle cheese on top and drizzle butter over all. Cover and refrigerate overnight. Bake at 325° for 1 hour. Serves 6 - 8.

Submitted by:

Serendipity, an Inn
407 71st Avenue North
Myrtle Beach, S.C. 29577
(803) 449-5268
Cos & Ellen Ficarra
$50.00 to $82.00

Continental breakfast
12 rooms, 12 private baths
Children, over 12
No pets
Restricted smoking
Mastercard, Visa, Am Ex

Award-winning Mission style inn, 1 1/2 blocks to ocean beach. Color television, air-conditioning, refrigerators, & daily maid service. Pool, jacuzzi, shuffleboard, table tennis. Near golf, tennis, restaurants and outlets. 90 miles to historic Charleston. 3 Diamond Triple A rating.

SUNDAY BRUNCH

16 slices white bread, crusts cut off
Ham, cut into small chunks
Shredded Velveeta Hot cheese (or your choice)
1 quart milk
6 eggs
Salt & pepper to taste
Note: May substitute broccoli for ham, for variation

Cut bread into 1" strips and cover bottom of 9" x 13" pan. Save some bread for top of casserole. Place a layer of cut-up ham, then a layer of cheese. Cover with a layer of bread strips. In bowl, mix milk, eggs, salt & pepper. Pour over top of bread. Refrigerate overnight. Bake 1 hour at 350°. Cool 15 minutes before serving.

Submitted by:

Mulberry Inn
512 Mulberry Street
Yankton, S.D. 57078
(605) 665-7116
Millie Cameron
$25.00 to $49.50

Full breakfast
Children allowed
No pets
Restricted smoking
Mastercard & Visa

1873 inn offers comfort and historic charm. Each guest room has its own distinctive features. Complimentary snacks in the 2 parlors or outside on the large porch. Minutes from the Missouri River and Lewis and Clark Lake.

TEXAS BRUNCH

- 6 eggs, beaten
- 1 - 17 oz. can cream-style corn
- 1 - 4 oz. can chopped mild green chilie peppers
- 1 cup shredded sharp Cheddar cheese
- 1 cup shredded Monterey Jack cheese
- 2 tablespoons quick-cooking grits
- 1 teaspoon Worcestershire sauce
- Dash of pepper

Condiments:
Sour cream
Picante sauce

In a bowl combine all ingredients except condiments. Pour into greased 8" x 8" x 2" baking dish. Bake at 325° for 45 minutes, or until knife inserted near center comes out clean. Let stand 10 minutes before cutting into squares and serving. Simply serve with fruit and muffins, or with tortillas for a Spanish flair. Serves 6 - 8.

Submitted by:

Michael's Bed & Breakfast
1715 35th Street
Galveston, Texas 77550
(409) 763-3760
Mikey & Allen Isbell
$85.00 to $100.00

Full breakfast
4 rooms
Children, over 12
No pets
No smoking
Mastercard & Visa

1915 red brick mansion on 1 acre: original greenhouse & fish pond, rose garden and gazebo. Antiques, contemporary pieces & original art. Host small weddings, receptions and luncheons. Featured on 1989 Galveston Historical Foundation's annual Historic Homes Tour.

THE VICTORIAN LADIES' BREAKFAST CASSEROLE

2 pkgs. frozen scalloped potatoes, thawed
1 pkg. chopped spinach, drained
1 1/2 cups diced ham
1/4 cup shredded Cheddar cheese
1/4 cup chopped onion, sautéed
12 eggs, scrambled
1 cup Hollandaise sauce
1 cup chopped tomatoes

Layer first 5 ingredients, in order listed, in large casserole dish. Bake at 350° for 20 - 30 minutes. Scramble and cook eggs and add to baked casserole. Drizzle Hollandaise sauce over scrambled eggs. Top with heated tomatoes. Serve immediately. Serves 8 - 10 people.

Submitted by:

The Victorian Ladies
63 Memorial Boulevard
Newport, Rhode Island 02840
(401) 849-9960
Donald & Hélène O'Neill
$85.00 to $125.00

Full breakfast
9 rooms, 9 private baths
Children, over 10
No pets
Smoking allowed
Mastercard & Visa

An 1850 Victorian house and carriage house. Air-conditioned with off-street parking. Within walking distance to beaches, harbor and many of Newport's attractions.

VEGETABLE CHEESE BAKE

- 2 tablespoons butter
- 2 shallots, chopped
- 1 large red bell pepper, chopped
- 3 cups chopped summer squash or zucchini , or both
- 1/4 teaspoon salt
- 1/4 teaspoon pepper
- 6 slices toasted bread
- Butter for bread slices
- 6 eggs
- 1 1/2 cups milk
- 1 tablespoon mustard
- 1 1/2 cups grated cheese

Melt butter; sauté shallots & red pepper until soft. Add squash and salt & pepper. Cook until most of moisture is out of squash. Set aside. Butter 1 side of bread. Lay in bottom of 9" x 12" baking dish. Spoon vegetables over bread. Blend eggs, milk and mustard in bowl. Pour over bread. Scatter cheese over the top. Refrigerate overnight. Bake at 350° for 40 - 45 minutes. Let cool 10 minutes before serving. Serves 8 - 10.

Submitted by:

Chesterfield Inn
Route 9
West Chesterfield, N.H.
03466
(603) 256-3211
Judy & Phil Hueber
$95.00 to $145.00

Full breakfast
9 rooms, 9 private baths
Children, over 10
No pets
Smoking allowed
Mastercard, Visa, Am Ex

Situated between Brattleboro, VT. and Keene, N.H., with beautiful views of the Green Mountain foothills. Luxurious guest rooms are newly renovated and furnished with antiques. Some fireplaces, balconies, sitting rooms or hand-stenciled walls.

WAKE UP CASSEROLE

- 2 cups seasoned croutons
- 1 cup shredded Cheddar cheese
- 1 - 4 oz. can mushroom pieces, drained
- 1 1/2 lbs. country-fresh sausage, browned & crumbled
- 1/2 cup chopped onion
- 6 eggs
- 2 cups milk
- 1/2 teaspoon salt
- 1/2 teaspoon pepper
- 1/2 teaspoon dry mustard
- 1 - 10 3/4 oz. can cream of mushroom soup
- 1/2 cup milk

Place croutons in greased 9" x 13" x 2" pan. Top with cheese and mushrooms. Brown sausage and onion; drain and spread over cheese. Beat eggs with 2 cups of milk and seasonings; pour over sausage. Cover and refrigerate overnight. (May be frozen at this point). Mix soup with 1/2 cup milk and spread on top. Bake at 325° for 1 hour. Serves 8.

Submitted by:

The Thorpe House
Clayborne Street
P.O. Box 36
Metamora, Indiana 47030
(317) 647-5425 or 932-2365
Mike & Jean Owens
$50.00 to $55.00

Full breakfast
5 rooms, 3 private baths
Children allowed
No pets
Smoking allowed
Mastercard & Visa

1840 Canal town home, in old Metamora, where steam engine still brings passenger cars, and gristmill still grinds cornmeal. Antiques and country accessories, family-style public dining room. Over 100 shoppes in quaint village. Country breakfast.

YUM YUM

4 tablespoons margarine
3 cups milk
4 large eggs
1/2 cup flour

Topping: grated carrots, chopped chives, julienne strip ham, cheese - your choice

Melt margarine in 9" x 13" pan. Mix milk and eggs lightly with beater, add flour. Pour mixed batter over melted butter. Bake at 450° for 20 minutes. Add any combinations of topping, and bake 5 - 10 minutes more.

Origin: An original recipe for Cape Neddick House.

Submitted by:

Cape Neddick House
1300 Route 1, P.O. Box 70
Cape Neddick, Maine 03902
(207) 363-2500
John & Dianne Goodwin
$50.00 to $70.00

Full breakfast
6 rooms
Children, over 6
No pets
Restricted smoking
Personal check - no credit cards

100 year old family Victorian farmhouse has antique bedsteads. Breakfast, served by 8th-generation Goodwins, is sprinkled with family tales of days past, & generous old-fashioned hospitality. Near beaches, boutiques, boat cruises, cultural & historical opportunities.

EGG/MEAT DISHES

BREAKFAST SAUSAGE HASH

1 medium onion, finely chopped
4 tablespoons butter, margarine or vegetable oil
4 cups sliced and peeled cold baked potatoes
1 lb. bulk sausage, browned & crumbled
2 teaspoons Worcestershire sauce
1 tablespoon chopped parsley
Salt & pepper to taste
8 beaten eggs
1 cup grated Cheddar cheese

Sauté onion in butter in large frying pan until transparent. Add potatoes, and turning frequently, cook over moderate heat until browned. Add sausage, Worcestershire, parsley and salt and pepper. Heat thoroughly. Pour eggs over top and cook until eggs start to set. Serve with grated cheese on top. Serves 8.

Submitted by:

Spring Bayou Inn
32 W. Tarpon Avenue
Tarpon Springs, Florida 34689
(813) 938-9333
Cher & Ron Morrick
$60.00 to $75.00

Continental plus breakfast
5 rooms, 4 private baths
No children
No pets
No smoking

Comfortable, turn-of-the-century home with spacious wraparound front porch, parlor, fireplace, and library. Near the sponge docks, restaurants, and shops of charming Greek-influenced "sponge capitol of the world".

CASTROVILLE/SMOKED TURKEY EGGS BENEDICT

6 English muffins
6 slices smoked turkey

Castroville Sauce:
1 - 3 cups half & half
2 - 3 teaspoons chicken stock paste
1 cup Gruyère cheese
Salt & white pepper to taste
2 cups artichoke hearts
1 diced pimiento
1 1/2 teaspoons thyme
1 1/2 tablespoons flour
Water for flour paste

Warm English muffins in 350° oven for 5 minutes. Place slices of turkey on muffins and return to oven for 2 minutes. Meanwhile, in double boiler, place half & half, chicken stock and cheese. After cheese has melted, add salt and pepper, artichokes, pimiento, and thyme. Just before mixture boils, thicken with flour paste. Cook for 10 minutes. Flour paste: Mix 1 1/2 tablespoons flour with enough water to make a medium paste. Add 1/4 cup of the double boiler mixture to the flour paste, and mix, before thickening the hot double boiler mixture. This will prevent lumps. Serve sauce over English muffins and turkey.

Submitted by:

The Martine Inn
255 Oceanview Boulevard
Pacific Grove, Calif. 93950
(408) 373-3388
Marion & Don Martine
$95.00 to $225.00

Full breakfast
19 rooms, 19 private baths
No children
No pets
Restricted smoking
Mastercard & Visa

Late 1890's ocean-front palace and carriage house, overlooks magnificent Monterey Bay. Former home of Laura & James Parke of Parke-Davis Pharmaceutical Company. Fireplaces, breakfast served on Old Sheffield silver, library, sightseeing, and gracious living.

CHICKEN CREPES BOMBAY

Crepes:
1 1/2 cups milk
2 tablespoons vegetable oil
3 eggs
1 1/2 cups all-purpose flour
1/8 teaspoon salt

Filling:
1/4 cup butter
1 cup celery, chopped
1/2 cup onion, chopped
2 tablespoons flour
1 teaspoon salt
1/2 teaspoon curry powder
1 chicken bouillon cube
1 1/2 cups milk
2 cups diced cooked chicken
1/2 cup pitted ripe olives, quartered
Parmesan cheese

Crepes: Blend all ingredients until smooth. Pour into warm buttered crepe pan just enough to cover bottom. Cook over medium heat until set and edges are slightly browned. Turn for only 30 seconds. Turn out onto waxed paper. Stack with waxed paper between each crepe. Can be refrigerated, tightly wrapped. Filling: Sauté celery and onion in butter to tender. Add flour & seasonings, and blend. Add milk gradually, cook until thickened. Fold in chicken and olives. Refrigerate overnight if you wish. Put 1/3 cup in center of each crepe, and fold to enclose. Sprinkle with Parmesan. Bake at 375° for 10 - 12 minutes, foil-covered. Makes 12 crepes.

Submitted by:

Arrowhead Inn
106 Mason Road
Durham, N.C. 27712
(919) 477-8430
Jerry & Barbara Ryan
$55.00 to $95.00

Full breakfast
8 rooms, 4 private baths
Children allowed
No pets (State law)
Restricted smoking
Mastercard, Visa, Am Ex

Restored 1775 manor house on 4 acres, near Duke University, a Civil War surrender site, & Research Triangle Park. Bountiful breakfasts in formal dining room, brick-floored keeping room or on terrace. Views & air-conditioning. Blend of modern comfort and old-time hospitality.

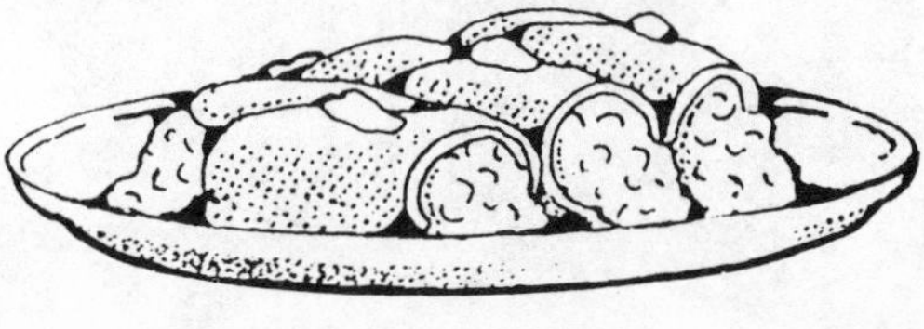

CODFISH FRITTERS

- **1 lb. salted dried codfish or fresh cod**
- **1/2 lb. flour**
- **2 teaspoons baking powder**
- **1 chopped onion**
- **1 egg**
- **2 tomatoes, finely chopped**
- **2 teaspoons margarine**
- **1/2 cup milk**
- **Dash of pepper or curry powder**
- **Hot oil for frying**

Wash and soak dried codfish overnight; flake and remove bones. (Fresh cod can be substituted, but add salt.) Mix in flour, baking powder, onion, egg, tomatoes and margarine. Add milk to bring to consistency for fritters. Add dash of pepper. Drop batter by tablespoonful in hot fat and fry until golden brown. These fritters freeze well, then microwave as needed. My guests come into the kitchen and devour them straight from the frying pan!

Origin: Jean is from Jamaica, and this is a version of the codfish fritters so popular in the Island for breakfast.

Submitted by:

Gilbert House Bed & Breakfast
P.O. Box 1104
Charles Town, W.V. 25430
(304) 725-0637
Jean & Bernie Heiler
$85.00 to $130.00

Full breakfast
3 rooms, 3 private baths
Children, over 10
Restricted smoking
Mastercard & Visa

Magnificent 1760 stone house on National Register, in quaint 18th century village. Fireplaces, air-conditioning, tapestries, master paintings, & fine antiques. Warm hospitality with fresh flowers, fruit and candy. Stream and gazebo nearby. Bridal suite. Gift certificates.

CREAMY SCRAMBLED EGGS EN BUTTERY CROUSTADES

8 hard rolls (3" diameter)
1/4 lb. plus 2 tablespoons butter
16 eggs
4 tablespoons milk
4 oz. cream cheese, softened
2 teaspoons salt
2 teaspoons pepper
1 lb. bulk sausage, browned
3 chopped Roma tomatoes
6 chopped green onions
1 tablespoon basil
Chopped parsley or fresh snipped chives

Preheat oven to 400°. Carefully slice tops off each roll, pinch out soft centers leaving 1/4" thick shell. Generously brush insides with melted 1/4 lb. butter. Place rolls on baking sheet, bake until crisp and lightly browned. Meanwhile beat eggs; add milk, cream cheese, 1 teaspoon salt and 1 teaspoon pepper. Put remaining 2 tablespoons butter in 2 - 3 quart Pyrex dish; cover with waxed paper. Cook at high heat in microwave for 2 minutes. Pour egg mixture into this dish. Microwave at medium heat 8 - 10 minutes, or until eggs reach desired firmness. While eggs cook, combine sausage, tomatoes, green onions, 1 teaspoon salt, 1 teaspoon pepper, and basil. Mix thoroughly. After eggs are cooked, combine sausage mixture and eggs, mix well. Spoon into buttery croustades and sprinkle with chopped parsley or fresh chives. Serve immediately. Serves 8.

Submitted by:

Micajah Davis House Inn
1101 Jackson Street
Lynchburg, Virginia 24504
(804) 846-5622
Bill & Bonnie Saunders
$58.00 to $85.00

Full breakfast
7 rooms, 5 private baths
Children, over 13
No pets
Restricted smoking
Mastercard & Visa

Uniquely designed with 3 houses: 1817 Federal style, each room as wide as the house, fireplaces; "one-of-a-kind" Weaver's Cottage, built as the kitchen dependency, 2 suites have fireplace & loft; Rose & Thistle is an 1890 Princess Anne with Victorian antiques & decor.

EASY EGG DISH

1 1/2 eggs per serving	**Seasonings to taste**
Water	**Velveeta cheese**
Oil to scramble eggs	**Canned ham patties**

Put oil in heavy skillet. Beat 1 1/2 eggs per serving. Add 1 teaspoon water per egg. Season to taste. Scramble eggs and pour into serving dish while eggs are quite moist. Place slices of Velveeta cheese to cover eggs. Add lightly fried canned ham patties on top of cheese. Place in warm oven until cheese is melted, and serve.

A favorite dish with our guests.

Submitted by:

The Kingsley House	Full breakfast
626 West Main Street	5 rooms, 5 private baths
Fennville, Michigan 49408	Children, over 6
(616) 561-6425	No pets
David & Shirley Witt	Restricted smoking
$50.00 to $65.00	Mastercard & Visa

Elegant 1886 Victorian home; the quiet, relaxing atmosphere of a bygone era. The Kingsleys introduced fruit trees to this lakeside area. Each of 5 guest rooms is named after an apple, and decorated to match its name. Enjoy the attractions of Saugatuck and Holland.

EDGEWOOD'S SOUTHERN SAUSAGE GRAVY AND BISCUITS

1 lb. sausage
2 tablespoons oil
2 teaspoons flour
Salt & pepper to taste
1 cup milk
1 can refrigerated or homemade biscuits

Cook sausage and drain grease. Add oil. Stir in flour, and salt and pepper to taste. Add milk and bring to a boil. Pour over cooked biscuits. Serves 6.

Submitted by:

Edgewood Plantation
Route #2, Box 490
Charles City, Virginia 23030
(804) 829-2962
Mr. & Mrs. Julian Boulware
$95.00 to $130.00

Full breakfast
6 rooms, 2 private baths
No children
No pets
Restricted smoking
Mastercard & Visa

Pre-Civil War home in Gothic Revival style, with an old mill at the back of the property built by Benjamin Harrison in 1725. Candlelight Southern breakfast, furnished in antiques. "It's like stepping back into time!"

EGGS À LA PIERRÓT

Eggs: (for 1)

1 croissant, spread gently with butter
2 slices ripe tomato
2 slices cooked bacon
2 poached eggs

Sauce Caterina: (for 8)
4 egg yolks
Dash of tarragon
1 teaspoon parsley
1 shallot
Juice of 1/2 lemon
1/4 lb. butter
Pinch of lemon peel

Slice croissant in half, butter gently and put a slice of tomato on each half. Top each tomato with bacon, and the bacon with a poached egg. Pour a little sauce on each egg and pop into moderate oven for about 2 minutes. Serve immediately. For Sauce Caterina: Place all ingredients in blender until smooth and creamy. Keep refrigerated until ready to use. Buon Appetito!

Origin: Catherine Forrestal's very own recipe!

Submitted by:

Pierrót-By-The-Sea
101 Centre Street
Beach Haven, N.J. 08008
(609) 492-4424
Catherine Forrestal
$65.00 to $100.00

Full breakfast
9 rooms, 3 private baths
Children, over 7
No pets
No smoking
Mastercard & Visa

A completely restored house with Victorian decor. Most rooms have ocean views; we are the closest B&B to the beach. Afternoon tea at 4:00 on our wraparound veranda. A charming stay, like going back in time.

GRILLED QUAIL & SAUSAGE ON VEGETABLE PANCAKE WITH BLUEBERRY COMPOTE

2 potatoes, grated
1 small onion, grated
1 parsnip, grated
1 carrot, grated
1/2 cup flour
2 eggs, beaten
Pinch of salt & pepper
2 oz. peanut oil
1 semi-boneless quail
2 - 2 oz. sausage patties
1 cup sugar
2 cups blueberries
1 cup water
1 oz. arrowroot, dissolved

Combine potatoes, onion, parsnip and carrot in large bowl. Dust with flour. Add egg and salt & pepper. Heat frying pan with oil. Place batter in pan and brown on both sides. Rub quail with salt & pepper and grill. Brown & drain sausage. Boil sugar, blueberries and water. Add arrowroot to thicken. Arrange on plate.

Submitted by:

Blair Creek Inn
P.O. Box 20, R. D. #2
Mertztown, Penn. 19539
(215) 682-6700
Carole Miller
$100.00 to $125.00

Continental breakfast
2 suites, 2 private baths
Children allowed
No pets
Smoking allowed
Mastercard & Visa

Historic inn & public restaurant, offers lunch Wednesday, Thursday & Friday, dinner Wednesday through Saturday, & a waiter-served Sunday brunch. 4 1/2 acres of land: manicured lawn, tranquil lake & flower gardens. Weddings in garden & gazebo or main dining room.

HAM & EGG OMELET CREPE

Basic Crepes:
3 whole eggs
1 cup sifted flour
1/2 teaspoon salt
1 1/4 cups milk
1/4 cup water
2 tablespoons melted butter for frying

Filling:
1/2 lb. diced, cooked ham
4 eggs, separated
1 cup sour cream
1/2 teaspoon lemon pepper
1/3 cup melted butter
Paprika

Combine all crepe ingredients except butter; beat until smooth. Cover bowl, let stand at room temperature for 1 hour. Pour scant 1/4 cup batter into center of hot buttered crepe pan. Lift and tilt pan in circular motion to cover bottom. Turn in about 30 seconds. Brown other side. Remove and stack between layers of waxed paper. Makes 12 - 14 crepes. They freeze well. For filling: Mix ham, egg yolks, sour cream and lemon pepper. Beat whites until they hold stiff peaks. Fold whites into ham mixture. Spoon 2 tablespoons onto each crepe. Roll and place seam side down in 2 buttered 9" x 13" x 2" pans. Brush tops with melted butter, sprinkle with paprika. Bake at 325° for 20 - 25 minutes.

Submitted by:

Fifth Street Mansion
213 South Fifth Street
Hannibal, Missouri 63401
(314) 221-0445
Mike & Donalene Andreotti
$50.00 to $75.00

Full breakfast
7 rooms, 7 private baths
Children allowed
No pets
Restricted smoking
Mastercard & Visa

1858 Victorian home in Italianate style, close to the Mississippi River, in "America's Hometown". Antiques, & old-fashioned hospitality with modern conveniences. Walk to Mark Twain Historic District, antique shops, and riverboat. Near parks, caves, golf, and water activities.

HOLDEN HOUSE EGGS FIESTA

2 eggs per serving
Snack-size flour tortillas
Cheddar cheese
Crumbled bacon
Sour cream
Mild salsa

Grease 5 - 8 oz. individual soufflé dishes (one for each person) with spray coating. Break 2 eggs into each dish. Cut tortillas in half with sharp knife and place in dish, curving each half around the dish, flat-cut side on bottom. Top eggs with generous slice of cheese and bacon bits. Bake at 375° for 20 minutes, or 400° for 25 minutes (high altitude), or until eggs are cooked and cheese is melted, with tortillas slightly browned. Do not overcook! Top eggs with a dab of sour cream and mild salsa. Serve in dish placed on plate, and garnished with parsley. Simple, yet pretty and festive.

Origin: Created by Sallie Clark, owner-innkeeper of Holden House.

Submitted by:

Holden House - 1902
Victorian Bed & Breakfast
1102 W. Pikes Peak Avenue
Colorado Springs, Col. 80904
(719) 471-3980
Sallie & Welling Clark
$50.00 to $85.00

Full breakfast
3 rooms, 3 private baths
No children
No pets
No smoking
Mastercard, Visa, Am Ex

Historic storybook Victorian with mountain views, antiques, and heirloom quilts. Honeymooner's suite boasts an open turret and 80-gallon tub. Near Pike's Peak area attractions. Warm hospitality in atmosphere of yesteryear.

HOLE IN ONE

2 tablespoons butter or margarine
1 slice firm wheat bread
1 egg
Salt & pepper to taste

Melt butter in hot skillet or on griddle. Cut a circle in the center of bread with a 3" cookie cutter. (Leave center piece in place.) Brown bread in butter, then turn & brown second side. Remove circle from center of bread & keep warm. Drop egg into hole. Cook until set, adding seasonings to taste. Turn and cook lightly on second side. Serve with toast round on top. Serves 1.

Submitted by:

Birch Hill Inn
Box 346
Manchester, Vermont 05254
(802) 362-2761
Jim & Pat Lee
$58.00 to $106.00

Full breakfast
6 rooms, 6 private baths
Children, over 6
No pets
Restricted smoking
Mastercard & Visa

In the innkeeper's family for over 70 years, on a hilltop, with mountain views from every room. 3 miles from town, yet secluded on a side road, where the only other house to be seen is our own farmhouse. Trout pond, walking and cross-country ski trails on premises.

JOSIE'S SOUR CREAM ENCHILADAS WITH HAM

Sauce:
1/2 cup butter
1/2 cup flour
4 cups milk
1 lb. diced Cheddar cheese
2 teaspoons dijon mustard
1 teaspoon salt
1/2 medium onion, grated

8 small flour tortillas

Filling:
1 cup chopped ham
1/2 lb. grated Monterey Jack cheese
1/2 cup diced green chilies
1/2 cup sour cream
6 tablespoons chopped fresh cilantro

In medium saucepan over low heat, melt butter, and add flour, stirring constantly for 3 - 5 minutes. Gradually add milk and cook, stirring until sauce is smooth and thick. Add Cheddar cheese and stir until cheese melts. Stir in mustard, salt and onion. Sauce may be made ahead and refrigerated. Reheat before assembling enchiladas. To assemble: Preheat oven to 350°. Mix all filling ingredients together. Place 1/8 of filling near the edge of each tortilla and roll tightly. Place seam down in an oiled baking dish. Pour sauce over enchiladas, covering them thoroughly. Bake for 35 - 40 minutes.

Submitted by:

Storybook Inn
P.O. Box 362
28717 Highway 18
Skyforest, California 92385
(714) 336-1483
Kathleen & John Wooley
$79.00 to $175.00

Full breakfast
9 rooms, 9 private baths, plus 3 bedroom, 2 bath cabin
Children, over 12
No pets
No smoking
Mastercard & Visa

Great escape to elegant mountain inn by Lake Arrowhead. Luxurious living room and den with wood-burning fireplaces and spectacular view. Morning paper, jacuzzi, fresh flowers. AAA 3-Diamond rating.

LA VISTA'S CREAMED VIRGINIA COUNTRY HAM

3 tablespoons butter
1/4 cup onion, chopped
1/2 cup green bell pepper, chopped
2 cups baked country ham, chopped
3 tablespoons flour
2 cups milk
Toast

Melt butter in frying pan over medium heat. Add onion and peppers and sauté until soft. Add country ham and stir until coated. Sprinkle flour over ham and stir until it disappears. Add milk and stir until thickened. Add more milk if necessary. Serve over hot toast. Serves 4 generously.

Origin: A creative way to use leftover country ham.

Submitted by:

La Vista Plantation
4420 Guinea Station Road
Fredericksburg, Vir. 22401
(703) 898-8444
Edward & Michele Schiesser
$55.00 to $70.00

Full breakfast
2 rooms, 2 private baths
Children allowed
No pets
Restricted smoking
Mastercard & Visa

1838 Greek Revival home, rich in Civil War history, set amid mature trees, farm fields & pond stocked with bass & sunfish. 2-story front portico, acorn & oak leaf moldings, wide heart of pine floors, and 6 fireplaces. Air-conditioned, bicycles, fresh eggs, homemade jams.

LOW CHOLESTEROL SCRAMBLED EGGS

1 - 14 oz. pkg. tofu
1/2 cup evaporated milk
1 tablespoon granulated chicken bouillon
1 teaspoon curry powder
1 tablespoon dried minced onion (optional)
6 eggs

Blend ingredients for 30 seconds at medium speed in blender. Cook as for scrambled eggs, in frying pan over low heat. Serve hot with toast or muffins.

Origin: Created by Gail for Wilson's Hostel.

Submitted by:

Wilson's Hostel
Box 969
Bethel, Alaska 99559
(907) 543-3841
Tom & Debbie Wilson
$59.00 to $79.00

Full breakfast
6 rooms, 2 private baths
Children allowed
No pets
No smoking
Mastercard, Visa, Diner's Club

A cozy chalet with a fire in the wood stove and comfortable furnishings. Accessible only by air to the Bethel jetport, we are quiet; near the Kuskokwim River. Light evening snacks and a hearty breakfast. Open year-round.

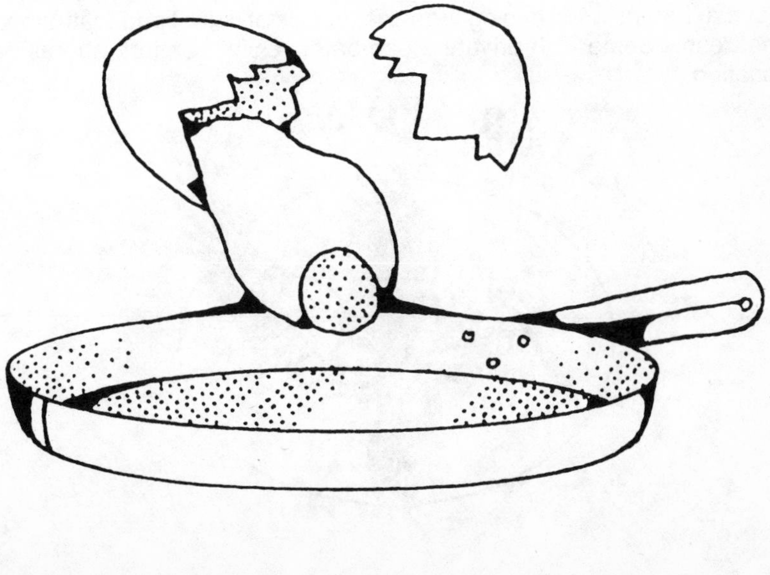

POACHED EGG FLORENTINE

2 pkgs. frozen chopped spinach, thawed & squeezed dry
8 oz. ricotta cheese
2 - 8 oz. pkgs. cream cheese
Sliced Canadian bacon
Poached eggs
Toasted English muffins
Cubed Monterey Jack or Cheddar cheese
Hot sauce

Blend spinach, ricotta and cream cheeses, pat into 2" ball. Flatten and hollow space for the poached egg. Place flattened ball on bacon slice, microwave for 30 - 40 seconds. Slide toasted English muffin under bacon, top with poached egg and garnish with teaspoon of melted cheese, spiced with hot sauce. Serves 20 - 22.

Origin: Recipe created to comply with local fire ordinance against "frying" in Bed & Breakfast inns.

Submitted by:

Pillar Point Inn
380 Capistrano Road
Princeton, California 94018
(415) 728-7377
Dick Anderton
$125.00 to $160.00

Full breakfast
11 rooms, 11 private baths
Children allowed
No pets
No smoking
Mastercard, Visa, Am Ex

A blend of Cape Cod and California architectural styles, all rooms have a harbor view, gaslog fireplace, television, VCR and featherbed mattress. Some with private steambath. Quiet comfort, shoreside location.

PILLAR POINT INN

RED FLANNEL HASH

3/4 lb. cooked corned beef
2 medium beets
1 medium potato
1 medium onion
Salt & pepper to taste
1 dash Tabasco sauce
2 tablespoons A-1 sauce or Pickapeppa sauce
1 tablespoon butter

Finely dice corned beef with knife. Boil, peel and shred beets and potatoes. Finely dice onions and sauté until translucent. Mix ail ingredients well, adjusting seasoning. Shape into 4 - 6 oz. patties and fry in butter 5 minutes on each side until crispy. Serve with eggs and toast.

Origin: My great-grandmother, "Nanna" Follansbee, served this at the Follansbee Inn.

Submitted by:

New London Inn
Main Street, P.O. Box 8
New London, N.H. 03257
(603) 526-2791
Maureen & John Follansbee
$70.00 to $90.00

Full breakfast
30 rooms, 30 private baths
Children allowed
No pets
Smoking allowed
Mastercard & Visa

Built in 1792, with no room for freezers. That suits us fine. Our food is made from ingredients as fresh and wholesome as our country mornings. Lakes, golf, tennis and skiing nearby to whet your appetites.

REDSTONE INN COOPER EGGS BENEDICT

3/4 cup butter
3/4 cup all-purpose flour
6 cups milk
1 lb. fully cooked ham, cubed
1 cup (4 oz.) shredded Cheddar cheese
8 hard-cooked eggs, quartered
1 lb. fresh or frozen asparagus spears, cut in 1" pieces & cooked until crisp-tender
Salt & pepper to taste
8 - 3" squares cornbread

Melt butter, stir in flour. Add milk all at once. Cook and stir until bubbly. Cook 1 minute more. Add ham and cheese to sauce. Heat on low to blend. Add eggs and asparagus, stir gently. Season with salt & pepper. Serve over warm corn bread. Makes 8 servings.

Submitted by:

The Redstone Inn
504 Bluff Street
Dubuque, Iowa
52001
(800) 331-5454
Manager - Debbie Griesinger
$62.00 to $160.00

Full breakfast
15 rooms, 15 private baths
Children allowed
No pets
Smoking allowed
Mastercard, Visa,
Am Ex, Diner's Club

1894 Victorian with whirlpools, marble and tile fireplaces, and "the most luxurious bridal suite in the Midwest". Maple and oak woodwork, beveled, leaded and stained-glass windows add to the elegance. English teas served daily. Open year-round.

SAUSAGE 'N' CHEESE TARTS

1/2 lb. bulk pork sausage
1 1/4 cups biscuit mix
1/4 cup margarine, melted
2 tablespoons boiling water
1 egg, slightly beaten
1/2 cup half & half
1/2 cup (2 oz.) shredded Cheddar cheese

Cook sausage over medium heat until browned, stirring to crumble. Drain and set aside. Combine biscuit mix, margarine and boiling water; stir well. Press about 1 tablespoon of dough into bottom and sides of well-greased and floured muffin cups. Spoon sausage evenly into cups. Combine egg and half & half. Stir well. Spoon about 1 1/2 tablespoons egg mixture into each cup. Bake at 375° for 20 minutes. Sprinkle cheese over tart, bake an additional 5 minutes. Yield: 1 dozen.

Submitted by:

The Banyan House
519 South Harbor Drive
Venice, Florida 34285
(813) 484-1385
Chuck & Susan McCormick
$35.00 to $75.00

Continental breakfast
9 rooms, 7 private baths
Children, over 8
No pets
Restricted smoking
No credit cards

Historic 1926 Mediterranean home with "Old World" charm. Lovely courtyard with enormous banyan tree, which shades the garden patio, pool and jacuzzi. Tour the quaint city and beaches on complimentary bicycles. Go shelling for prehistoric shark teeth.

SAUSAGE-APPLE RING

1 lb. hot sausage
1 lb. mild sausage
1 1/2 cups cracker crumbs
2 eggs, beaten
1/2 cup milk
1/4 cup chopped onion
1 cup chopped apples
Scrambled eggs

Mix all ingredients, except scrambled eggs, together. Put in a ring mold. Bake 1 hour at 350°. Can be baked 30 minutes and frozen. Then bake another 30 minutes when ready to serve. Fill center with cooked, scrambled eggs. 1 ring serves 8. Recipe can be halved.

Submitted by:

Buttonwood Inn
190 Georgia Road
Franklin, N.C. 28734
(704) 369-8985
Liz Oehser
$48.00 to $60.00

Full breakfast
4 rooms, 3 private baths
Children, over 10
No pets
Restricted smoking

Country rustic charm: quilts, primitive country antiques, a common room and desk for guests. Built in late 1920's, with tung & groove white pine paneling interior and batten board exterior. Next to public golf course, with mountains in view.

SAUSAGE-BISCUIT PINWHEELS À LA GOOSE & TURRETS

3 1/2 cups flour, plus 1/2 cup later
1 rounded teaspoon baking powder
1/2 teaspoon baking soda
1/4 teaspoon salt
1 cup Crisco
1 1/2 cups buttermilk
2 lbs. bulk sausage

Sift 3 1/2 cups flour into large mixing bowl. Make well in center and add baking powder, soda and salt. Mix. Cut in Crisco. Add buttermilk and mix well. Add last 1/2 cup flour. Blend completely until smooth and not sticky. Wrap dough in waxed paper and chill for 1 hour. Divide dough in half. Roll each half on floured surface to 1/4" thick, a roughly 18" x 8" rectangle. Spread each half thinly with sausage. (12 oz. - 1 lb. each) Leave 1/2" on 1 long edge free of sausage. Roll long edge up jelly roll fashion, ending with plain edge so that it seals, leaving 2 log-shaped cylinders. This can be done 1 day ahead and refrigerated. If not, still allow 30 minutes to chill logs. Preheat oven to 450°. Cut across logs with a bread knife in approximately 1/2" slices. Bake 15 minutes or until sausage is cooked and dough is golden. Bake on broiling pan if sausage is fatty. Serves 10 - 15.

Submitted by:

The Goose & Turrets
835 George Street
P.O. Box 937
Montara, Calif. 94037-0937
(415) 728-5451
Raymond & Emily Hoche-Mong
$70.00 to $85.00

Full breakfast
5 rooms, 1 private bath
Children allowed
No pets
No smoking
Mastercard, Visa, Am Ex

1908 Italian villa-style in small village where the surf is the loudest thing in town! Common area with woodstove, piano, and books. Afternoon tea, German down comforters, & bathrobes. Our mascot geese welcome guests.

SAUSAGE BOATS

1 lb. lean sausage
8 eggs
2/3 cup tomato sauce
1/3 cup picante sauce

Press sausage into 4 small greased au gratin dishes. Bake until almost done (10 minutes) at 375°. Remove from oven and break 2 eggs into each dish. Return to oven and bake an additional 10 - 15 minutes. Remove sausage and egg from dish and place on top of spicy tomato sauce (combine tomato sauce & picante sauce). Makes 4 servings.

Origin: Created by our chef, Eileen Black.

Submitted by:

Interlaken Inn
15 Interlaken Avenue
Lake Placid, New York 12946
(518) 523-3180
Carol & Roy Johnson
$100.00 to $140.00

Full breakfast
12 rooms, 12 private baths
Children, over 5
No pets
Smoking allowed
Mastercard, Visa, Am Ex

Victorian inn in the heart of Lake Placid. Individually decorated rooms, 3 with private balconies. Gourmet dining room with tin ceiling and lots of lace! A family-owned inn whose desire is to please our guests.

SUSAN'S CHEESE EGGS

1 teaspoon butter
4 large eggs
1 tablespoon half & half
1 teaspoon dried or fresh cilantro
1/2 teaspoon garlic salt
1/4 cup shredded medium Cheddar cheese

Melt butter in frying pan. Beat (scramble) eggs with half & half, then pour into frying pan. Begin to cook over medium heat, sprinkle with cilantro and garlic salt. Continue to mix/scramble in pan until almost done. Add cheese as eggs finish cooking, and remove as soon as cheese melts and is mixed through eggs. Serve with toast, fruit and bacon. Serves 2 and may be multiplied proportionately.

Origin: Developed by Susan Wynne, owner- innkeeper, Old Miners' Lodge.

Submitted by:

The Old Miners' Lodge - A Bed & Breakfast Inn
615 Woodside Avenue
P.O. Box 2639
Park City, Utah 84060-2639
(801) 645-8068
Hugh Daniels, Susan Wynne & Jeff Sadowsky
$40.00 to $165.00

Full breakfast
10 rooms, 10 private baths
Children allowed
No pets
Restricted smoking
Mastercard, Visa, Am Ex, Discover

Built in 1893 to house local silver miners, and thoughtfully restored by its owners, who feel staying at the Lodge is "more like staying with friends than at a motel". Close to historic Main Street and 3 world-class ski areas. Comfort in antique-filled rooms.

SWISS MUSTARD EGGS

3 eggs
2 tablespoons milk
1 tablespoon stone-ground mustard
1/8 teaspoon pepper
2 strips bacon
1 English muffin, halved, buttered & toasted
1/2 tablespoon butter
1/4 cup grated Swiss cheese
1 tablespoon grated Parmesan cheese

Mix eggs with milk, mustard and pepper, using wire whisk. Cook bacon until crisp, crumble and set aside. Spread muffin with butter and toast under broiler. Melt 1/2 tablespoon butter in skillet. Add egg mixture and scramble. When almost done, add Swiss cheese and bacon. Cook until cheese melts. Place muffin on plate, spoon eggs onto both halves, sprinkle with Parmesan. Garnish plate with quartered tomato slices and sprouts.

Submitted by:

Amber House
1315 22nd Street
Sacramento, California 95816
(916) 444-8085
Jane & Michael Richardson
$65.00 to $135.00

Full breakfast
5 rooms, 5 private baths
Children, over 10
No pets
No smoking
Mastercard, Visa, Am Ex

Stately mansion sheltered by towering elm trees, near restaurants, major business districts, museums, shopping & historical attractions. Oriental rugs, fragrant flowers, antique pocket doors, library, jacuzzi, and skylight. Works of famous poets found in "namesake" rooms.

TARTLETS WITH SCRAMBLED EGGS & CAVIAR OR CANADIAN BACON

Pastry:
2 cups sifted all-purpose flour
1/4 lb. unsalted butter, very cold, cut into small pieces
1/2 teaspoon salt
1 egg yolk
1/4 cup ice water

Topping for tartlets:

12 eggs
Cream
Salt to taste
Freshly ground pepper
1 tablespoon basil
Canadian bacon or caviar

Place flour, butter and salt in medium mixing bowl and mix with electric mixer at medium speed for 8 minutes, until consistency is like fine cornmeal. Add egg yolk and combine; increase speed and gradually add ice water, 1 tablespoon at a time. When pastry leaves sides of bowl and forms a ball, remove it to lightly floured surface and reshape into ball. Refrigerate covered for 45 minutes. Roll out on floured surface and cut to size of tartlet pans, usually about 2" - 4" circles. Line each pan with pastry and prick with fork. Place on baking sheet and bake at 425° for 8 - 10 minutes, until edges are golden brown. Topping: Scramble 12 eggs with a little cream, the salt, pepper and basil. Divide eggs among tartlets, and top each with slices of bacon or 1 teaspoon of caviar. Serve immediately.

Submitted by:

Ridgebury Inn & Hunt Club
RD #1, Box 342
Ridgebury Road
Slate Hill, New York 10973
(914) 355-4868
Jean & Bob Yonelunas
$65.00 to $125.00

Full breakfast
7 rooms, 1 private bath
Children, over 10
No pets
Restricted smoking
Mastercard, Visa, Am Ex

Small and cozy, with an English country flair. Guests retain privacy, but feel included in a warm atmosphere of friendly relaxation. Spa and gym, or walk or bike 87 acres of fields and ponds. Stable space for horses @ $15.00 per night.

THE TESUQUE SKILLET BREAKFAST

1 oz. butter
1 baked potato, cubed
1/2 cup black beans, cooked until tender
4 eggs, over-easy
1/2 cup New Mexican red chilie sauce
White Cheddar cheese

Melt butter and sauté potatoes to golden brown. Place in 6" cast iron skillet, add drained black beans. Place 4 over-easy eggs on top of beans. Pour chilie sauce over eggs and top with white Cheddar cheese, and melt under broiler. Serves 2.

Submitted by:

Rancho Encantado
Route #4, Box 57-C
Santa Fe, New Mexico 87501
(505) 982-3537
Elisabeth T. Egan &
John T. Egan
$95.00 to $300.00

Full breakfast
80 rooms, 80 private baths
Children allowed
No pets
Smoking allowed
Mastercard, Visa, Am Ex

Tucked away in the foothills of the Sangre de Cristo Mountains, a secluded ranch/resort with pristine atmosphere for horseback riding, swimming and tennis, as well as gourmet dining. Open year round.

OMELETS, QUICHES & SOUFFLÉS

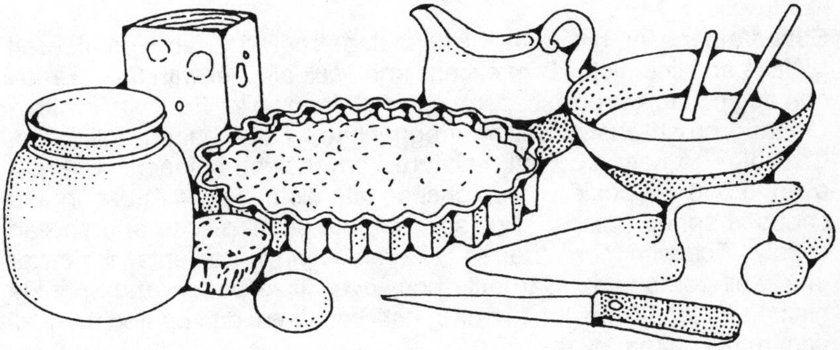

ALWAYS RELIABLE QUICHE

1 sheet frozen puff pastry (thawed in refrigerator overnight)
6 eggs
5 rashers low-salt bacon
1 pkg. frozen chopped spinach (thawed)
2 cups shredded Swiss cheese
1 bunch spring onions, sliced
1 cup heavy cream
1/2 cup milk
Salt, pepper, sprinkle of marjoram, 1 teaspoon dijon mustard, 1 tablespoon wheat germ, and other herbs or spices of your choice

Garnish: Nutmeg

Butter quiche or pie dish. Roll out defrosted pastry on floured surface and line dish. Trim excess and prick all over with fork. Break one egg into mixer bowl separating white from yolk. Beat white with a fork and brush pastry well with egg white. Cook bacon until crisp. Crumble. Squeeze out all moisture from thawed spinach. Preheat oven to 350°. Sprinkle 1 cup cheese into dish. Top with bacon and chopped spring onions. Pull spinach into small pieces and spread evenly. Top with more cheese. Mix remaining ingredients with mixer until well combined. Carefully pour over filled pastry and sprinkle nutmeg on top. Bake for 1 hour or until set. It will puff up and then fall after removal from oven.

Submitted by:

Almond View Inn
912 Walnut Drive
Paso Robles, Calif. 93446
(805) 238-4220
Dick & Robina Conway
$75.00 to $80.00

Full breakfast
3 rooms, 3 private baths
Children, over 16
No pets
No smoking
Mastercard & Visa

Spanish Mission Revival home, 52 years old, sits high on a hill with magnificent views in every direction. Decorated in soft pastels, very quiet and comfortable. Spa available for guests. Minutes from town.

A SUMMER QUICHE

Pie crust:
Pinch of salt
2 cups unbleached flour
6 tablespoons butter
1/3 cup cold water

Quiche filling:
1/2 lb. country sausage, cooked & crumbled
1 cup grated Swiss cheese
1 tomato, peeled & sliced very thin
3 eggs, plus 1 yolk
1 tablespoon flour
2 cups light cream
Salt & pepper to taste
Fresh basil leaves

Pie crust: Mix salt and flour, cut in butter until it resembles coarse cornmeal. Add water and mix only until the dough forms a ball. Roll out and place in 9" pie plate. Quiche filling: Place sausage in pie crust and then the cheese. Arrange tomatoes in a neat pattern over the cheese. Beat together eggs, flour, cream, and salt & pepper to taste. Pour the batter slowly over tomatoes. Place basil leaves in a flower pattern on top, spacing them about 1" apart. Bake 30 - 35 minutes at 350° until knife comes out clean, and top is lightly browned and puffy.

Submitted by:

Pig Hill Inn
73 Main Street
Cold Spring, New York 10516
(914) 265-9247
Wendy O'Brien
$90.00 to $145.00

Full breakfast
8 rooms, 4 private baths
Children, over 12
No pets
No smoking
Mastercard, Visa, Am Ex

An 1830's brick Georgia townhouse filled with antiques and whimsical details. Fabulous home-cooked breakfast served in bed, in front of your fireplace, on trays laden with hand-pressed linens & fine china.

BAKED EGG RAMEKINS FOR TWO

Pam or vegetable spray
4 eggs
2 tablespoons cream or half & half
2 slices bacon, cooked and crumbled
3 tablespoons grated Swiss cheese
2 teaspoons chopped parsley
2 dashes paprika

Coat ramekins with spray vegetable oil. Crack 2 eggs in each. Put 1 tablespoon cream on each egg to seal the yolk and white. Top each with 1/2 of bacon, Swiss cheese, parsley and paprika. Bake at 450° 12 - 15 minutes, until eggs are cooked.

Submitted by:

House on Cherry Street
1844 Cherry Street
Jacksonville, Florida 32205
(904) 384-1999
Carol Anderson
$60.00 to $75.00

Full breakfast
4 rooms, 3 private baths
Children, over 10
No pets
Restricted smoking

Award-winning, restored Colonial home on St. John's River, near downtown and airport. Period antique canopy beds, decoys, baskets, coverlets and other collectibles. Air-conditioning, flowers in room, gourmet breakfast.

BLUEBELLE HOUSE CHRISTMAS SOUFFLÉ

1 large loaf white bread
1 1/4 lb. Cheddar cheese
1 1/4 lb. Monterey Jack cheese
5 eggs
3 1/2 cups milk
1 1/2 teaspoons dry mustard

Trim crusts and cube bread. Grate cheeses. Line greased 9" x 13" (or slightly larger) casserole with bread cubes. Layer grated cheeses and bread and top with another layer of cheeses. Mix eggs, milk and mustard. Pour over top of casserole. Cover with Saran Wrap and refrigerate for 1 - 2 days. Bake in pan of hot water at 325° for 45 minutes - 1 hour. Test for firmness after it sits 10 minutes. Our family favorite for Christmas or any festive breakfast. Serve with fruits, bacon or sausages, and muffins. Reheats or microwaves beautifully.

Submitted by:

Bluebelle House
P.O. Box 2177
263 South State Highway 173
Lake Arrowhead, Calif. 92352
(714) 336-3292
Rick & Lila Peiffer
$70.00 to $105.00

Continental plus breakfast
5 rooms, 3 private baths
Children, over 12
No pets
No smoking
Mastercard & Visa

Cozy elegance of European decor in an alpine setting. Immaculate housekeeping, warm hospitality, relaxing by the fire or on the deck. Walk to lakeside village, boating, swimming, restaurants. Private beach club, ice skating nearby. Winter sports 30 minutes away.

CAJUN POTATO PIE

12 oz. frozen hash brown potatoes (thawed)
3 medium or 2 jumbo eggs, beaten
1/2 cup milk
1/4 - 1/2 cup picante sauce
1 cup shredded mozzarella cheese
1/2 cup shredded Cheddar cheese
2 chopped green onions
1/4 cup chopped cilantro or parsley
1/4 teaspoon salt
1/4 lb. chopped tasso (Cajun ham) or plain ham

Combine all ingredients, mixing well. Pour into greased 9" pie plate. Bake at 350° for 50 - 60 minutes, until the mixture is set and golden brown. Remove, let sit 5 minutes and cut into 8 pieces. Serve with scrambled eggs, Eggs Benedict or other breakfast dishes. Makes 8 servings.

Submitted by:

Barrow House
524 Royal Street
P.O. Box 1461
St. Francisville, Louis. 70775
(504) 635-4791
Shirley & Lyle Dittloff
$50.00 to $75.00

Continental breakfast
Full breakfast, $5.00 extra
4 rooms
Children, over 8 preferred
No pets
Smoking allowed
No credit cards

Wicker rockers on front porch, in quiet neighborhood of antebellum homes. Rolling hills and live oaks. 1860's antiques, private gourmet candlelight dinners. Tour six area plantations and enjoy a cassette walking tour of our historic town prepared for our guests.

CARILYN'S BREAKFAST SOUFFLÉ

4 slices white or wheat bread without crust
3 slices ham, bacon or sausage
2 slices Kraft Old English cheese
9 eggs
3/4 - 1 cup milk
Sprinkle of salt & pepper
1/2 tablespoon each of minced chives and another herb of your choice
Sprinkle of cinnamon

Make individual servings or 1 large dish. Spray 2 - 3 1/2" or a 6 1/2" soufflé dish with Pam. Place pieces of bread to cover bottom, then layer meat and cheese. Mix eggs, milk and seasonings together, pour over bread, meat and cheese. Refrigerate overnight, and next morning put into a 350° oven for 10 - 12 minutes. Serve hot.

Origin: One of my great-grandmother's recipes from Italy.

Submitted by:

Captain Samuel Eddy House
609 Oxford Street South
Auburn, Mass. 01501
(508) 832-5282
Jack & Carilyn O'toole
$50.00 to $85.00

Full breakfast
5 rooms, 5 private baths
Children, over 2
No pets
Restricted smoking
Mastercard & Visa

1765 home with warmth and charm of 18th century. Meals cooked on the hearth and in beehive oven in our period costumes. Candlelight and music, with just a little "gourmet". Unique antique bedchambers with canopy beds. Herb gardens & shop in pool area.

CORNER OAK GARDEN FRESH OMELETS

1/4 cup grated sharp Cheddar cheese
1/4 cup grated Swiss (or Jarlsberg, etc.)
1/4 cup grated Monterey Jack (or mozzarella)
1/4 cup freshly grated Parmesan
2 tablespoons chopped fresh basil
2 tablespoons chopped chives
1 tablespoon fresh thyme leaves (or oregano)
2 tablespoons Italian parsley, chopped
2 large vine-ripened tomatoes
4 chopped green onions
2 tablespoons butter
8 eggs, room temperature
4 tablespoons water

Mix cheeses and herbs in bowl, set aside. Peel & chop tomatoes, allow to drain. Briefly sauté green onions in 1 tablespoon butter. Add to tomatoes and set aside. In a non-stick omelet pan over medium-high heat, melt 1 tablespoon butter and coat pan. Beat 2 eggs and 1 tablespoon water with fork until well blended. Pour into hot pan. Tilt pan and lift edges of omelet to allow egg mixture to flow underneath. When omelet is almost set, spread 1/4 of tomato mixture across half of omelet. Top with about 1/4 of cheese. When omelet is set, gently tilt pan onto plate, vegetable & cheese half on the plate. Fold plain half over the top. Sprinkle with a little more cheese and garnish with fresh herbs. Repeat to make 4 omelets.

Submitted by:

Corner Oak Manor
53 St. Dunstans Road
Asheville, North Carolina 28803
(704) 253-3525
Karen & Andy Spradley
$65.00 to $95.00

Full breakfast
4 rooms, 4 private baths
Children allowed (Under 12 in cottage suite)
No pets
No smoking
Mastercard & Visa

Renovated & redecorated 1924 English Tudor with oak antiques, handmade items, oval drop ceiling, baby grand piano, fireplace and outdoor jacuzzi. Near Biltmore Estate, Blue Ridge Parkway, Great Smoky Mountains and shopping.

CORN-FOR-BREAKFAST QUICHE

16 oz. fresh or frozen corn niblets
1 lb. grated Cheddar
1 stick melted butter
8 eggs
2 cups half & half
1 teaspoon salt
1/2 teaspoon pepper
1/2 teaspoon nutmeg
Dash of cayenne pepper
1/4 cup Parmesan cheese

Layer corn and grated cheese in greased 9" x 13" baking dish. Beat together butter, eggs, half & half, and seasonings, and pour over dish. Sprinkle with Parmesan cheese & bake at 350° for 45 minutes, or until lightly browned. Cool slightly before cutting. Serves 8.

Submitted by:

Colonial Pines Inn
Route 1, Box 22B
Hickory Street
Highlands, N.C. 28741
(704) 526-2060
Chris & Donna Alley
$55.00 to $75.00

Full breakfast
7 rooms, 7 private baths
Children allowed
No pets
Restricted smoking
Mastercard & Visa

Quiet country guest house on 2 acres with a lovely mountain view. Near famous shopping and dining, and waterfalls, hiking trails, spectacular views. Bounteous breakfast with homemade breads our specialty. Enjoy our cool mountain air at 4,118' elevation!

CORN SOUFFLÉ

4 eggs, separated
2 cups fresh corn, cut from cob
1 cup lowfat or skim milk
1 tablespoon flour
1/2 tablespoon honey or maple syrup
1 teaspoon salt (or less)
1/2 teaspoon pepper
1/3 cup grated sharp cheese

Separate eggs. Combine egg yolks, corn, milk, flour, maple syrup, and salt and pepper in blender. Beat egg whites until stiff. In bowl fold together corn mixture, egg whites and cheese. Pour into lightly oiled 8" - 9" soufflé dish. Bake in preheated 350° oven for 35 - 40 minutes until golden in color. Serves 6 - 8.

Origin: Adapted from old Midwestern recipe. I prefer using maple syrup as it gives a more New England character.

Submitted by:

Seekonk Pines Inn
142 Seekonk Cross Road
Great Barrington, Mass. 01230
(413) 528-4192
Linda & Chris Best
$60.00 to $90.00

Full breakfast
7 rooms, 2 private baths
Children allowed
No pets
No smoking

1830's homestead amid lovely gardens and meadows with pool & picnic tables. Large common room with fireplace, piano and library. Antiques, quilts, stenciling, original artwork. Whole-grain, reduced fat breakfast menu. Near Tanglewood & skiing. Bicycles also available.

COUNTRY SALMON PIE

1 sheet puff pastry
Parmesan cheese
1 large onion, diced
1 clove garlic, chopped fine
1 cup sautéed, chopped mushrooms
2 tablespoons butter
3 cups sour cream
4 eggs
1 lb. can salmon, clean and broken
1 1/2 cups shredded Swiss cheese
1 teaspoon dill
1/4 teaspoon salt

Roll puff pastry out to fit 9" springform pan, leave at least 2" up the side. Sprinkle with Parmesan cheese. Set aside. Sauté onions, garlic and mushrooms in butter until soft. Beat sour cream and eggs together until well blended. Stir salmon, mushrooms, garlic & onion, 1 cup Swiss cheese, dill and salt into sour cream mixture. Pour into pastry. Top with remaining 1/2 cup cheese. Turn sides of dough to form edge. Bake at 400° for 10 minutes and at 375° for 40 - 50 minutes, until set.

Submitted by:

The Gosby House Inn
643 Lighthouse Avenue
Pacific Grove, Calif. 93950
(408) 375-1287
Shelley Claudel
$85.00 to $125.00

Full breakfast
22 rooms, 20 private baths
Children allowed
No pets
No smoking
Mastercard, Visa, Am Ex

Queen Anne Victorian mansion in the heart of Pacific Grove, one of Four Sisters Inns. Individually decorated rooms, with beautiful antiques. Afternoon hors d'oeuvres, bathrobes, morning newspaper and complimentary beverages.

CREAMY BAKED OMELETTE

8 oz. softened cream cheese
1/4 cup melted butter
2 teaspoons dried basil
1/2 teaspoon salt
1/2 teaspoon ground pepper
25 large eggs
5 cups extra-rich milk
1 cup finely diced ham (optional)
1 cup shredded Swiss or Cheddar cheese
Paprika for garnish

Beat together cream cheese, butter, basil, salt and pepper. Add eggs and beat. Mixture need not be smooth. Stir in milk, and ham if desired. Pour into 4 quart greased baking dish, large rectangular size works best. Bake at 350° for 50 minutes. Sprinkle with shredded cheese and paprika. Bake for an additional 5 minutes.

Submitted by:

Grey Whale Inn
615 North Main St.
Fort Bragg, California 95437
(707) 964-0640
John & Colette Bailey
$60.00 to $140.00

Full breakfast
14 rooms
Children, over 12
No pets
No smoking
Mastercard, Visa, Am Ex

1915 Clearheart redwood inn. 1 room with fireplace, 4 with ocean views, 1 with whirlpool tub and sun deck. Lounge with fireplace, TV room with VCR, recreation room with pool table. Near Skunk Train, state parks, beaches, fishing and hiking trails.

CRUSTLESS BACON & EGG QUICHE

8 strips bacon, diced
1 1/2 cups milk
1/2 cup prepared biscuit mix
3 eggs
1/4 cup melted butter
Dash of pepper
1 cup shredded Cheddar cheese

Fry or microwave bacon until crisp; crumble and set aside. In blender combine milk, biscuit mix, eggs, butter and pepper. Blend for 15 seconds. Pour into greased 9" pie pan. Sprinkle bacon and cheese on top of egg mixture, gently press below surface with a fork. Bake at 350° for 30 minutes or until knife inserted halfway between center and edge comes out clean. Let stand 10 minutes before serving. Yield: 4 - 6 servings.

Submitted by:

White Rock Farm
154 White Rock Road
Kirkwood, Penn. 17536
(717) 529-6744
Les & Lois Hershey
$45.00 to $60.00

Full breakfast
3 rooms
Children allowed
No pets
No smoking

A 150 acre working beef cattle and crop farm in Lancaster County. Overlooks scenic Octorara Creek & historic covered bridge. Hiking, biking, spacious lawn, rolling fields and typical farm pets. Near Amish crafts, antiquing, orchards, parks, boating and botannical gardens.

EGG SAUSAGE SOUFFLÉ

8 - 10 slices of bread, torn apart
5 eggs
1 1/2 cups milk
1/4 teaspoon salt
1/4 teaspoon pepper
1/2 teaspoon dry mustard
1 lb. country sausage (removed from casings)
1 can cream of mushroom soup or 1 cup thick white sauce with 1/2 cup sautéed mushrooms added
1/2 cup milk
1 cup grated Gruyère & Emmanthaler cheese, mixed (can be frozen)

Break bread up and distribute evenly over bottom of 9" x 13" baking dish. Mix eggs with 1 1/2 cups milk and spices. Pour over bread and allow to stand. Meanwhile, brown sausage & drain. Spread sausage evenly over bread. Combine soup, 1/2 cup milk, and cheese, and spread this over the sausage. Bake at 350° for 3/4 of an hour until brown. Allow to stand 5 minutes before serving. Serves 6 - 8.

Submitted by:

Swiss Woods Bed & Breakfast
500 Blantz Road
Lititz, Pennsylvania 17543
(717) 627-3358
Werner & Debrah Mosimann
$55.00 to $95.00

Full breakfast
5 rooms, 5 private baths
Children allowed
No pets
No smoking
Mastercard & Visa

Overlooks Speedwell Fordge Lake, in Pennsylvania Dutch country. Flowering perennials and annuals, sandstone fireplace in living room, with natural woodwork, and sunny windows. Queen beds, patios or balconies. Great view, refreshing quiet, & a touch of the continent.

EMERALD BAY QUICHE

1 - 10" pie shell with high fluted sides
8 slices crisply cooked bacon, cut in small pieces (optional)
2 oz. grated Cheddar cheese
1 medium tomato, thinly sliced
2 large ripe avocados
3 whole eggs
1 cup milk, or half & half, or cream
Salt to taste
White pepper to taste
Tabasco sauce

Preheat oven to 375°. Place bacon (if desired), then grated cheese evenly in pie shell. Next add layer of sliced tomato. Slice 1 avocado and arrange slices evenly over tomato. Mash second avocado.and add remaining ingredients. Beat well, so avocado is well beaten in*. Pour mixture into pie shell. Bake for 30 minutes. Serves 4 generously. (*Due to tendency of avocados to oxidize, this quiche must be eaten fresh out of the oven. You can use a blender to combine avocado with other ingredients.)

Origin: From Frank De Haan, our "breakfast chef extraordinaire."

Submitted by:

The Captain's Alpenhaus
6941 West Lake Boulevard
P.O. Box 262
Tahoma, California 95733
(916) 525-5000
Joel & Phyllis Butler
$40.00 to $115.00

Full breakfast
9 rooms, 8 private baths, plus 5 - 2 bedroom cottages
Children allowed
No pets
Restricted smoking
Mastercard, Visa, Am Ex

Cozy, quaint, European-style country inn, with gourmet quality restaurant, stone fireplace, cottages nestled in pine trees. On Lake Tahoe's unspoiled West Shore. Near skiing, water sports, fishing, golf, tennis, and hiking.

"HEART HEALTHY" BREAKFAST SOUFFLÉ

3/4 lb. LEAN ground pork
3/4 teaspoon Italian seasoning
1/4 teaspoon fennel seeds, crushed
2 cloves garlic, minced
1 cup skim milk
4 eggs plus 8 egg whites (or 2 - 8 oz. boxes frozen egg substitute, thawed)
1/4 cup (1 oz.) shredded low-fat Cheddar cheese
3 chopped green onions
3/4 teaspoon dry mustard
1/4 teaspoon salt
1/4 teaspoon ground red pepper
6 (1 oz.) slices stone-ground whole wheat bread, cut in 1/2" cubes

Coat skillet with cooking spray; add pork, Italian seasoning, fennel seeds and garlic; cook until meat is well-browned, stirring to crumble. Drain in colander, pat dry with paper towel and set aside. Combine milk and next 6 ingredients in large bowl, stir well. Add pork mixture and bread, stirring until well-blended. Spray 6 individual ramekins with cooking spray, and divide mixture evenly amongst them. Refrigerate 8 - 12 hours. Bake at 350° for 30 - 45 minutes or until set and browned. Serve immediately. Serves 6.

Submitted by:

The Manor at Taylor's Store
Route #1, Box 533
Smith Mountain Lake, Virginia 24184
(703) 721-3951
Lee & Mary Lynn Tucker
$50.00 to $80.00

Full breakfast
6 rooms, 4 private baths, plus 3 bedroom - 2 bath cottage
Children in cottage only
No pets
Restricted smoking
Mastercard & Visa

Historic 130 acre estate nestled in foothills of the Blue Ridge Mtns. Private porches, fireplaces, antique decor, hot tub, billiard room, movies, exercise room, and guest kitchen. On premises swimming, canoeing, fishing and hiking. A special place for special people!

HOT SPINACH QUICHE

1 cup flour
1 teaspoon salt
1 teaspoon baking powder
2 eggs, beaten
1 cup milk
1/4 lb. melted oleo
1/2 onion, chopped fine
1 pkg. frozen spinach, thawed & blotted, or 3/4 pkg. fresh torn spinach
1 lb. sharp grated cheese

Sift flour, salt and baking powder. Add beaten egg, milk, melted oleo and stir well. Add other ingredients. Spread in well-greased 9" x 13" pan. Bake in 350° oven for 30 minutes. Cool. Cut in squares.

Origin: My mother-in-law gave me this recipe. She was always trying something new.

Submitted by:

Bed & Breakfast at Ludington
2458 S. Beaune Road
Ludington, Michigan 49431
(616) 843-9768
Grace & Robert Schneider
$40.00 to $50.00

Full breakfast
3 rooms, 2 private baths
Children allowed
Pets allowed
No smoking

A country place near Lake Michigan, on 15 private acres. Surrounded by a canopy of shade trees, with a spring-fed creek. Relaxed, homey atmosphere, where your comfort is a priority. Woods and creekside trails, hot tub, tree swing, and ping-pong.

JANE'S CRUSTLESS QUICHE

1/2 cup bacon, fried & crumbled
1/2 cup chopped onion
1 cup shredded Swiss cheese
2 cups milk
1/2 cup Bisquick
4 eggs
1/4 teaspoon salt
Dash of pepper

Combine bacon, onion and cheese, and spread in well-greased 10" pie pan. Blend milk, Bisquick, eggs, salt and pepper on high in blender or processor and pour over bacon mixture in pan. Bake at 350° for 50 minutes, until knife comes out clean. Let set 5 minutes before serving.

Origin: From Liza's mother, Jane Deignan, who otherwise didn't cook a thing!

Submitted by:

The Woodstocker
Bed & Breakfast
61 River Street, Route #4
Woodstock, Vermont 05091
(802) 457-3896
Liza Deignan &
Romano Formichella
$60.00 to $100.00

Full breakfast
9 rooms, 9 private baths
(includes 2 suites)
Children allowed
No pets
Restricted smoking
Mastercard & Visa

Located at the west end of historic Woodstock village. Hearty buffet breakfast with homebaked goodies and, of course, quiches! Elegant living room and luxurious whirlpool after a day of relaxing, cycling or skiing.

MAGIC CANYON QUICHE

Filling:
24 oz. Swiss cheese
1 lb. cooked salmon, fresh or canned
1 lb. fresh broccoli heads
Salt
Garden fresh chives, shredded
6 cups milk
9 eggs
Fresh cracked pepper

Pie crust:
3 cups whole wheat pastry flour
1 cup wheat germ
1 tablespoon salt
1 cup shortening
1 egg
1 tablespoon vinegar
1 tablespoon honey
Warm water to total 1 cup of liquid

Prepare pie crust: Mix dry ingredients, cut in shortening. Mix with combined liquids. Form into 3 balls, wrap each in plastic, chill overnight. Roll out dough between sheets of waxed paper. Line 3 quiche pans, cover bottom with some of shredded cheese. Fill with salmon, broccoli, salt, chives and remaining cheese. Blend 2 cups milk and 3 eggs for each quiche. Top with cracked pepper. Bake at 375° for 15 minutes, then at 350° for 45 more minutes. Cool before serving. Quiches refrigerate and reheat well, but do NOT freeze. You can substitute shrimp, crab or halibut for salmon.

Submitted by:

Magic Canyon Ranch
Bed & Breakfast
40015 Waterman Road
Homer, Alaska 99603
(907) 235-6077
Carrie & Ted Reed
$60.00 to $85.00

Full breakfast
4 rooms, 1 private bath
Children allowed
No pets
Restricted smoking

Enjoy Kachemak country from green fields to sparkling glaciers, with superb views & total seclusion. 75 acres of space to explore or enjoy area recreation. Country crafts & antiques in the house and guest cottage. Hearty breakfasts of fresh eggs and seafood of the season.

Magic Canyon Ranch

MAINE CRABMEAT BREAKFAST PIE

- 1 bunch chopped scallions
- 1 large chopped red pepper
- 6 oz. crabmeat
- 1 cup grated Swiss cheese
- 1 cup grated Cheddar cheese
- 8 large eggs
- 2 cups half & half
- 1 teaspoon salt
- 1/2 teaspoon pepper
- 1 cup fresh bread crumbs

Butter quiche pan well. Mix all ingredients together. Pour into pan and bake at 350° until set. Serve hot. Cut into pie-shaped pieces. Serves 8.

Origin: Basically a quiche recipe with a seacoast twist. Quite popular with guests to New England.

Submitted by:

Arundel Meadows Inn
P.O. Box 1129
Kennebunk, Maine 04043
(207) 985-3770
Mark Bachelder &
Murray Yaeger
$70.00 to $125.00

Full breakfast
7 rooms, 7 private baths
Children, over 12
No pets
Restricted smoking
Mastercard & Visa

165 year old farmhouse with uniquely decorated guest rooms; three with working fireplaces. Located in Arundel, Maine, on the Kennebunk River, minutes from Kennebunkport, home of President George Bush.

MASON HOUSE BREAKFAST QUICHE

1 - 9" unbaked pie shell
1/2 cup real mayonnaise (light)
2/3 cup milk
3 eggs
1 tablespoon cornstarch
1 1/2 cup shredded sharp Cheddar cheese (or 1/2 mozzarella or Swiss)
1/2 lb. browned sausage (sweet Italian is best) or diced ham
1/3 cup finely chopped onion
1/8 teaspoon white pepper
1/2 cup finely chopped mushrooms

Mix mayonnaise, milk, eggs, and cornstarch. Layer remaining items into pie shell. Pour mixture over all. Bake at 325° for 40 - 45 minutes until center is firm. Let stand for 5 - 10 minutes before cutting into 8 servings.

Submitted by:

Mason House Inn/Bentonsport
Route #2, Box 237
Keosauqua, Iowa 52565
(319) 592-3133
Sheral & Bill McDermet
$40.00 to $50.00

Full breakfast
8 rooms
Children allowed
No pets
No smoking

Charming 1846 steamboat river inn, our tradition of quality hosting continues into the 1990's. In National Historic District, near antique shops, state park and state forest, canoeing and cross-country skiing.

MUSHROOM AND RED PEPPER PIE IN A POTATO CRUST

1 - 2 potatoes, sliced thinly
Salt to taste
12 - 15 large mushrooms
1/4 cup onion
1/2 of a red pepper
Garlic to taste
1 1/4 cups whole milk
3 eggs
1/4 teaspoon nutmeg
1/8 teaspoon pepper
1 1/4 cups grated cheese
4 oz. cream cheese

Grease pie tin with butter. Place potatoes in pan, so no pie tin is showing, and you get a scalloped-edge effect. Salt to taste. Sauté other vegetables and garlic and place in pan evenly. Mix milk, eggs, nutmeg, and pepper, and pour over vegetables. Spread grated cheese over mixture. Dollop small pieces of cream cheese on top and bake at 350° for 1 1/4 hours.

Submitted by:

The Cottonwood Inn
123 San Juan
Alamosa, Colorado 81101
(719) 589-3882
Julie & George Mordecai-Sellman
$38.00 to $54.00

Full breakfast
4 - 5 rooms, 2 private baths
Children allowed
No pets
Restricted smoking
Mastercard & Visa

Lovely, historical turn-of-the century home. Local artwork and antiques, hearty breakfast. Visit Great Sand Dunes, cross-country ski, ride the Cumbres-Toltec Railway, bike, hike, fish, hunt or visit nearby bird sanctuaries.

MUSHROOM OMELETTE

2 eggs
1/4 cup grated Cheddar cheese
1/2 cup fresh mushrooms
3 tablespoons melted butter

Beat eggs. Add cheese and mushrooms. Place in frying pan with butter. Turn over until both sides are golden brown. Makes 1 omelette.

Origin: Anne's own recipe.

Submitted by:

Meadow Spring Farm
201 East Street Road
Kennett Square, Penn.
19348
(215) 444-3903
Anne Hicks
$50.00 to $65.00

Full breakfast
6 rooms, 3 private baths
Children allowed
No pets
Restricted smoking
No credit cards

Wind down a picturesque country lane with cows grazing in the field. Pool, hot tub in solarium, breakfast served in dining room or "breakfast in bed". Game room, or see our animals on the farm. Near museums, skiing, tennis, golf, & hot air ballooning. Warm hospitality.

OVEN BAKED OMELET

6 eggs
1/2 cup low-fat cottage cheese
1/2 cup sour cream
1/2 cup mild salsa
1 cup shredded Monterey Jack cheese
1 cup shredded Cheddar cheese

Mix the first 3 ingredients with a whip. Spray 9" pie pan with no-stick cooking spray. Spread salsa in pan and add cheese. Pour egg mixture over cheese. Bake at 350° for 45 minutes. Serves 5 - 6.

Submitted by:

Gate House Inn
1330 Jackson Gate Road
Jackson, California 95642
(209) 223-3500
Stan & Bev Smith
$75.00 to $105.00

Full breakfast
5 rooms, 5 private baths
Children, over 12
No pets
Restricted smoking
Mastercard & Visa

Charming turn-of-the-century Victorian offering 3 rooms, a 2-room suite or a private summer house. Step into the past with lace curtains, brass or Early American queen-size beds and Victorian furnishings, which complete our comfortable decor.

QUICHE LAFAYETTE

Pillsbury prepared pie crust
2 cups diced, cooked ham
1 small can chopped mushrooms
3 cups shredded Cheddar cheese
6 eggs
1 can Pet evaporated milk
Additional cheese

Prepare pie crust according to directions. Layer ham and drained & rinsed mushrooms, and cheese. Beat eggs well. Add Pet milk, beat again. Pour egg mixture over layers. Sprinkle additional cheese on top. Bake at 350° for 30 - 45 minutes until set.

Origin: Created by Sarah at Lafayette House.

Submitted by:

Lafayette House
2156 Lafayette Avenue
St. Louis, Missouri 63104
(314) 772-4429
Sarah & Jack Milligan
$35.00 to $60.00

Full breakfast
5 rooms, 2 private baths
Children allowed
No pets
Restricted smoking
No credit cards

1876 Queen Anne mansion "in the center of things to do in St. Louis". Antiques, collections, library, special breakfasts. Close to the Arch, zoo, convention center, medical centers, baseball, symphony, and botannical gardens.

SALSA SUPREME OVEN OMELET

1/2 cup hot salsa or picante sauce
1 cup chopped artichoke hearts (may use canned)
1 cup shredded Monterey Jack cheese
1 cup shredded sharp Cheddar cheese
6 eggs
8 oz. carton sour cream
Dill weed (optional)
Tomato wedges (optional)
Parsley sprigs (optional)

Preheat oven to 350°. Pour 1/2 cup salsa into bottom of lightly greased 10" quiche dish. Sprinkle artichokes over salsa. Sprinkle cheeses over artichokes. In blender container, place eggs and blend well. Add sour cream to eggs and blend until smooth. Pour egg mixture over cheeses. Sprinkle lightly with dill weed. Bake uncovered for 30 - 40 minutes, or until knife inserted near middle comes out clean. Cut into wedges. Garnish with tomato wedges and parsley, and serve. Serves 6.

Submitted by:

The Heartstone Inn & Cottages
35 Kingshighway
Eureka Springs, Ark. 72632
(501) 253-8916
Iris & Bill Simantel
$51.00 to $85.00

Full breakfast
12 rooms, 12 private baths
Children allowed
No pets
Restricted smoking
Mastercard, Visa, Am Ex

Award-winning inn with charm of yesteryear, yet modern conveniences. Rooms feature antiques, fresh flowers, television, private entrances, and air- conditioning. In historic district, close to all area attractions. New York Times says "best breakfasts in Ozarks."

SCRAMBLED EGGS SUPREME

4 eggs, beaten
2 tablespoons cottage cheese
1/8 teaspoon garlic powder
Salt & pepper to taste

Beat all ingredients to fluffy state with rotary or electric beater. Grease glass or ceramic baking dish with butter or margarine. Bake uncovered in 300° oven until set, approximately 20 minutes. Do not undercook.

Origin: Concocted by accident while preparing lunch for my farm-hands in Montana.

Submitted by:

Sleeping Place of the Wheels
3308 Lodgepole Road
Coeur d'Alene, Idaho 83814
(208) 765-3435
Donna & Wallace Bedord
$22.00 to $35.00
Special family rates

Full breakfast
2 rooms
Children allowed
No pets
Restricted smoking
Mastercard & Visa

An acre of lawn, gardens, and small orchard with off-street parking, near Freeway #90, yet isolated. We "kater" to kids: swings, sandbox, highchair and crib. Guests may wander at will, inside or out. Accommodations for RV or boat.

WESTWAYS' SOUTHWESTERN SOUFFLÉ

- 2 cups shredded Monterey Jack cheese
- 2 cups shredded medium sharp cheese
- 3 - 4 oz. cans whole green chilies
- 6 large fresh eggs
- 1 cup flour
- 4 cups whole milk
- Salt to taste
- Pepper to taste

Butter bottom of 3-quart soufflé dish. Cut chilies into 1" pieces. Layer the cheeses and chilies in bottom of dish. Beat together eggs, flour, milk, salt and pepper. Pour over cheeses and chilies. This should fill approximately half of the dish. Bake in preheated 350° oven for 1 hour. Let stand 5 minutes before serving. Serve with homemade guacamole, sour cream, homemade salsa, and warm fresh corn or flour tortillas. Serves 8.

Origin: Our Hispanic housekeeper's grandmother, a native of the Southwest.

Submitted by:

Westways "Private" Resort Inn
P.O. Box 41624
Phoenix, Arizona 85080
(602) 582-3868
Brian Curran & Darrell Trapp
$49.00 to $125.00

Full breakfast
6 rooms, 6 private baths
No children
No pets
Restricted smoking
Mastercard, Visa, Am Ex

Fashioned after the world's finest 5-star resorts, with casual western comfort and a touch of Southwest class. 1989-90 Arizona state award of hospitality. Guests preserve their privacy in deluxe guest rooms.

ZUCCHINI OMELETTE

Butter
1/2 onion, sliced
3 tablespoons chopped parsley
6 - 8 small zucchini, sliced
Salt to taste
4 eggs, beaten
2 tablespoons grated Parmesan cheese

In medium skillet, fry onion and parsley in butter until onion is golden brown. Add sliced zucchini and let cook, covered, until tender. Salt to taste. Add beaten eggs and Parmesan cheese and lower heat to let eggs cook thoroughly. Turn often while eggs are cooking.

Origin: "I ate this as a young girl in Italy. It was considered a recipe of the poor people in my small southern Italian town." Gina Glass, owner, The Village Inn.

Submitted by:

The Village Inn
407 El Camino Real
Arroyo Grande, California
93420
(805) 489-5926
Fred & Susan Patrick
$75.00 to $125.00

Full breakfast
7 rooms, 7 private baths
Children, over 10
No pets
No smoking
Mastercard, Visa,
Am Ex, Discover

Victorian farmstyle revival house with charming English country decor. Queen beds and sitting areas, afternoon buffet. Resident managers entertain guests with music. Near quaint shops, bicycling, horseback riding on the beach, tennis, golf, and Hearst Castle.

FRUITS, SOUPS & BEVERAGES

APPLE CIDER SYRUP

- 1 cup sugar
- 2 tablespoons cornstarch
- 1 teaspoon cinnamon
- 2 cups fresh apple cider
- 2 tablespoons lemon juice
- 1/4 cup butter or margarine

Mix all ingredients except margarine or butter, and cook, stirring constantly, until mixture thickens and boils. Boil and stir 1 minute. Remove from heat and stir in margarine. Store in refrigerator. Wonderful served on French Toast made with cinnamon bread or on Apple Pancakes.

Submitted by:

Derby Village Inn
46 Main Street
Derby Line, Vermont 05830
(802) 873-3604
Tom & Phyllis Moreau
$35.00 to $55.00

Full breakfast
5 rooms, 5 private baths
Children allowed
No pets
No smoking
Mastercard & Visa

Fine lodging in an elegant 1900 Victorian home. We are located in a charming country village facing the Canadian border. Near golf, skiing, lakes and peace and tranquility. Come and enjoy our warm hospitality and delicious home cooking. Year-round recreation.

BAKED APPLES WITH FRENCH CREAM

4 large apples, halved & cored
Butter
2 cups your favorite granola
1 cup heavy whipping cream
1 teaspoon vanilla extract
3 tablespoons sugar

Place halved and cored apples in shallow, buttered baking dish. Sprinkle generously with granola, to cover each apple half. Place dab of butter on top of granola. Bake at 350° for 45 minutes. While apples are baking, whip heavy cream with vanilla and sugar until thick and creamy, but still of a pouring consistency. When apples are done, place in individual serving bowls and pour French cream over the top. Serve while apples are hot from the oven. Serves 6 - 8.

Submitted by:

Howard Creek Ranch
40501 North Highway One
P.O. Box 121
Westport, (Mendocino Coast)
California 95488
(707) 964-6725
Charles (Sunny) & Sally Grigg
$50.00 to $90.00

Full breakfast
6 rooms, 3 private baths
Children allowed, by prior arrangement only
Pets allowed, by prior arrangement only
Restricted smoking
Mastercard & Visa

Historic 1867 farm bordered by beach & mountains in wilderness area. Flowers, antiques, fireplaces, redwoods, 75 foot swinging footbridge over Howard Creek, cabins, hot tub, sauna & cold pool, plus masseuse, combined with comfort, hospitality, and good food.

BAKED CURRIED FRUIT

1 - 16 oz. can pineapple chunks
1 - 16 oz. can pear halves
1 - 16 oz. can apricot halves
1 - 16 oz. can peach slices
1 - 6 oz. jar maraschino cherries
2/3 cup blanched slivered almonds or pecan halves
3/4 cup light brown sugar
1/3 cup butter or margarine
3 or 4 tablespoons curry

Drain and place all fruits and nuts in large flat Pyrex baking dish. Mix brown sugar, butter and curry and drizzle over fruit. Then cover, in plastic for microwave, foil for oven. Bake 20 minutes on High in microwave or 1 hour at 350° in conventional oven. Refrigerate overnight. Reheat before serving over 1/2 of a day old bran muffin. (We use Jiffy Bran Muffin mix with dates.) Serve in small bowls and wait for the "Ah's. . ." Serves 8 - 10.

Origin: We modified this recipe to suit our taste, and have often served it at our New Year's Day brunch - a very popular dish.

Submitted by:

Abbie Hill Bed & Breakfast
P.O. Box 4503
Richmond, Virginia 23220
(804) 355-5855
Barbara & Bill Fleming
$45.00 to $95.00

Full breakfast
3 rooms, 2 private baths
Children, over 12
No pets
No smoking

Early 1900's Federal Townhouse near Museum of Fine Arts, State Capitol, St. John's Church, Maymont Park. Antique furnished & newly decorated; our baths retain old-fashioned charm. Virginia breakfast in our aviary-dining room. Private veranda or main porch.

BAKED PEARS

Fresh pears, halved
Butter
Brown sugar
Lemonade

Core the pears, and halve them. Put in baking dish appropriate for number of pears you are baking. Dot with butter and sprinkle with brown sugar. Pour lemonade into baking dish until about 1/4" covers bottom of dish. Bake at 350° for 45 minutes.

A delicious change from baked apples.

Submitted by:

Center Lovell Inn
Route 5
Center Lovell, Maine 04016
(207) 925-1575
Bil & Susie Mosca
$52.00 to $145.00

Full breakfast
11 rooms, 7 private baths
Children allowed
No pets
Smoking allowed
Mastercard, Visa, Am Ex

1805 farmhouse with 1830 Norton Annex overlooks Kezar Lake Valley, with 180° sunsets over the White Mtns. & Presidential Range. Year round activities: outdoor sports, antiques, arts & crafts, beautiful fall foliage and the Fryeburg Fair. 1 of 4 Master Chef Inns in Maine.

BROILED GRAPEFRUIT

1 grapefruit (halved)
1 - 1 1/2 tablespoons butter
1/2 teaspoon sugar
2 tablespoons cinnamon-sugar mixture (4 parts sugar to 1 part cinnamon)
2 cooked chicken livers

Fruit should be at room temperature. Cut around each section of grapefruit half, close to membrane. Fruit should be completely loosened from shell. Cut membrane around center of grapefruit. Fill center with butter. Sprinkle sugar over each half, then sprinkle each with cinnamon-sugar mixture. Broil grapefruit on shallow baking pan 4 inches from heat about 8 - 10 minutes or just long enough to brown tops and heat bubbling hot. Sauté a chicken liver coated with flour, and seasoned with salt & pepper, in butter. At end of broiling time, place cooked chicken liver in center of each grapefruit half. 1/2 grapefruit = 1 serving.

Submitted by:

Chalet Suzanne
P.O. Drawer AC, U.S. Highway 27 & County Road 17A
Lake Wales, Florida 33859
(813) 676-6011
Carl & Vita Hinshaw
$85.00 to $165.00

Full & continental breakfast
30 rooms, 30 private baths
Children allowed
Pets allowed
Smoking allowed
Mastercard, Visa, Am Ex, Discover

"Fairy tales can come true. . ." Storybook inn with an "around-the-world" look to its clustered cottages and fountain courtyards. Family owned & operated since 1931. Private airstrip, pool, gift shop, ceramic studio and soup cannery, award-winning gourmet restaurant.

CHOKECHERRY SYRUP OR JELLY

3 1/2 cups chokecherry juice
1/2 cup lemon juice
2 cups apple juice
1 box pectin
7 cups sugar
1 1/2 teaspoons almond extract

Combine juices and pectin and bring to a boil. Add sugar and boil 4 minutes or until thick enough to slowly drop from a spoon. Remove from heat and add almond extract. Skim and pour into sterilized jars. For syrup: Double all ingredients except pectin.

Origin: I've used this recipe for several years. It's delicious on pancakes and waffles.

Submitted by:

Hillard's Bed & Breakfast & Guest House
11521 Axtell Gateway Road
Bozeman, Montana 59715
(406) 763-4696
Larry & Doris Hillard
$60.00 (2 people) - Weekly & family rates available

Full breakfast
6 rooms, 2 private baths
Children allowed
Pets allowed (Limited)
Restricted smoking
Mastercard

A lovely 3 bedroom home and 3 bedroom guest house located on 11 acres. Walking distance to "Blue Ribbon" trout stream. We are situated between 2 major ski resorts. Have a heated pool in summer. Peaceful setting, yet close to airport and city.

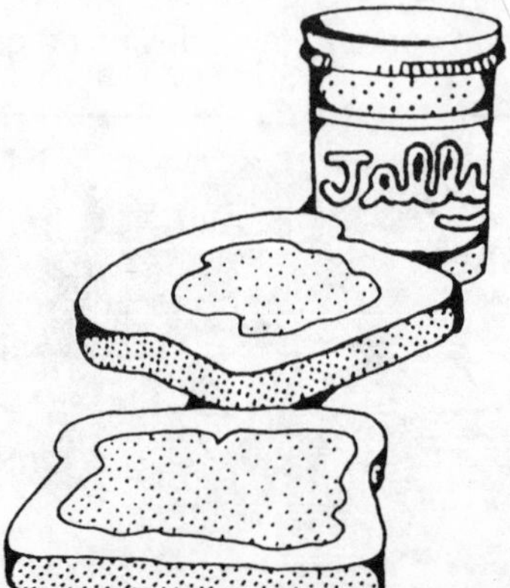

CITRUS COMPOTE

- 1/3 cup white grape juice
- 1/4 cup fresh orange juice or frozen concentrate
- 1/4 cup clover honey (or sugar)
- 1/8 - 1/4 teaspoon ground cinnamon
- 1 1/2 cups oranges, peeled & sectioned (3)
- 1 1/2 cups grapefruit, peeled & sectioned (2)
- 1/4 cup finely chopped, toasted almonds

Combine grape juice, orange juice, honey, and cinnamon in saucepan. Cook over medium heat until blended. Add citrus fruit sections, heat 1 minute. Pour into serving dish. Sprinkle with almonds. Serve hot or cold. Makes 4 - 6 servings.

Origin: Recipe is an old family favorite.

Submitted by:

Hostess House
5758 NE Emerson
Portland, Ore. 97218-2406
(503) 282-7892
Milli Laughlin
$25.00 to $40.00

Full breakfast
4 rooms
Children allowed
No pets
Restricted smoking

Warmth & quiet hospitality in a contemporary setting. 5 minutes from Portland's airport, 10 minutes from Lloyd Center, and easy access to I-5, I-84 and I-205. Near antique and specialty shops, museums, parks, boating, golf, ice skating, skiing, swimming and tennis.

CRANAPPLE FRAPPÉ

2 cups Cranapple Juice
1 cup orange juice
1/4 cup whipping cream
1 large banana
3/4 cup crushed ice
Garnish: Fresh apple wedge with peeling, and fresh mint

Combine all ingredients except ice and garnishes in blender container. Blend until smooth. Add crushed ice and blend on high speed one minute. Serve in frosted, stemmed goblets. Garnish with fresh apple and mint.

Origin: Began as an alternative to fresh juice each morning.

Submitted by:

Maple Leaf Cottage Inn
P.O. Box 156
Historic Elsah, Illinois 62028
(618) 374-1684
Mrs. Patty Taetz
$65.00 Single or Double

Full breakfast
6 rooms, 6 private baths
Children, over 12
No pets
Restricted smoking
Mastercard & Visa

Private grounds cover one village block, surrounded by an English garden, facing the spectacular limestone bluffs of Elsah. Stenciling & lace tablecloths add to country elegance. Screened front porch, with wicker chairs and swing, is a great place to enjoy a peaceful evening.

CREAMY FRUIT DRESSING

8 oz. cream cheese, room temperature
1/4 cup orange juice (increase to make sauce desired thickness)
2 tablespoons sugar
1/2 teaspoon ginger
Chill fresh fruits: Strawberries, raspberries, bananas, kiwi, melon, blueberries, etc.

Frost goblets or bowls by placing in freezer at least one hour before serving. Whirl all ingredients, except fresh fruits, in blender or food processor until smooth. Additional juice may be used if a more pourable sauce is desired. Place fresh fruits in frosted goblets. Sauce may be poured over fruit before serving or placed in small crystal pitcher and served on the side.

Origin: An original recipe. I cook "by ear," and have difficulty committing recipes to paper, since they're rarely made the same way twice.

Submitted by:

The Inn At Wildcat Mountain
Bed & Breakfast
Highway 33, P.O. Box 112
Ontario, Wisconsin 54651
(608) 337-4352
Patricia & Wendell Barnes
$35.00 to $55.00

Full breakfast
4 rooms
Children, over 10
No pets
No smoking
Mastercard & Visa

1910 Greek Revival home on the Kickapoo River. Massive pillars, turn-of-the-century furnishings and a rolling lawn. Near Wildcat Mtn. State Park, & the Elroy-Sparta National Trail. Canoe, hunt, fish, cross-country ski. Handcrafts and baked goods from Amish community.

FRESH FRUIT & YOGURT CRUNCH

1 cup granola
1 cup fresh fruit
1 1/2 cups vanilla yogurt

Line 4 small fruit dishes with 1/4 cup granola each. Mix yogurt with fresh fruit cut into bite-sized pieces. Any fruit or berries will do. Carefully place fruit and yogurt mixture on granola. Let set in refrigerator about 30 minutes before serving, to mix flavors and moisten granola.

Origin: This is an original recipe idea.

Submitted by:

Anton Boxrud
Bed & Breakfast
57 South, 600 East
Salt Lake City, Utah 84102
(801) 363-8035
Ray & Margaret Fuller
$40.00 to $55.00

Full breakfast
4 rooms, 2 private baths
Children allowed
No pets
Restricted smoking
Mastercard & Visa

Stay with us in a beautiful historic Victorian home. Many of the original furnishings grace the rooms. You will be within walking distance of downtown and a 30 minute drive or bus ride to the ski slopes. Come and be pampered.

FROZEN FRUIT CUP

2 - 10 oz. pkgs. frozen strawberries
5 mashed bananas
1 large can crushed pineapple
3/4 cup sugar
1 small can frozen orange juice
1 small can frozen lemonade
2 cups ginger ale

Stir all ingredients together. Freeze in Tupperware container. Set out 20 minutes before serving. Serve like a frozen slush.

Submitted by:

The Travelling Companion
4314 Main Street
Elk Horn, Iowa 51531
(712) 764-8932
Duane & Karolyn Ortgies
$40.00 double

Full breakfast
3 rooms
Children allowed
No pets
No smoking

Velkommen (Welcome). This charming 1909 home is nestled in a peaceful town in the heart of the largest Danish settlement in the U.S. Comfortable furnishings. The inn's name is from Hans Christian Andersen's fairy tales, with each room named after a different story.

FRUIT SOUP

3 cantaloupe melons
1 honeydew melon
2 - 13 oz. cans canned peaches (undrained)
2 large cans apricot nectar
1/4 cup honey
1/2 cup brown sugar
3 cups sour cream
2 teaspoons cinnamon
Garnish: Mint leaves or kiwi fruit

Puree the fruit in Cuisinart. Leave it a little chunky. Add the rest of the ingredients. Mix well and chill. Garnish with mint leaves or piece of kiwi fruit.

Submitted by:

The Victorian Inn
1229 Seventh Street
Port Huron, Michigan 48060
(313) 984-1437
Sheila Marinez
$45.00 to $60.00

Continental breakfast
4 rooms, 2 private baths
Children, over 10
No pets
Smoking allowed
Mastercard, Visa, Am Ex, Discover

1 hour north of Detroit, find fine dining & guest rooms in authentically restored Victorian elegance. A timeless ambiance, classically creative cuisine and gracious service. All food is prepared with the utmost attention to detail, which was the order of the day in a bygone era.

HERONCREST FARM PEACH SHORTCAKE

1 cup stoneground whole wheat flour
1 cup unbleached white flour
2 teaspoons baking powder
Grating of nutmeg
1 teaspoon brown sugar
2 tablespoons margarine & 2 tablespoons butter (have very cold)
2/3 - 3/4 cup buttermilk
1 - 2 peaches per person
Lemon juice for fruit
White sugar
Heavy cream
Vanilla

Buttermilk Biscuits: Preheat oven to 450°. Sift together flours, baking powder, nutmeg,and brown sugar. Cut in with pastry cutter or 2 knives the margarine, butter and buttermilk. Stir quickly until just mixed. Drop onto greased cookie sheet, dividing into 6 or 8 biscuits. Have dough higher in center. Bake until golden, 10 - 12 minutes. Peaches: Peel peaches just before serving, as they turn brown quickly. Sprinkle with a little lemon juice to protect the fruit somewhat. Slice 1 - 2 peaches per person into a bowl. Sprinkle with a little white sugar. Whip heavy cream, flavor with vanilla. Split biscuits, fill with peaches, put more peaches on top, then whipped cream.

Submitted by:

Spring House
Muddy Creek Forks
Airville, Pennsylvania 17302
(717) 927-6906
Ray Constance Hearne
$60.00 to $85.00

Full breakfast
5 rooms, 2 private baths
Children allowed
No pets
No smoking

Welcome to country luxury: cozy featherbeds in winter, fragrant breezes in summer, and a spacious front porch with swing, all overlooking a sparkling river. We feature regional specialties for breakfast. House is authentically restored, with original stenciling.

HOT MULLED CIDER

1/2 cup brown sugar
1/4 teaspoon salt
1 gallon cider
Dash of nutmeg
1 teaspoon allspice (2 teaspoons whole)
2 teaspoons whole cloves
2 - 3" sticks of cinnamon

Combine first three ingredients. Tie spices in cheesecloth. Simmer 20 minutes. Makes 20 servings.

Origin: For generations, the fragrance of this, left steaming on the stove, has warmed guests throughout the Midwest, even before their cups are filled.

Submitted by:

Avery Guest House
606 S. Prospect St.
Galena, Illinois 61036
(815) 777-3883
Flo & Roger Jensen
$40.00 to $60.00

Continental plus breakfast
4 rooms
Children allowed
No pets
No smoking
Mastercard, Visa, Am Ex

In the Historic District, this pre-Civil War home is a short walk from antique shops and historic buildings. Enjoy the scenic view from our porch swing; play the piano or just visit. Breakfast is served in the sunny dining room with bay window overlooking Galena River Valley.

MAPLE POACHED PEARS

6 - 8 pears, peeled, cored & quartered
1 cup maple syrup
1/2 cup orange juice
Juice from 1/2 small lemon
Rind from 1/2 orange, cut into julienne strips (all white removed)
Garnish:
Chopped fresh mint

Combine all ingredients, except mint, in saucepan. Bring to boil, reduce heat, and simmer gently 10 minutes. Cool slightly and pour into glass serving bowl or individual dishes. Serve warm, garnished with mint. Makes 4 - 6 servings.

Origin: An original recipe. Chef & co-owner, Mary Phillips' breakfast always includes a fruit course, Bayfield-grown whenever possible.

Submitted by:

Old Rittenhouse Inn
P.O. Box 584
301 Rittenhouse Avenue
Bayfield, Wisconsin 54814
(715) 779-5111
Jerry & Mary Phillips
$69.00 to $159.00

Continental plus breakfast
21 rooms, 21 private baths
Children allowed
No pets
Restricted smoking
Mastercard & Visa

Elegant Victorian dining and lodging overlooking Lake Superior and the Apostle Islands National Lakeshore. Guest rooms furnished with antiques and working fireplaces. Creative menus change daily featuring area fresh produce, homemade breads and desserts.

MICROWAVE FRUIT SALAD

1 pkg. reg. vanilla pudding
1 pkg. reg. tapioca pudding
3 cups juice from peaches & pineapple
Water
29 oz. can peaches, cut up
1 can pineapple chunks
1 can mandarin oranges, drained (don't use juice)

Add water to juice from fruit to make 3 cups. Mix juice and pudding and cook in microwave on high speed for 8 minutes, stirring occasionally. Let cool and add to fruit. Let stand several hours in refrigerator. Serve in attractive fruit bowls. Quick, delicious and easy to do.

Submitted by:

Calmar Guesthouse
R.R. #1, Box 206
Calmar, Iowa 52132
(319) 562-3851
Art & Lucille Kruse
$35.00 to $40.00

Full breakfast
5 rooms
Children allowed
No pets
Restricted smoking

Fully restored, newly remodeled, 1890 Victorian home. Northeast Iowa is beautiful. Near world famous Bily Clocks, Niagara Cave, Norwegian Museum, smallest church in the world, antique shops, state parks, golf, tennis, hunting, fishing, and swimming - welcome!

ORANGE CREAM FRUIT

1 - 3 oz. pkg. instant vanilla pudding
1 1/2 cups milk
1/2 of 6 oz. can frozen orange juice concentrate
3/4 cup sour cream
20 oz. can drained pineapple chunks
16 oz. can drained sliced peaches
11 oz. can drained mandarin oranges
3 medium bananas, sliced
2 medium apples, chopped

Combine pudding, milk and orange juice concentrate. Beat 1 - 2 minutes, until thick. Add sour cream and gently blend. Fold in all fruit. Chill.

Submitted by:

The Inn at Coit Mountain
HCR 63, Box 3
Newport, N.H. 03773
(603) 863-3583 or
(800) 367-2364
Dick & Judi Tatem
$70.00 to $150.00

Full breakfast
5 rooms, 1 private bath
Children allowed, crib available
No pets
Restricted smoking
Mastercard & Visa

Most people say "Ohhh. . ." when they come into the inn - it's more beautiful than our brochure can describe. Enjoy the Lake Sunapee area all year round in our elegant, but most comfortable inn. Some bedrooms have fireplaces for your pleasure.

RICOTTA FIGS

1 cup ricotta cheese
4 tablespoons sugar
Zest of 1 lemon
1 egg white
8 large fresh figs
8 large fig leaves
Pomegranate seeds or slivered almonds

In Cuisinart, blend cheese, 2 tablespoons sugar and zest. Whip egg white until stiff peaks form. Add 2 tablespoons sugar, fold in cheese mixture. Refrigerate. Wash and dry figs and fig leaves. Cross-cut figs, place on fig leaf. Spoon in cheese mixture, top with 3 pomegranate seeds or slivered almonds. Makes 8 servings.

Submitted by:

Hersey House
451 North Main Street
Ashland, Oregon 97520
(503) 482-4563
Gail Orell & Lynn Savage
$60.00 to $100.00

Full breakfast
4 rooms, 4 private baths
Children, over 12
No pets
Restricted smoking

Restored turn-of-the-century Victorian has individually decorated rooms: Wildflower, Sunshine Terrace, Eastlake and Rose Victorian. Walk to theaters. English country garden & player piano. Front porch with wicker furniture and game table. Family china , silver, and linens.

SAILORS' SUNRISE

1 ripe banana
1/2 cup powdered milk
1/2 cup plain yogurt
2 cups apple juice
1 pkg. (10 oz.) frozen strawberries or 1/2 - 1 teaspoon dry strawberry Jello

Mix ingredients in blender. Serve in chilled glasses. Makes four servings.

Submitted by:

Duke House Bed & Breakfast
618 Maiden Street
Mineral Point, Wis. 53565
(608) 987-2821
Tom & Darlene Duke
$40.00 to $50.00

Full breakfast
2 rooms
No children
No pets
No smoking

Recently redecorated to create a bright and airy feeling. Spacious rooms have hardwood floors, oriental rugs and wing-backed chairs. Homemade baked goods are our specialty, and classical music fills the air during breakfast. A hearty welcome and gracious hospitality.

SAND PLUM JELLY

3 cups sand plum juice
1 box fruit pectin
2 3/4 cups honey

For clear jelly, cook plums and let juice drip through a bag. Cook pectin and juice to a boil, skimming off foam. Add honey and boil 5 to 10 minutes. Pour into prepared jars and seal with paraffin.

The town of Guthrie celebrates this little fruit with a Sand Plum Festival during the summer.

Submitted by:

Harrison House
124 W. Harrison
Guthrie, Oklahoma
73044
(405) 282-1000
Phyllis Murray
$40.00 to $80.00

Continental breakfast
23 rooms, 23 private baths
Children allowed
Well-behaved pets allowed
Restricted smoking
Mastercard, Visa, Am Ex, Discover, Diner's Club, Carte Blanche

A delightful Victorian inn in a restored bank building located in the center of historic Guthrie, Oklahoma. Charmingly decorated, beautifully appointed, and invitingly warm. Rooms furnished with antiques.

SCANDINAVIAN FRUIT SOUP

1 lb. dried fruits (apples, prunes, apricots, pears, peaches)
1/2 cup tapioca
1/2 cup raisins
1/4 lb. dried cherries
2 quarts water
1 stick cinnamon
1 lemon, sliced
1 orange, sliced

Soak dried fruits and tapioca overnight in water. Next day add remaining ingredients. Simmer gently until flavors blend, tapioca is clear, and soup is slightly thickened, about 1 hour. Serve warm in winter, chilled in summer. Serves 14 - 18.

Origin: Scandinavians were among the first and most prominent settlers in our Door County region of Wisconsin. This dish is very traditional.

Submitted by:

Inn at Cedar Crossing
336 Louisiana Street
Sturgeon Bay, Wis. 54235
(414) 743-4200
Terry Wulf
$65.00 to $109.00

Continental plus breakfast
9 rooms, 9 private baths
Children, over 5
No pets
Restricted smoking
Mastercard, Visa, Discover

1885 brick vernacular inn in downtown Historic District. Lovingly restored in 1986, with elegant antique-filled guest rooms, double whirlpool tubs, & inviting fireplaces. 95-seat Victorian dining rooms feature fireplaces and "homemade exquisite" cuisine 3 meals a day.

STRAWBERRY BUTTER

- 1 cup unsalted butter, (2 sticks, softened)
- 1/2 cup sifted confectioner's sugar
- 1 - 10 oz. carton frozen sliced strawberries, thawed and drained (reserve juice)

Whip the butter until fluffy. Beat in the sugar and add the strawberries. Gradually beat in the reserved strawberry juice. Store in refrigerator. This butter freezes well. Serve on hot biscuits or rolls. Makes 1 3/4 cups.

Origin: Handed down by my great-grandmother, Minnie Webb.

Submitted by:

Hamilton Place
105 E. Mason Avenue
Holly Springs, Miss. 38635
(601) 252-4368
Linda & Jack Stubbs
$55.00 to $65.00

Full breakfast
4 rooms, 4 private baths
Children allowed
No pets
Smoking allowed
Mastercard & Visa

Antique-filled antebellum home built in 1838 and listed on the National Register of Historic Places. Pool and hot tub for guests to enjoy, also an antique shop in the carriage house. Three blocks from historic town square.

STRAWBERRY CHIFFON HONEYDEW WEDGES

1/2 cup cold water
2 teaspoons unflavored gelatin
1 cup strawberry yogurt
1/2 cup frozen strawberries
1 honeydew melon, halved & seeded

In small saucepan bring water to a boil, remove from heat; dissolve gelatin in water. Add yogurt, mix well. Stir in strawberries. Chill, stirring occasionally, until thickened. Beat until fluffy on low speed. Spoon mixture into melon halves. Cover and chill 3 hours or until firm. Cut melon half into wedges to serve. Garnish with strawberries.

Submitted by:

Autumnwood Bed & Breakfast
165 Autumnwood Lane
Madison, Indiana 47250
(812) 265-5262 or 265-5272
Jae Breitweiser
$50.00 to $75.00

Continental plus breakfast
9 rooms, 1 private bath
Children allowed
No pets
Restricted smoking
Mastercard & Visa

An 1840 home nestled among large old trees overlooking the Ohio River Valley. A relaxing and beautiful fountain for quiet summer evenings. Minutes away from historic homes, antique shops, and restaurants.

SWEDISH TOSA APPLES

- **4 large baking apples (or pears), peeled, sliced & cored**
- **1 tablespoon lemon juice sprinkled over apples**
- **6 tablespoons butter**
- **8 tablespoons sugar**
- **1 1/2 tablespoons flour**
- **2 tablespoons cream (or half & half)**
- **1/2 cup slivered almonds**

Put apples in buttered baking dish. Sprinkle with juice. Melt butter. Add sugar & flour, cook over medium heat until thick & smooth, 4 - 5 minutes. .Stir in cream and almonds. Pour over apples. Bake at 400° about 20 minutes or until brown.

Origin: Received this from a friend; we've modified it to include fresh pears as well as apples.

Submitted by:

Jefferson-Day House
1109 Third Street
Hudson, Wisconsin 54016
(715) 386-7111
Wally, Sharon & Marjorie Miller
$75.00 to $135.00

Full breakfast
3 rooms, 3 private baths with whirlpools
Children, over 9
No pets
Restricted smoking

An 1857 Italianate home on a quiet, tree-lined, historic street, is 2 blocks from the St. Croix River. Afternoon snacks, 3-course fireside breakfasts, and antique collections. Near museum, live theatre, biking, ballooning, boating and skiing. 30 minutes from Minneapolis.

WILLIAM KLINGER'S STRAWBERRY SOUP

1 - 15 oz. pkg. frozen strawberries
1 - 15 oz. carton sour cream
1 tablespoon grenadine syrup
1 tablespoon lemon juice
1 tablespoon vanilla
1 tablespoon sugar
3 oz. sifted powdered sugar
3 pints whipping cream
Garnish: Strawberry halves & mint leaves

In blender mix strawberries and sour cream, beat slowly till well mixed. While mixing, add grenadine syrup, lemon juice, vanilla, and sugars. When very smooth, add whipping cream, mix on high for 5 seconds. Chill and shake well before serving. Use a strawberry half with a mint leaf as garnish. Makes 8 - 1/2 cup servings.

Origin: I serve soups with my breakfasts, and love to create good recipes.

Submitted by:

William Klinger Inn
108 East Second Street
Hermann, Missouri 65041
(314) 486-2410
Laverne Rickher
$86.62 to $121.08

Full breakfast
7 rooms, 7 private baths
No children
No pets
No smoking
Mastercard & Visa

An 1878 Victorian townhouse in the Historic District. Antiques, private patio, and carriage house for mini-conferences. Historic museums, antique shops, specialty shops, park, tennis, swimming, boating and golf nearby.

CEREALS, PUDDINGS & MISCELLANEOUS

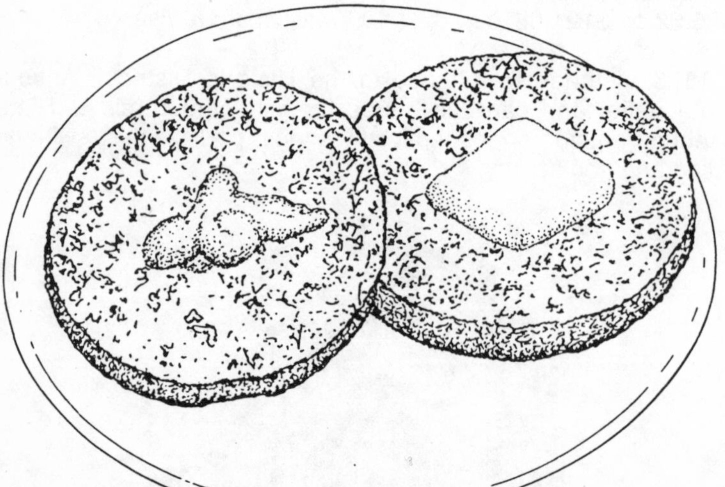

BIRCHERMUESLI THORNROSE HOUSE

2 cups old-fashioned rolled oats
1/3 - 1/2 cup golden raisins
Milk to cover cereal
1 grated apple (Granny Smith, preferably)
Juice of 1 lemon
Whipped heavy cream or Cool Whip (opt.)
Fresh fruits (in season)
Toasted almonds to taste

Combine oats, raisins and milk just to barely cover in bowl and refrigerate overnight. Next morning add grated apple and lemon juice; fold in just enough cream to give a nice consistency. (May be omitted for cholesterol-conscious guests.) Spoon into individual serving bowls and top with fresh fruit and toasted almonds.

Origin: Created by a Swiss physician for his heart patients; I have modified it.

Submitted by:

Thornrose House at Gypsy Hill
531 Thornrose Avenue
Staunton, Virginia
24401
(703) 885-7026
Carolyn & Ray Hoaster
$45.00 to $55.00

Full breakfast
3 rooms, 3 private baths
Children allowed, except weekends
No pets
No smoking
Personal checks

Thornrose House, circa 1912, is in an historic, Victorian town in the heart of the Shenandoah Valley. Shops, restaurants and historic sites nearby. 300 acre park with golf, swimming, tennis, exertrails. Air-conditioned, comfortable sitting room and fireplace for chilly days.

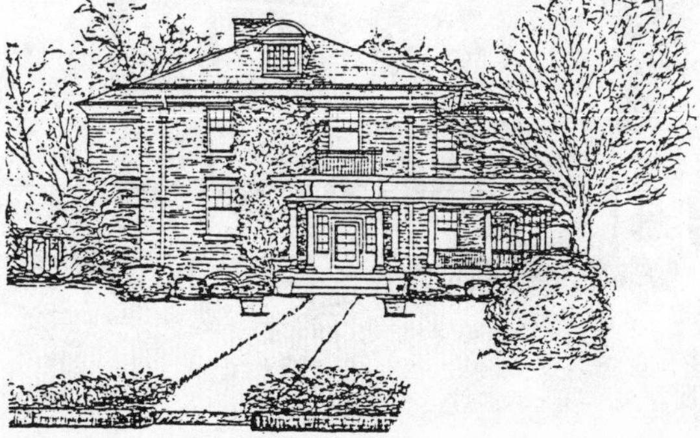

BLUEBERRY PUDDING FROM MAINE

2 cups blueberries
2 tablespoons butter
1 1/2 cups sugar
1 cup flour
1 teaspoon baking powder
Pinch of salt
1 cup milk
1 cup hot water

Butter a square baking dish. Place blueberries in dish. In a bowl, beat butter, 3/4 cup sugar, flour, baking powder, salt and milk. Pour over blueberries. Sprinkle with remaining sugar. Pour 1 cup hot water over the top. Bake at 375° for 40 minutes. Serve with heavy cream.

Submitted by:

Broad Bay Inn and Gallery
P.O. Box 607
Waldoboro, Maine 04572
(207) 832-6668
Jim & Libby Hopkins
$40.00 to $65.00

Full breakfast
5 rooms, 3 private baths
Children, over 10
No pets
Restricted smoking
Mastercard & Visa

Restored 1830 inn, in Midcoast village, near Medomak River. Near a lighthouse, tennis, golf, antique shops, theatre, boating, swimming, and an art gallery, with nationally-known artists and limited edition prints. Candlelight dinners, canopy beds, Victorian furnishings.

CAPTAIN SAWYER'S GRANOLA

8 cups old-fashioned oatmeal
2 cups wheat flakes
1 cup coconut
1 cup sunflower seeds
1 cup sesame seeds
2 handfuls sliced almonds
Wheat germ
Bran
Cinnamon, nutmeg (opt.)
1 cup honey or 1/2 honey & 1/2 molasses
1/3 cup oil
Grape Nuts
All Bran
Wheaties
Raisins
Dates
Peanuts
Walnuts

Mix dry ingredients in large baking pan. Add honey and oil. Bake at 250° for 1 hour, stirring every 15 minutes. Then add and mix any or all of the remaining cereals, raisins, dates, or nuts.

Submitted by:

Captain Sawyer's Place
87 Commercial Street
Boothbay Harbor, Maine
04538
(207) 633-2290
Doreen Gibson
$65.00 to $100.00

Continental plus breakfast
10 rooms, 10 private baths
Children, over 12
No pets
No smoking
Mastercard & Visa

An 1878 sea captain's home, in the heart of one of Maine's most beautiful fishing villages. Overlooking the busy harbor, we are only steps away from fine restaurants, sailing and boat cruises, fishing, shops, galleries and theater.

CARAMEL MUFFINS

1/2 cup softened margarine
1 cup brown sugar
1/2 cup sliced almonds, chopped pecans or walnuts
English muffins, halved

Combine margarine and brown sugar. Beat well and add nuts. Spread on the halves of English muffins. Place on ungreased cookie sheet. Broil in oven for 2 - 3 minutes or until bubbly on top. Serve piping hot.

Submitted by:

Queen Anne Inn
420 W. Washington
South Bend, Indiana 46601
(219) 234-5959
Pauline & Bob Medhurst
$65.00 to $85.00

Full breakfast
5 rooms, 5 private baths
Children allowed
No pets
Restricted smoking
Mastercard, Visa, Am Ex

1893 Victorian noted for its leaded glass, Frank Lloyd Wright-designed bookcases and Italian imported oak staircase. Furnished in antiques & reproductions. Homemade coffee cakes, omelets or Belgian waffles for breakfast. Near downtown and Notre Dame.

CHEESY-PEAR MUFFINS

4 cups shredded Swiss cheese
1/2 cup mayonnaise
3/4 teaspoon dry mustard
8 split English muffins, toasted
3 tablespoons prepared mustard
16 slices ham
8 Bartlett pears, cored and sliced
Nutmeg

Combine cheese, mayonnaise, and dry mustard. Spread each toasted muffin with prepared mustard. Top with ham slices and sliced pears. Cover with cheese mixture and finish with a dash of nutmeg. Broil 6 inches from heat until cheese melts and is lightly browned. We serve these muffins with soft boiled eggs and fresh fruit bowls. Serves 8.

Origin: My mother served this popular dish with soup for Sunday supper or on special school days when she knew I needed a treat.

Submitted by:

North Coast Country Inn
34591 S. Highway #1
Gualala, California 95445
(707) 884-4537
Loren & Nancy Flanagan
$95.00 to $115.00

Full breakfast
4 rooms, 4 private baths
No children
No pets
No smoking
Mastercard & Visa

Rustic redwood buildings on a forested hillside overlooking the Pacific Ocean. Fireplaces, mini-kitchens, decks, authentic antiques. Romantic hot tub under the pines, and hilltop gazebo garden. Near beaches, hiking, golf, tennis, state parks, and restaurants.

CHILIE-CHEESE RICE

1/2 stick butter
1 bunch scallions, most of green tops removed, finely chopped
1 jalapeno chilie, finely chopped (optional)
3 cups cooked rice
1 1/4 teaspoons salt
1 1/2 cups sour cream
2 cups (8 oz.) cubed Monterey Jack cheese
2 - 4 oz. cans chopped, drained green chilies

Preheat oven to 350°. Generously butter a 2-quart casserole dish. In small sauté pan, sauté scallions and jalapeno in butter until translucent. Stir into cooked rice; add salt, sour cream, cubed Monterey Jack and green chilies. Pour into prepared casserole dish. Sprinkle with Cheddar. Bake for 30 minutes, or until cheese topping is melted and casserole is bubbly.

Submitted by:

Grant Corner Inn
122 Grant Avenue
Santa Fe, New Mexico
87501
(505) 983-6678
Louise Stewart & Pat Walter

Full breakfast
13 rooms, 7 private baths
Children, over 6
No pets
Smoking allowed
Mastercard & Visa

A colonial manor home with lush gardens, 2 blocks from Santa Fe's Historic Plaza. Beautifully appointed guest rooms with antiques and collectibles. Public restaurant serving gourmet breakfast and brunch is open daily.

CLAFOUTE

8 oz. stale sourdough French bread, cut 3/4" thick
1/2 cup raisins
2 eggs
1/3 cup granulated sugar
3 cups 1% milk
2 teaspoons vanilla extract
1 teaspoon grated nutmeg
Powdered sugar
Warm Berry Sauce:
2 cups fresh berries (strawberries, raspberries, wild blackberries, or a mixture)
1/4 cup granulated sugar
1/2 cup orange juice

Slice bread and arrange one layer deep, snugly fitted, in a 9" x 13" glass baking dish. Sprinkle top with raisins. Mix eggs, sugar, milk, and vanilla in bowl and pour over bread. Sprinkle top with nutmeg. Cover and refrigerate overnight. Remove from refrigerator 15 minutes before baking. Bake at 350° for 45 minutes, or until lightly browned. Remove from oven and let pudding settle for 15 minutes. Sprinkle with powdered sugar. Cut into 8 serving size rectangles. While pudding is baking, mix berries, sugar and orange juice together in sauce pan. Bring to boil and immediately turn to low heat. Cook for 20 minutes. Serve in a bowl to be ladled over pudding.

Submitted by:

Moon & Sixpence Inn
3021 Beaverton Valley Road
Friday Harbor, Wash. 98250
(206) 378-4138
Evelyn & Charles Tuller
$65.00 to $90.00

Full breakfast
5 rooms
Children, over 12
No pets
Restricted smoking
Personal checks

Early 1900 farmhouse, fully restored with family antiques. Comfortable rooms, a weaving studio, breakfast in sunny dining room with various German-Dutch delights, and classic country service.

INDIAN PUDDING

1 quart milk
1/4 cup "minute" tapioca
1/3 cup cornmeal
1/2 cup molasses
1 cup sugar
1/4 teaspoon cinnamon
1/4 teaspoon sugar
Salt to taste
1 beaten egg
1 cup raisins

Put milk and tapioca in double boiler and cook until tapioca softens a little. Mix next 6 ingredients together in bowl, and add to the milk mixture. Cook until it is somewhat thickened. Take from stove and add egg and raisins. Put in greased casserole and bake at 375° for 1 hour. Serve with cream.

Origin: From one of our guests. It's a wonderful winter morning treat.

Submitted by:

Fairhaven Inn
North Bath Road
Bath, Maine 04530
(207) 443-4391
Sallie & George Pollard
$45.00 to $70.00

Full breakfast
7 rooms, 2 private baths
Children allowed
Pets allowed
Restricted smoking
Mastercard & Visa

1790 Colonial nestled into the hillside overlooking the Kennebec River. 27 acres of country sights and sounds. Beaches, golf, Maine Maritime Museum, cross-country ski trails, fires burning, candlelight dinners on weekends, and gourmet breakfasts.

OLD-FASHIONED BREAD PUDDING

4 cups bread, muffins, croissants, coffee cake, etc. - in 1/2" cubes
2 cups milk, scalded with 1/4 cup butter
1/2 cup sugar
3 eggs, slightly beaten
Dash of salt
1 teaspoon cinnamon
1/2 cup raisins

Mix all ingredients together, pour in baking dish. Set dish in another dish with 1/2" of water in it. Bake at 350° for 1 hour.

Origin: Created from necessity to use leftover bread & pastry items.

Submitted by:

Grandmére's Inn
449 Broad Street
Nevada City, California 95959
(916) 265-4660
Annette Meade
$95.00 to $135.00

Full breakfast
6 rooms, 6 private baths
Children, over 14 (any age in Guest Room)
No pets
No smoking
Mastercard & Visa

An 1856 three-story Colonial Revival home on the National Register, our inn is furnished in elegant Country French decor. Large lawns and Victorian flower garden, queen-sized beds, and a country breakfast. Short stroll into historic gold mining town of Nevada City.

POTATO PATTIES

2 large potatoes
1 tablespoon butter
1 teaspoon finely chopped onion
Salt & pepper to taste

Mash cooked and drained potatoes, adding other ingredients. Form into patties and fry in bacon drippings. Makes 4 - 6 patties.

Submitted by:

The Catlin-Abbott House
2304 East Broad Street
Richmond, Virginia 23223
(804) 780-3746
Dr. & Mrs. James L. Abbott
$72.50 to $140.00

Full breakfast
5 rooms, 3 private baths
Children, over 12
No pets
No smoking
Mastercard, Visa, Am Ex

The luxury of triple-sheeting, goose down pillows and nightly turn-down service. Antiques, family heirlooms, fresh flowers & fireplaces. Coffee or tea arrives upon awakening; breakfast is served in the dining room or in your room. Your comfort is of primary importance.

SCARLETT'S SUPER STARTER

2 cups old-fashioned oatmeal
4 cups low fat milk
1/4 - 1/2 teaspoon salt
1 fresh ripe nectarine
1 apple
1 banana
1/4 cup raisins

Put all ingredients into medium saucepan and let soak for several minutes. Cook over low heat bringing mixture slowly to a simmer, stirring frequently. Simmer slowly until mixture thickens, about 10 minutes. Serve in bowls accompanied by wheat toast or English muffins, and homemade jellies. Serves 6.

Submitted by:

Scarlett's Country Inn
3918 Silverado Trail
Calistoga, California 94515
(707) 942-6669
Scarlett Dwyer
$85.00 to $125.00

Continental breakfast
3 rooms, 3 private baths
Children allowed
No pets
Smoking allowed
Mastercard & Visa

Secluded 1890 farmhouse set on green lawns with tall pines overlooking the vineyards. Breakfast in room or by woodland swimming pool. Near spas. Queen-sized beds, private entrances, air-conditioning, afternoon refreshments, one suite with fireplace.

SEVEN WIVES INN GRANOLA

8 cups regular oats (not quick)
1 1/2 cups wheat germ
1 1/2 cups brown sugar
8 oz. coconut (wide, unsweetened)
8 oz. almonds
3 oz. sunflower seeds
8 oz. cashews (raw or salted)
1/2 cup water
1/2 cup oil
1/2 cup honey
1/2 cup peanut butter
2 teaspoons vanilla
1 cup raisins (optional)

Mix the first seven "dry" ingredients in large bowl. Mix well and bring to a boil the next five "wet" ingredients. Add wet to dry. Blend well. Spread on 2 large cookie sheets. Bake about 2 hours in 200° oven (until coconut is brown around edges). Add 1 cup raisins after baking if desired. Makes about 5 lbs.

Origin: A power outage proved that a hot breakfast might not always be possible. Served every day since; it's our most requested recipe.

Submitted by:

Seven Wives Inn
217 North, 100 West
St. George, Utah 84770
(801) 628-3737
Donna & Jay Curtis,
Allison & Jon Bowcutt
$35.00 to $65.00

Full breakfast
13 rooms, 13 private baths
Children allowed
No pets
No smoking
Mastercard, Visa, Am Ex

2 side-by-side pioneer homes built in 1873 and 1883. It has massive wood-grained moldings bearing their original paint; antiques fill all the rooms. Swimming pool on the premises. Near Utah's National Parks: Zion, Bryce & north rim of the Grand Canyon. 2 hours to Las Vegas.

SPINACH CHEESE GRITS

4 cups water
1/2 teaspoon salt
1/2 teaspoon granulated garlic or more
1 cup quick grits
2 cups grated Cheddar cheese
1 - 8 oz. pkg. chopped frozen spinach
4 whole eggs

Boil water and add salt and garlic. Stir in quick grits. Cook about 2 minutes. Remove from heat. Stir in 1 cup grated cheese. Stir in defrosted spinach. Beat eggs slightly and stir into the mixture. Pour in oiled baking dish and bake at 350° for 30 - 45 minutes or until grits are puffy and not loose in the center. Top with grated cheese and keep in warm oven until cheese melts.

Submitted by:

The Great Southern Hotel
127 West Cedar
Brinkley, Arkansas
72021
(501) 734-4955
Stanley & Dorcas Prince
$36.00 to $40.00

Full breakfast
4 rooms, 4 private baths
Children allowed by special arrangement
No pets
Restricted smoking
Mastercard, Visa, Am Ex, Discover

Grand times & Southern hospitality, in Victorian elegance. A quaint, homey atmosphere reminiscent of "by-gone days". 1989 award for Best Restaurant of Southeast Arkansas by Arkansas Times. 1985 Arkansas Heritage Award; on National Register of Historic Places.

INDEX OF INNS
